EDGE OF EMPIRE

Rome's Frontier on the Lower Rhine

By Jona Lendering and Arjen Bosman

Karwansaray Publishers
2012

Published in 2012 by

Karwansaray BV

Weena 750

3014 DA Rotterdam

The Netherlands

www.karwansaraypublishers.com

© KARWANSARAY BV 2012-10-08

The cover design incorporates elements symbolizing the Roman presence along the Lower Rhine. Over the stark landscape of a river delta, we superimposed three face-masked helmets which belonged to troopers of the Roman cavalry units based, and in some cases recruited, in this area. From left to right, they were found on the Nijmegen Kops Plateau, in the river Waal near the same city, and in the Canal of Corbulo near Leiden. The background consists of the text of a funerary inscription of a soldier buried "at the dam at Carvium" (modern Herwen, NL), an extra indication of Roman attempts to engineer the waterways in this region of the empire. More information on this stone at: http://tinyurl.com/9rkuca9

ISBN 978-94-90258-05-4

Translated and expanded English edition of Jona Lendering and Arjen Bosman, *De rand van het Rijk* (© Athenaeum-Polak & Van Gennep; Amsterdam 2010).

Translation by Marie Smit-Ryan

Copy-editing by Duncan B. Campbell

Maps designed by Carlos García

Unless otherwise indicated, all photos © Livius.org, Military Legacy, or Karwansaray BV

Illustrations José Antonio Germán, Johnny Shumate, and Graham Sumner

Design and typesetting by MeSa Design, Elst, the Netherlands

Cover design by Andrew J. Brozyna, Longmont, CO, USA

Printed by High Trade BV, Zwolle, the Netherlands

Printed in the EU

Contents

List of maps

Introduction

Half a million pages, printed on both sides: a twenty-five-metre high paper tower could be built from the number of reports Dutch archaeologists wrote between the first publication of this book in Dutch, in 2000, and the revised edition, in 2010. The data explosion is not only confined to the Netherlands. In the Dutch speaking part of Belgium, the number of excavations carried out between 2005 and 2011 increased sevenfold. There appears to be no end to the information coming to light about the Roman Empire's border along the Lower Rhine, the daily life of the province of Germania Inferior and its preoccupation with supplying the needs of the Roman army, and the later transformation of this region into a powerful Frankish kingdom.[1] Nor can two authors know everything. Nevertheless, they thought it worth the effort to weave the many different strands into a compact, accessible history of the Low Countries in Roman times.

In the first centuries of our era, the area between Cologne and Boulogne-sur-Mer developed into one of the most prosperous parts of Europe. On a number of occasions, its potential was converted into power: in AD 69, it became the Emperor Vitellius' power base when carrying out his coup d'état; in the third century AD, as the Gallic Empire, its emperors taught their colleagues in the Roman Empire how to reorganize the Empire's defence; in the fifth century, the Frankish rulers of this region guaranteed that Late-Roman tradition was continued and created a mighty kingdom.

This rise to power is remarkable, because in the Roman Empire, the provinces of Germania Inferior and Belgica had been outlying districts. They were particularly important because they were part of the Rhine border as well as being its hinterland, thereby forming the buffer protecting Gaul. The texts from this period written about the region make fascinating reading, even though, more often than not, they are about war.

What strikes one is that writers had a very poor knowledge of these provinces. Their stories are full of stereotypes, and anyone making a study of the Low Countries in Antiquity would be well advised to first separate facts from fantasy. This works best when sources are continually compared with the actual archaeological finds.

However, it is these very preconceptions that make the texts so entertaining. Even before Caesar subdued Belgica, his countrymen were convinced that there, on the edge of the world disc, very brave barbarians lived: valiant warriors who fought their enemies ruthlessly and without mercy. In his book about the Gallic War, Caesar manipulates the expectations of his readers by referring, over and over again, to barbarian customs, thereby giving his victory over the Belgic tribes an extra brilliance. And not even one hundred and fifty years after Caesar, Tacitus portrays the leader of the Batavian Revolt as a noble savage, although this Julius Civilis had received a Roman upbringing, had served for twenty-five years in the Roman armies and enjoyed Roman civil rights. A few centuries later, the Christian writer Salvian attempted to drive home to his readers the evil of their ways by pointing out that even the barbarians in the Low Countries led purer lives, since they did not commit all sins at the same time!

The authors of *Edge of Empire* have given many lectures in which the preconceptions of classical Antiquity about the population of Germania Inferior have been discussed. After the lectures there were always people who maintained that one still finds this kind of stereotyping today, in reports about the inhabitants of unfamiliar parts of the world. It is true, we can only recognize the preconceptions in Antiquity because we experience similar ones in our own time. Conversely, the realization that certain misconceptions that exist today were also to be found in Antique society, impresses on us just how deeply they are rooted. A study of these is one reason to read about the Low Countries under in Roman times, but the reader must feel free not to take this all too seriously and, we hope, just find pleasure in reading *Edge of Empire*.

1 Preconceptions

• The Entry of a God

The entry of a god: that is how it must have seemed to the inhabitants of the Low Countries when, in the summer of 57 BC, the army of Gaius Julius Caesar marched into their lands. As tens of thousands of heavily-armed Roman legionaries trekked through the countryside of the Scheldt and the Meuse, the natives were awe-struck. One group of warriors surrendered at the first sight of a Roman siege tower. The sentiments of these Belgian tribes must have been similar to those of the German chieftain two generations later, who, on seeing a Roman army for the first time, requested a meeting with the enemy general. For a while he was silent in the general's presence and then declared his joy at having the privilege of looking upon a god.

Yet, the invaders were not complete strangers to the natives. Through trading contacts, the Belgians had already developed a taste for Mediterranean products. A chieftain who wanted to cut a dash poured Italian wine for his guests. From merchants' tales, they must have known that the Romans lived many days' journey to the south on the shores of a big sea. The merchants, however, had never been there themselves; they had learned this from other merchants who had also heard it at second hand. The native inhabitants will have heard that Rome was a town, and in their minds' eye they will have pictured it as an immense village with houses of stone, but much more would have been beyond the realms of their understanding. That the population of Rome's capital lived in tenements of four or five storeys – if indeed they ever came to hear of this – would have been dismissed by them as a great joke.

Now that they were confronted by the race that, a year earlier, had only been a name to them, it turned out that the tall tales they had heard were based on fact. More than that, they must have realized that even the wildest tale did not do justice to the reality. And this was just the beginning. Up to now, they had only seen the Roman legionaries, the objects they lugged with them, and the wooden camps they built. Nobody in their wildest dreams could have foreseen the changes that they were about to face.

• Carthaginian, Greek and Roman Geographical Knowledge

The Romans were just as much in the dark about their opponents. Worse still, the geographical knowledge they possessed had not been accumulated through any effort of their own, but had been picked up second-hand from the races they had conquered in the course of centuries, such as the Greeks and the Carthaginians. The latter were regarded as excellent seafarers who had even ventured onto the hazardous Atlantic Ocean. In the sixth century BC, one explorer, whose name has been passed down to us by the Romans as Himilco, went in search of the region where tin came from. His quest was important because this metal was (and is) essential for the manufacture of bronze. Although his own account of his travels has been lost, we know from Roman sources that the Carthaginian sea captain reached his goal and must therefore have landed in Brittany or Cornwall.[2] It is not reported anywhere that he sailed the North Sea, but it is possible that he also went in search of the place where amber came from. That would explain why, from the sixth century BC, Greek authors speculated about a northern amber river with the name Eridanus.[3] As we shall see, this soft mineral probably came from Heligoland and the Baltic Sea region, from where a trade route ran to Bratislava and northern Italy.

The Carthaginians jealously guarded the secret of the sea route to the Tin Islands. Operating out of the ports of Malaga, Tangier and Cadiz, they saw to it that not one foreign ship managed to reach the Atlantic Ocean. Any strange ships they encountered to the west of Sardinia were sunk with no quarter given.[4] In a treaty that the Carthaginians concluded with the still-small city state of Rome in the sixth century BC, the latter agreed that they would not venture into western waters, and we can assume that there were similar treaties agreed between Carthage and other cities.[5]

Despite these measures, the Carthaginians did not manage to completely monopolize ocean-going trade, as the Greeks had an outpost in Marseilles from which merchants travelled up the Rhône to the north. In settlements such as Lyon they exchanged their goods with native traders, some of whom transported tin up the Loire or the Seine, while others came along the Rhine and Saône with amber.

Nevertheless, the Greeks knew precious little about the lands to the northwest. This is not surprising as these regions were virtually inaccessible. They could not be reached overland – it is not very likely that merchants from Marseille ever got further north than Lyon – or by sea, as the Carthaginians blocked the sea passage. Still, there *were* reports about the far west. One of these was *The Ocean* by Pytheas of Marseilles. This Greek seafarer claimed that, in around 325 BC, he had succeeded in slipping past the Carthaginian blockade and had sailed the northern seas. Modern scholars assume that he did indeed reach the British Isles. However, Pytheas also claimed that, further north, he had seen drift-ice that had come from a 'frozen sea', and that he had reached a place where amber could be found.[6]

The Roman encyclopaedist Pliny the Elder writes that

Pytheas maintained that amber came from the German tribe of the Guiones, who lived on the coastal plain along the Ocean. This plain was called Metuonis and was 1000 kilometres long. At one day's sail lay the island of Abalus where amber was washed up in spring. Pytheas went on to say that this was refuse from the frozen sea and that the inhabitants used it as fuel and sold it to the neighbouring Teutons. The Greek scholar Timaeus also believed this, but he called the island 'the Royal Island'.[7]

We would have to look for Abalus near Jutland, where the Teutons lived. The most obvious candidate is Heligoland, where amber is indeed to be found and which lies about a day's sail from the north-German coast. That amber was used for fuel poses more of a problem, as it is most unlikely that the inhabitants of Abalus were not aware of the value of the product they sold. A possible explanation is that Pytheas was talking about turf and that Pliny got matters confused.

On the way to Heligoland, the Greek explorer must have sailed along the Flemish and Dutch coasts, but his description has been lost. However, his younger contemporary Ephorus of Cyme, an historian, remarked that in the northern coastal region more people died in the struggle against the water than in fights with their fellow men,[8] and it is plausible that he picked up this interesting piece of information from Pytheas. Be that as it may, it is a description that typified the Low Countries and it has lost little of its validity throughout the centuries.

This is the sum total of what the Greeks knew for sure about the Low Countries. The Romans adopted this very scant knowledge after they conquered the Greeks in the second century BC. Of course, the Romans had their own ideas about the tribes of the north, usually referring to them as 'Gauls'. Although these tribes lived across a large area on both sides

The Romans were fascinated by the haircut of the barbarians of the north. Independent Gaul was called Gallia Comata, 'Long-haired Gaul'; Tacitus was to comment on the painted hair of the Batavian leader Julius Civilis, and Sidonius Apollinaris would, as late as the fifth century AD, notice the peculiar hair style of the Frankish warriors. This coin, minted by Julius Caesar, shows a British warrior with a remarkable haircut (private collection).

of the Alps, they all spoke the same Celtic language and had a material civilization which archaeologists categorize under the La Tène cultures.

In 387 or 386 BC, Gauls from the Po valley had, without any warning, invaded and sacked Rome. The terror this inspired in the Romans was not easily erased and they never quite lost their fear of the northerners. Notwithstanding this, at the end of the third century BC, the Romans extended their rule to the area they called Cisalpine Gaul ('on this side of the Alps'), namely the Po valley. A century later, they annexed the region to the west of the Alps and formed it into a Roman province, which still today is called Provence. The more northerly regions remained unexplored, and the Romans called the inhabitants of these regions slightly 'long-haired Gauls'.

Gauls, Celts and La Tène

The word 'Celts' is one of the most problematic expressions in ancient anthropology. Perhaps the word originally referred only to the peoples immediately north of Marseilles, but as early as the fifth century BC, the Greek researcher Herodotus used the name for the inhabitants of a much larger area which embraced both present-day Port-Vendres (at the foot of the east Pyrenees) and the source of the Danube (in the Black Forest).

A century later, Ephorus used the same word for everyone from the west.

Later writers use the term 'Celtic' as a synonym for 'barbarian'. In this way, the Greek author Cassius Dio refers to the tribes east of the Rhine as Celts, although these peoples are called Germans in almost all other sources. (When Dio talks about Germans, he is referring to the inhabitants of the Roman provinces of Germania Inferior and Germania Superior.) Following on from Dio's choice of word is the use of the term 'Celts' by Christian writers of the Middle Ages, to refer to the peoples of all the regions not subjected to the Romans, such as the inhabitants of Ireland.

The use of the word 'Celts' in this way would have caused raised eyebrows amongst the classical writers, because in all this linguistic confusion there was one thing that everyone agreed upon: the inhabitants of the British Isles were *not* Celts. It was Caesar's opinion, for example, that they were Belgian tribes who had sailed westward, and although we do not have to accept this unquestioningly, his remark proves that he did not see the Britons as Celts. The geographer Strabo also distinguishes the Britons from the Celts.

From ancient times, the Romans called the races living in the Po valley and in central France 'Gauls', but Caesar asserts that they called themselves Celts (see page 10). Presumably, it was the other way around: the people who called themselves Gauls were called Celts by others. Be that as it may, it is pretty certain that the region Caesar referred to as Celtic was linguistically distinct from the Aquitanian-speaking region in the southwest and the Belgian-speaking region in the north (see page 10-11). The language spoken by Caesar's Celts is related to a number of ancient languages that linguists began referring to as the Celtic language group. The distribution of these races corresponds roughly with that of the small number of Iron Age cultures that fall under the 'La Tène' umbrella.

Therefore, one cannot actually use the term 'Celtic' at all, let alone use it to refer to people who, from an archaeological point of view, belong to the La Tène culture but speak a German language. When the word is used by the authors of this book, it is usually to designate the language group.

Besides Gauls, the Romans also identified Germans. At the end of the second century BC, two tribes of Germans, referred to in our sources as Cimbri and Teutoni, had left their motherland, Jutland, to trek south. There, they were defeated in battle by the Romans, who noted that the migrants had a much simpler way of life than the Gauls and spoke a different language. As a consequence, the Romans began to differentiate between these two peoples. In the following chapters you will see that this differentiation is open to question.

To sum up: in the northwest there lived barbarian Gauls and even more savage Germans, and somewhere in their lands, tin and amber were mined. This was all the Romans knew of the area north of the Alps. They did not even know about the existence of the Rhine before the beginning of the first century BC.

● Civilization and Barbarism

The Greeks and the Romans may not have known much about the northwest of Europe, but what they did not know, they made up. An example is the Greek author, Xenophon of Lampsacus, who, around 100 BC, gave the first ethnological description of the people in the far north. He tells that

at a three days' sail from the northern coast there is an island of immense size called Balcia. Pytheas calls it 'the Royal Island'. The Bird Islands are also mentioned – there, the inhabitants live on birds' eggs and oats – and other islands where people are born with horses' hooves and so they are called 'Horse footers'. On other islands again, you can find the 'All ears' people: the inhabitants have ears of such extraordinary size that they cover the rest of their otherwise naked bodies.[9]

Pure fantasy, as you can gather. Fortunately, there were Romans who saw through such unreliable accounts. The quote here has been passed down to us by Pliny, who mentions at the same time that Xenophon had a doubtful reputation. Nevertheless, this did not stop Pliny from passing it on, and we may assume that such ideas were always in circulation. Even critical minds were influenced by them. In this way, leading ancient scholars sometimes entertained quite strange ideas about social geography.

The central theme in these accounts was always the contrast between the civilized Greeks and Romans on the one hand, and the rest of the human race – the barbarians – on the other. Further, the world was divided up roughly into a number of concentric rings. The inner ring consisted of Greece and Italy, which were almost completely surrounded by the Mediterranean Sea. Encircling this group were the continents of Europe, Asia and Africa. And, finally, there was an outer ring consisting of the large world sea, the Ocean. The civilized world was in the centre, and the ancients assumed that, where the earth bordered on the Ocean, there lived barbarians and wild people who were hardly distinguishable from the freaks and monsters that lived beyond the edge of the world. Every Greek and Roman knew the stories about the monsters in the world sea and knew that, in this place, primordial chaos reigned.

Civilization and barbarism were in many respects the antitheses of each other. To start with, there was a question of contrasting geography. The civilized Greeks and Romans lived along rivers and on coastal plains; the barbarians, on the other hand, lived in forests and mountains. (The logical conclusion was that the shore of the Ocean resembled a forested fjord landscape.) The different geography translated into contrasting modes of production: while the civilized areas had a fertile soil which made agriculture possible, the poor soil of the barbarians only supported stock-breeding. Counterposed to the civilized, bread-eating people were the nomadic barbarians with a diet of meat and dairy products.

It goes without saying that their way of life was also very different. The Greeks and Romans could live in towns and did not need to carry weapons because they lived in peace with their neighbours. In their free time, they could relax, for instance, by studying. (The Greek word *scholê* means "free time".) The barbarians, on the other hand, never remained in one place for long. They were constantly on the move with their herds through the wild, mountainous countryside. They always had to be on the alert for cattle thieves; that is, if they were not on cattle raids themselves. Consequently, they always carried weapons. While the life of the civilized town-dweller was regulated by laws and ethics, the barbarians lived in isolated villages and did not put much store by laws and morals. By the same token, the barbarians did not respect the laws of hospitality and did not baulk at either seeing their guests as edible delicacies for their own consumption, or offering them as sacrifices to appease their gods.

Naturally, good taste only existed in the towns around the Mediterranean Sea. There, people were well-coifed and wore chitons, tunics or chic togas, while on the edge of the world, barbarians had moustaches and beards and dressed – that is, if they did not go naked – in trousers. You could not get anything more uncivilized than that!

According to this view, the barbarians found themselves in a vicious circle. They lived in an inhospitable wilderness where it was impossible to till the land. Consequently, they had to go on raids to survive, and, because of that, lived in a permanent state of war. If it should occur to any of them to grow crops, it would be a futile exercise, as it would not be long before they would have to abandon their land. Under these existential circumstances, any form of cultural activity was impossible. In the view of the Greeks and Romans, this would surely lead to social disorder, causing the barbarians to avoid human company and to prefer the isolation of the inhospitable countryside. The only escape from all this misery was to be defeated by the Romans, who were then quite willing to teach civility and morals to those they defeated.

Until it came to that, the barbarians were belligerent, hot-headed and unreliable. Because they were always fighting, there was no time for reflection. That is why they valued strength above reason and adhered to a simple warrior ethic. Their lives centred on values such as honour and courage. Because they never took time to think deeply, they quickly warmed to any undertaking where they could display their courage and thus gain fame. Generally speaking, they were always impatient for change. They never stayed long in one area, and replaced their leaders frequently; they did not abide by agreements, and marital fidelity was unknown to them.

At least, that is how the Romans thought about the tribes that lived on the northern coast of the European continent. In the first place, their view was based on partly or wholly distorted information about the inhabitants of remote lands. In the second place, this caricature sprang from the reversal of what the Greeks and Romans regarded as normal. A reader in Antiquity was not surprised if a writer stated that the men of some peripheral tribe did not shave their faces but the back of their heads.[10] In the third place, this image was based on transferring the customs and characteristics of one barbarian tribe to another. Nobody thought it was unusual that Tacitus applied to the Germans the Persian custom of making important decisions when inebriated.[11]

How little of what they concluded actually corresponded to the truth is evidenced by the fact that not one of the writers in Antiquity ever mentioned the hunting weapons used by the inhabitants of the Low Countries. If they had really seen the hunters of the north, they would certainly have described their weapons: after all, their boomerangs must have been quite striking. But not one source mentions them, so that the archaeologists who dug them up were completely unprepared for such a find.

Even critical minds, such as the geographer Strabo, were influenced by these caricatured descriptions of the lives of the people in the north. They did, however, shade some nuances into their picture. They recognized that the barbarians displayed noble characteristics, while

Reconstruction of an Iron Age boy from the area of The Hague. He uses a boomerang (Drawing by Johnny Shumate).

in the civilized world there was the temptation to descend into decadence and unmanly behaviour. Moreover, they recognized that absolute barbarism did not exist anywhere and that, even in the Graeco-Roman world, there were illiterate peasants. But Strabo and like-minded intellectuals also knew that the people living on the periphery led simple lives and were tempestuous fighters.

What the Romans who marched into the Low Countries in 57 BC knew about the territory of their campaign came down to this: there was ebb and flow; the days were not always the same length as they were in the south; and aggressive Gauls, and even more war-hungry Germans, lived there. And because the inhabitants were not really home-loving and were wont to trek south every now and then, a preventive attack on their homelands could be seen as a legitimate form of self-defence for the Romans.

The Romans' decision to attack must have been made in the last months of 58 BC. General Gaius Julius Caesar had carried out successful operations along the Saône in the previous summer and had defeated a group of Germans near the Rhine. Full of self-confidence, he decided to proceed further north as far as the Ocean. Some time earlier, he had impressed the Senate by marching along the ocean coast of Portugal as far as Galicia. Here, he had found gold mines and had returned a rich man. Who would not want to repeat such successes?

The push to the edge of the world was the metaphorical leap into the void. We already discussed how little the Romans knew of this area – a place that had never been visited by Mediterranean merchants and was only known from the accounts of seafarers who, centuries before, had sailed along its coast. It is no coincidence that Caesar's *Gallic War* begins with a number of explanatory remarks about the land of the long-haired barbarians.

2 War on the Edge of the World

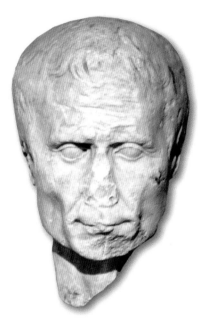

Bust of Julius Caesar. The provenance is not known, but it was probably found in Nijmegen (Leiden, Rijksmuseum van Oudheden, National Museum of Antiquities).

• Gauls and Germans

The whole of Gaul is divided into three parts, one of which the Belgae inhabit, the Aquitani another, and the third a people who in their own language are called 'Celts', but in ours, 'Gauls'. They all differ among themselves in respect of language, way of life and laws. The River Garonne divides the Gauls from the Aquitani, and the Marne and Seine rivers separate them from the Belgae.

Of these three, the Belgae are the bravest, for they are furthest away from the civilization and culture of the Province. Merchants very rarely travel to them or import such goods as make men's courage weak and womanish. They live, moreover, in close proximity to the Germans who inhabit the land across the Rhine, and they are continually at war with them.[12]

The opening words of Caesar's *Gallic War* are justifiably famous. It is one of those passages in which something is so clearly expressed that it is impossible to hold a different opinion. The Rhine is the border between the Gauls and the Germans – that is how simple it is.

Oh, wouldn't it be great if it were really so simple? Archaeologists have now ascertained that the material culture of Central Gaul – the La Tène civilization – also existed on the other side of the Rhine. It is impossible, therefore, to speak of a border. Further northwards, the situation is even less clear, and there is good reason to think that the Rhine did not form the border here, either.

The whole idea came into being with Caesar's well-written single-paragraph description, by which he created a pretext for himself to rid the country west of the big rivers of

---

The Northwest Block

Linguists suspect that the inhabitants of the region between the rivers Somme and Weser had their own language, referred to as 'Belgian' or the 'Northwest Block'.[13] This language came into existence before Celtic and German, and took on more and more German features from the late second century BC.

Archaeologists are also reluctant to include the northwest of the European continent amongst the La Tène or German Iron Age cultures, because certain characteristic artefacts have not been found either to the southwest or the northeast of the Lower Rhine. It seems that there are parallels in the development of the material culture for the germanization of the language from the late second century BC.

Much about this cultural region is unclear and the situation is possibly even more complex than adherents of the 'Northwest Block hypothesis' think. In fact, the idea may one day go out of fashion again. What is certain, however, is that the northwest of Europe, both linguistically and culturally, had a lot more to offer than just Celtic and German cultures.

German-speaking intruders. Great credibility was attached to this propaganda for a long time. As recently as the peace negotiations after the First World War, the French politician Clemenceau claimed the western Rhineland as part of France, with the argument that, from ancient times, the river formed the border between Gaul and Germania and thus between France and Germany. After all, that was what Caesar had written! Because Caesar's impressive report, the *Gallic War*, will be quoted many times in the following pages, it cannot do any harm to say a little more about this work, so that it becomes clearer what a curious fabric of facts and insinuations Caesar constructed.

● Facts and Propaganda

Caesar was a politician and wrote his report on the wars in northwest Europe with political intent. One of his purposes was to justify his military actions and the other was to impress the home front. This is obvious from the opening words of the *Gallic War*. The three parts into which Gaul could be divided are recognizable archaeologically. Besides the La Tène culture of the "people who in their own language are called 'Celts', but in ours, 'Gauls'", there were areas in the southwest and in the north with a recognizable character of their own. That would seem to confirm what Caesar says about the Aquitani and the Belgae.

But it is only part of the story. The borders that he mentions do not comply with the dividing lines that archaeologists have observed. Caesar draws the border of the area of the Belgae too far to the south. It goes without saying that, by expanding the area of the bravest of all the Gauls in this way, his own military operations appear all the more impressive.

The reader has to be on his guard against this sort of misrepresentation. And yet, Caesar does not always set out to deceive. In the following passage, written in the winter of 55/54 BC, it looks as if he simply made a mistake:

The Meuse flows from the Vosges mountain range in the territory of the Lingones, and is joined by a distributary of the Rhine called the Waal, so forming the island of the Batavi. It flows into the Rhine no more than 120 kilometers from the Ocean.[14]

Caesar here confuses the Meuse (in Latin, *Mosa*) with the Moselle (*Mosella*). In those days, the Meuse flowed into the branch of the Rhine which we call the Waal, while it is the Moselle that rises in the Vosges. This mistake just goes to show how unfamiliar Gaul was to Caesar, even when he had been there for more than three years.

Inserting descriptions like these served to increase the writer's credibility. That is also the reason why Caesar speaks about himself in the third person: it looks more objective. Very few people will have doubted the truth of the following words, in which Caesar describes the coalition of Belgae that he had to deal with in 57 BC.

When Caesar asked the two envoys about the Belgian states – how many were under arms, and what their strength in war was – he discovered that most of the Belgae were of German extraction, and had long ago crossed the Rhine and settled on the western side because of the fertility of the soil. They had forced out the Gauls who dwelt there. In our fathers' time, when the Cimbri and Teutoni were harassing the whole of Gaul, only the Belgae had stopped them entering their own territory. So it transpired that they had acquired an aura of great authority and courage in military matters by the memory of this achievement. The Remi claimed to have complete information about the Belgae's numerical strength, because they were closely connected both by physical proximity and ties of marriage: they knew how many men each leader had pledged for the war at the general council of the Belgae.

The strongest people among the Belgae in terms of bravery, influence, and numbers were the Bellovaci: they could supply 100,000 armed men, and had promised to select 60,000 from that number. At first they demanded command of the entire campaign for themselves. Their neighbours the Suessiones had pledged 50,000 armed men. The Nervii, a people dwelling far off, and considered particularly fierce by the Gauls themselves, pledged a similar number. The Atrebates pledged 15,000, the Ambiani 10,000, the Morini 25,000, the Menapii 7,000, the Caletes 10,000, the Veliocasses and Viromandui 10,000 between them, and the Aduatuci 19,000. The Remi thought that the Condrusi, Eburones, Caeroesi, and Paemani (who are collectively known as Germans) could supply about 40,000 men.[15]

Caesar went to great lengths to let it be known that he was about to take on a very formidable opponent. The catalogue of enemies, the (exaggerated) numbers, and his mention that, at some time in the past, these tribes had been able to withstand attacks of the Cimbri and the Teutoni, were all unambiguous. He emphasizes that the Nervii are the most dangerous of all the Belgians, pointing out, predictably, that they lived furthest from civilization.

The word 'tribe' (*civitas*) used by Caesar, was (and is) somewhat disparaging. By the use of this word, the Romans conveyed that there was something primitive about these communities. The term often referred to a loose form of collaboration between local leaders who did not share much more than a dialect, ownership of a more or less defined territory and the cult of certain gods. Only under particular circumstances, such as in times of war, was there a question of central leadership. In more peaceful times, however, power rested with the big landowners who had their land farmed by semi-free peasants.

Central Gaul had a more advanced society than Caesar cared to admit. Many of the political units which he referred to as 'tribes' would be called 'states' today, as they had, for example, annually chosen magistrates who regularly officiated at meetings in town halls especially built for this purpose. These estates could mobilize well-organized armies, and they emphasized their political independence by issuing their own coins.

In comparison, the Belgian north was less developed. Caesar's impression of a 'tribal community' can indeed be applied to this area. But here, too, the people engaged in trade. That the Nervii minted coins, like all the other northern peoples, is a fact that Caesar chooses to omit, because it does not fit into the Roman conception that, the farther a tribe lived from the Mediterranean Sea, the more uncivilized it was.

One last device that the author of the *Gallic War* uses to indicate the savageness of his opponents is the insertion of ethnological asides. An example of such an ethnographic intermezzo is the horror story about the human sacrifices that Gallic druids made to their gods.[16] Archaeologists have confirmed that such gruesome rituals did indeed take place. All over northwestern Europe, bog bodies have been found: the remains of people who had been drowned with violence, such as the 'Weerdinge Couple' and the 'Yde Girl', both found in the north-eastern part of the Netherlands. Further south, large numbers of bones have been discovered at different sacred places, dating to before the arrival of the Romans. There is truth in what Caesar says about human sacrifices; but, of course, he has an ulterior motive in mentioning it. And so we see that, to characterize the enemy as barbarians, even the truth was brought into play.

The readers of the *Gallic War* should, therefore, be on their guard not to accept anything as being unquestionably true. (Of course, this applies to all ancient sources.) Sometimes, Caesar massages the facts to magnify his own talent as a commander. Furthermore, he was able to legitimize his operations by portraying the Gauls and the Belgae as savages. That was not without meaning in a time when influential philosophers like Athenodorus Calvus began to justify Roman imperialism by postulating that Rome's mission was to subdue the barbarians for their own good.

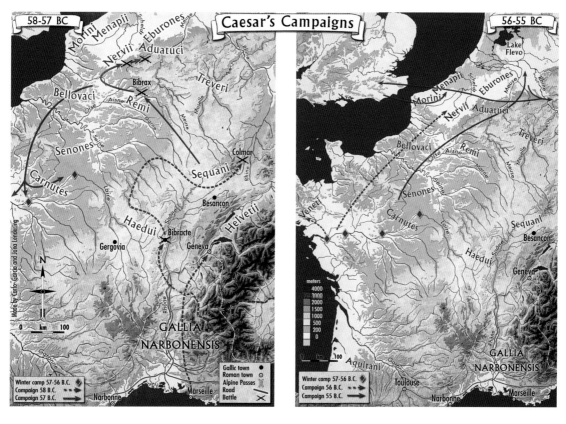

Caesar's Campaigns

58-57 BC

Morini
Menapii
Nervii
Aduatuci
Eburones
Bellovaci
Bibrax
Remi
Treveri
Colmar
Senones
Sequani
Carnutes
Besançon
Haedui
Bibracte
Gergovia
Geneva
Helvetii

GALLIA NARBONENSIS

Made by Carlos García and Jona Lendering

N

0 km 100

| Winter camp 57-56 B.C. |
| Campaign 58 B.C. |
| Campaign 57 B.C. |

Gallic town	●
Roman town	◉
Alpine Passes	)(
Road	
Battle	✕

Narbonne
Marseille

56-55 BC

Lake Flevo
Menapii
Morini
Eburones
Nervii
Aduatuci
Treveri
Bellovaci
Remi
Senones
Sequani
Veneti
Carnutes
Besançon
Haedui
Geneva

meters
4000
3000
2000
1500
1000
500
200
0

0 km 100

Aquitani
GALLIA NARBONENSIS

| Winter camp 57-56 B.C. |
| Campaign 56 B.C. |
| Campaign 55 B.C. |

Toulouse
Narbonne
Marseille

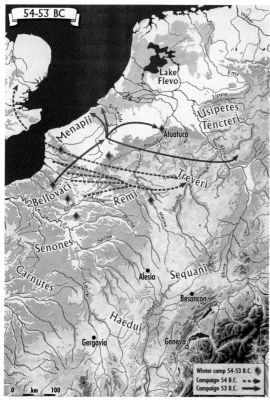

54-53 BC

Lake Flevo
Ems
Lippe
Menapii
Scheldt
Usipetes
Tencteri
Atuatuca
Treveri
Bellovaci
Remi
Oise
Aisne
Moselle
Senones
Carnutes
Alesia
Sequani
Besançon
Haedui
Gergovia
Geneva

0 km 100

| Winter camp 54-53 B.C. |
| Campaign 54 B.C. |
| Campaign 53 B.C. |

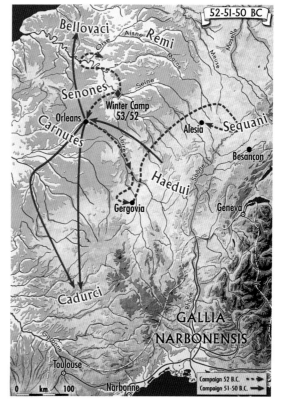

52-51-50 BC

Bellovaci
Oise
Aisne
Remi
Marne
Meuse
Senones
Seine
Orleans
Winter Camp 53/52
Alesia
Sequani
Carnutes
Besançon
Haedui
Gergovia
Geneva

Cadurci

GALLIA NARBONENSIS

0 km 100

| Campaign 52 B.C. |
| Campaign 51-50 B.C. |

Toulouse
Narbonne

• The Nervii

The war in Gaul had started in the spring of 58 BC, when a group of Helvetii prepared for an incursion into the Roman Province, and a German tribe from Alsace attacked a number of Rome's allies in central Gaul. As governor of the Gallic provinces on both sides of the Alps, Caesar was forced to intervene with his four legions. He called up two extra units, forced the Helvetii to retreat, and subsequently beat the Germans, who, he maintained, had no right to be west of the Rhine. This latter battle took place in Alsace, on the borders of the world that was known to the Romans.

After this, the troops moved to their winter quarters around Besançon and the general wrote the first part of his *Gallic War*, in which he summarized the events with the modest observation that, in just one summer, he brought to a close two important wars. At this time, rumours reached him that the Belgae had formed a federation against the Romans, because they were afraid that

our army would march against them now all the rest of Gaul had been subdued; secondly, they were being stirred up by a number of the Gauls, some of whom had been unwilling for the Germans to have any further involvement in Gaul, and were equally reluctant for the army of the Roman people to overwinter and become established there. Others were of a volatile and unstable disposition – the sort of men who delight in changes of rule. Yet another group incited the Belgae to conspire because it was common in Gaul for men who possessed some degree of power and the means to hire support to seize regal power – something which would be more difficult to achieve under our rule.[17]

This was no idle threat by the Belgae, and their preparations were understandable, as Caesar did indeed intend to invade the unexplored area in the north of the lands of the long-haired Gauls. As is often the case in Caesar's *Gallic War*, what the author says is less interesting than what he leaves out – in this case, a denial of the Belgian claim that the Roman general was planning to advance with his legions into the lands of the Belgae.

Thus, Caesar's legionaries marched on the Remi, whose lands were surrounded by the tribes of the anti-Roman coalition. Confronted by the presence of eight legions, the Remi hastily chose the side of the Romans. In the years that followed, they would be among Caesar's most reliable allies.

Caesar defeated the alliance in a marshy area where the Gauls could not exploit their numerical advantage. However, it was a hard-won victory, and further advance would have been abandoned if, at the same time, Caesar's Gallic allies had not taken to plundering the defenceless lands of the Belgian tribes. Some of the latter decided to stop fighting, so the Romans were able to continue marching on into the unknown area in the north, which was the source of so many fanciful stories.

Legions and Legionaries

A legion was a professional army of nominally 4,800 infantry who were armed with javelins, swords and daggers, and protected by a mail vest, a helmet and a shield (see picture on page 52). Legionaries officially served for six campaigns, and, when their unit was disbanded, they were often rewarded with a piece of land. Because many of Caesar's soldiers served him longer, and later re-enlisted to avenge his death, his legions acquired a permanent character. In this way, a professional army gradually came into being.

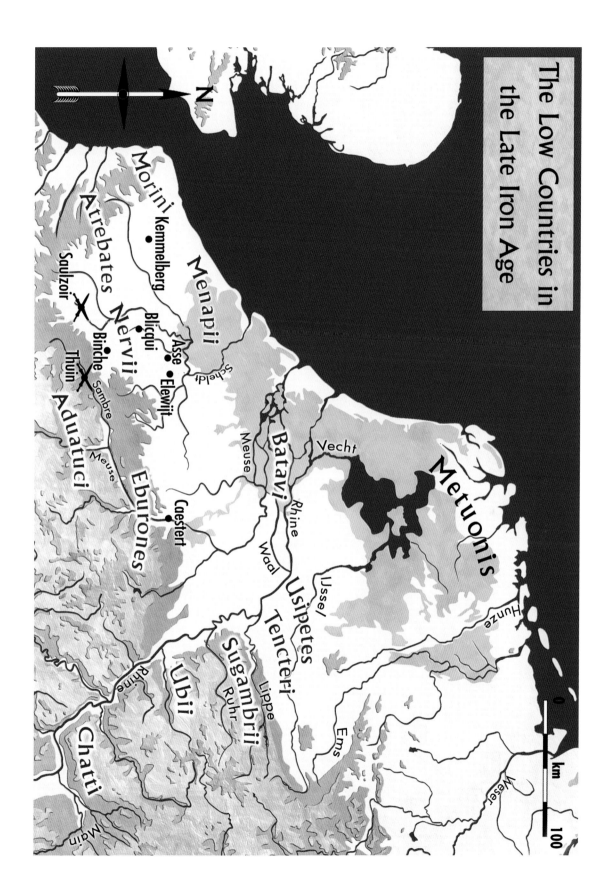

The Low Countries in the Late Iron Age

N

Morini
Atrebates
Kemmelberg
Saulzoir
Blicqui
Asse
Binche
Elewijt
Thuin
Sambre
Aduatuci
Meuse
Nervii
Menapi
Scheldt
Eburones
Meuse
Caestert
Batavi
Vecht
Rhine
Waal
Metuonis
IJssel
Usipetes
Tencteri
Hunze
Sugambri
Ubii
Lippe
Ruhr
Rhine
Ems
Chatti
Main
Weser

0
km
100

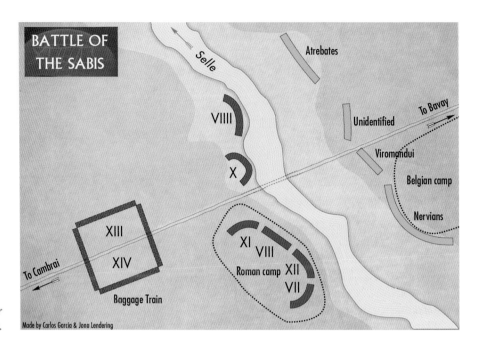

BATTLE OF
THE SABIS

Selle

Atrebates

VIIII

Unidentified

To Bavay

X

Viromandui

Belgian camp

Nervians

XIII

XIV

XI

VIII

Roman camp

XII

VII

To Cambrai

Baggage Train

Made by Carlos García & Jona Lendering

The Battle of the Sabis (the Selle near
Saulzoir in France).

Even those who had spread the tales were not familiar with the country of the Nervii on the Scheldt or the Aduatuci on the Sambre. Caesar began, therefore, to collect information about the Low Countries and the Nervii from the Ambiani who were living around present-day Amiens.

When Caesar enquired about their character and customs, he discovered the following: they permitted no merchants within their borders; they did not allow the import of wine and other luxury goods, because they believed such things enfeebled their spirit and weakened their courage. They were fierce men, and very brave, who reproached and condemned all the other Belgae for surrendering to the Roman people and casting aside their ancestral courage: they declared that they would send no envoys, and accept no peace terms.[18]

Here Caesar is serving up a, by now, familiar cocktail: a selective description of the local way of living, duly laced with what the Romans would associate with dangerous enemies.

In the summer, he marched quickly from the Ambiani up to the northeast along an ancient road. This made the direction of his march predictable and afforded the Belgian tribes the chance to pick the place of the battle. On the third day, Caesar learnt that the Nervii, with two other tribes, the Atrebates and the Viromandui, were lying in wait for him on the Sabis,[19] a tributary of the Scheldt.

The general sent ahead a cavalry unit to look for a place where the Roman army could set up camp directly across from the enemy, with the intention of doing battle the following day. After the cavalry came six well-trained legions, who marched without baggage so that they could be at their destination as quickly as possible and pitch camp. Bringing up the rear were the baggage trains and two newly-recruited legions. However, the mounted advance guard was operating too far ahead of the main army, and this gave the Nervii the opportunity to finish them off before the legions arrived. In this way, the Nervii were able to make use of their one chance to put parts of the enemy army out of action before it had reached full strength. After all, with eight legions and as many as 40,000 men, the Romans were numerically much stronger. Having first defeated the Roman cavalry, the Nervii managed to engage with the legions that arrived first. Caesar writes that

our cavalry, slingers, and archers crossed the river and engaged with the enemy cavalry, who continually retreated into the woods and rejoined their comrades before coming out from the trees and attacking our men again. Meanwhile, the six legions arrived, measured out the camp, and began the work of fortification. As soon as our army's baggage came into view of the enemy hidden in the woods (the moment they had agreed for joining battle) they suddenly rushed out in full force and launched an attack on our cavalry, which was easily repulsed and scattered.[20]

Caesar's plan to first assemble his army and build a camp, and then to engage in battle on the following day, had been thwarted. That the fight did not end in disaster was because his soldiers were so well-trained, and his colonels did not wait for orders but took their own decisions.

Once he had given all the appropriate orders Caesar ran down where luck would take him to speak his encouragement to the men – and ended up among the Tenth Legion. His speech was long enough only to urge them to remember their long-established record for bravery, and not to lose their nerve but to resist the enemy assault with courage: for the enemy was within missile range of the Roman army. Then he gave the signal for battle.

When Caesar moved to the other side to give encouragement he found the men already fighting. Everything happened so quickly, and the enemy was so determined to fight, that there was no time for our men to fit on their emblems or even to put on helmets and take the covers from their shields. Wherever each man ended up after stopping work on the defences, and whichever signal he saw first, there he took his stand, so as not to waste fighting-time in looking for his comrades.

The Roman army was drawn up so as to take account of the natural terrain, the slope of the hill, and the need of the moment, rather than in accordance with any theoretical military formation. For the legions were resisting the enemy in different directions and different places, while thick barrier hedges got in their way and obscured the view. It was impossible to allocate assistance, or see what was needed where, or for one man to co-ordinate all commands. The difficult circumstances, therefore, were matched by a number of different outcomes.

The soldiers of the Ninth and Tenth Legions had placed themselves on the left flank: they threw their spears and charged upon the Atrebates, whom they happened to be facing. The Atrebates were fatigued and exhausted after running, and suffering from their wounds. Our men, who had the higher ground, quickly forced them into the river. The Atrebates tried to get across but their way was blocked: our men caught them up, drew their swords, and slaughtered many of them.

Then our men crossed the river without hesitation. They advanced on to unfavourable ground: the enemy resisted. Battle began again, and again they routed the enemy.[21]

The commander of the Tenth Legion was Titus Labienus, who was to become the hero of the day. Less fortunate were the troops from the Eleventh and Eighth that had been drawn up in the middle. They did manage to put their opponents to flight but, in doing so, advanced so far ahead that they left a gap between them and the right flank. Boduognatus, the commander of the Nervii, did not hesitate for a moment and ordered his men to advance through the opening, up to the unfinished Roman camp. From here, he attacked the legions in the rear. The following quote is one sentence in Latin:

After his words of encouragement to the Tenth, Caesar made his way to the right flank. There he saw that his soldiers were hard pressed. Because their standards were crowded together the men of the Twelfth were packed so close that they obstructed one another in the fighting. All the centurions of the fourth cohort were dead, the standard-bearer was slain, the standard lost; all but a few centurions from the rest of the cohorts were wounded or dead. Among the casualties was a senior centurion called Publius Sextius Baculus, a man of immense courage, who was suffering from numerous serious wounds. He could no longer stand upright, and the rest of the men were weakening: some of those at the rear were leaving the battle and retreating to avoid missiles, while the enemy did not slacken but pressed on up the hill in front, and continued to attack on both flanks. Caesar realized that the outcome rested on a knife-edge – there was no hope of reinforcements – so he snatched a shield from one of the soldiers at the rear (he had come out without his own shield) and made his way to the front line. There he called upon the centurions by name and encouraged the men, ordering them to advance and open ranks, so they could use their swords more easily.[22]

Caesar does not disguise the fact that it looked bad for the Romans. Nor did the arrival of the two legions whose responsibility it was to protect the army supplies bring about a reversal. Meanwhile,

Titus Labienus, who had taken over the enemy camp and from his vantage-point saw what was happening in our camp, sent the Tenth Legion to our men's assistance. Their arrival transformed our fortunes, so much so that our men – even those who lay wounded – supported themselves on their shields and began the fight afresh. The orderlies now observed that it was the Nervii who were afraid and, weaponless as they were, they charged upon the armed enemy. So too the cavalry tried to wipe out the shame of its desertion by fighting everywhere in an attempt to outdo the legionaries. The enemy, however, even at this critical moment, showed such determination in their bravery that when those in the front rank had fallen the men behind them stood upon the slain and continued the fight from on top of the corpses. When they were overthrown the pile of bodies grew higher, while the survivors used the heap as a vantage-point for throwing missiles at our men, or catching their spears and throwing them back. Not without good reason were they judged to be men of enormous bravery. For they had dared to cross a very wide river, climb its steep banks, and advance on extremely difficult ground: the Nervii's courage had made light of these obstacles.[23]

In other words, Labienus' actions saved the legions that tried to resist the fury of the Nervii on the Roman side of the river. Caesar does not appear to be very grateful: he gives a nev-

Oppida

In order to create the impression that the Belgae were formidable opponents, Caesar calls their settlements *oppida*, a word that was familiar to the Roman public from the almost endless Iberian wars. (The singular is *oppidum*.) At that time, the word had referred to heavily-fortified, practically impregnable hillforts. The hillforts of the Gauls resembled these; but, for the sake of convenience, Caesar does not mention that, in many Gallic oppida, the civil aspect was more important than the military one. They were often built alongside trade-routes and formed the administrative centres of the political units that Caesar calls 'tribes' – deliberately using an archaic word.

The religious aspect of these oppida was also significant. After the Romans assumed power, temples arose on practically all of them. There was a conscious political strategy behind this: by taking over the centres of ritual, the Romans laid claim to the local gods, subjugating the local populations spiritually as well.

er-ending description of his own actions, and mentions Labienus only once. After all, the author of the *Gallic War* could not afford to give anyone except himself credit for the victory.

When the battle was over, the name and fighting strength of the Nervii were almost wiped out. The elders were gathered together in inlets and marshes along with the women and children; when news came of the battle, they assumed that nothing stood in the way of the victors, and that for the vanquished nothing was secure. So all the survivors agreed to send envoys to Caesar and surrender to him. Describing the disaster which had befallen them, the Nervian envoys declared that they had been reduced from 600 senators to three, from 60,000 men capable of active service to a mere 500.[24]

With the remarkable use of the word 'senators', Caesar must have been referring to the chiefs and big landowners of the Nervii, who were expected to fight at the head of their warriors. That only three of them survived is credible, but the second number of casualties must be incorrect, if only for the fact that Caesar mentions somewhere else that, in 52 BC, the Nervii could muster 5,000 warriors.[25] Another reason is that the lands of the Nervii could never have fed 60,000 people. Ten thousand Nervian warriors at the Sambre would be a more realistic estimation. Naturally, the fact that Caesar heavily exaggerates does not mean that the meeting of the Nervii with the Romans was not a catastrophe for the former.

• The Aduatuci

After his victory, Caesar sent troops to the southwest to demand the submission of the tribes who lived on the shore of the Ocean. They were not anti-Roman and one legion turned out to be sufficient to enable the Roman general to state that he had pushed the boundaries of the Roman sphere of influence as far as the Ocean.

With the other legions, Caesar himself marched along the Sambre and the Meuse. It is

Wall of the oppidum south of Thuin. This is possibly the place where Caesar fought against the Aduatuci.

impossible to estimate to what extent the Roman troops were still at their full strength following the battle against the Nervii, but, even if the seven legions had lost a quarter of their men, Caesar still had the use of 25,000 legionaries. The Romans were thus more numerous than the Aduatuci, who, according to the statistics Caesar gives on page 12, had the use of 19,000 warriors. However, Caesar inflates the campaign of September 57 BC to epic proportions.

The Aduatuci were on their way to assist the Nervii in full force when news of the battle made them give up their march and return home. They abandoned all their towns and strongholds and brought all their property to one town (oppidum) which had superb natural defences. All along its circumference it presented sheer cliffs and heights, which at one spot left a gently sloping approach, no more than 200 feet wide. This the Aduatuci had strengthened by a high double wall and were even now putting heavy rocks and sharpened stakes along its length.

The Aduatuci were descendants of those Cimbri and Teutoni who, when marching into our Province and Italy, had left all the cattle and baggage they could not drive or carry with them on this side of the Rhine: they left a guard – 6,000 of their own men – to protect it. Following the destruction of the main force, these men were harassed by neighbouring peoples for many years (sometimes attacking, sometimes defending). Eventually peace was made by common consent and they selected this place to settle in.[26]

Ancient writers were very creative in blowing up etymologies into historical facts. The whole story about the origins of the Aduatuci seems to be based on no more than the similarity of the words Aduatuci and Teutoni, which are both derived from *θευδô, an old word that meant 'people' in different languages. The purpose of Caesar's historical reconstruction was, of course, to bring his attack on the Aduatuci in line with the war against the Teutoni, who, in Rome, still had the reputation of national bogeyman.

The Aduatuci, whose only mistake was that they had shown solidarity with the tribes that Caesar had attacked, hid in an oppidum which has very recently been identified and whose location was probably south of modern Thuin in Belgium. The besieged watched with dismay as the enemy stormed up towards them.

As soon as our army arrived, the Aduatuci began making frequent sallies from the town and skirmishing with our men. Later, when they were shut in by a rampart almost seven kilometers in length, with numerous forts along it, they remained in the town. Moveable shelters were drawn up, an earthwork built, and when the Aduatuci saw a siege-tower constructed in the distance, at first they stood on the wall, mocking and jeering that such a large apparatus was being put together so far off. What hands, what strength were men of such puny stature relying on to move this huge and heavy tower against their wall? (For the main part, Gauls are very tall, and hold our slighter build in contempt.)

But when they saw the tower being moved, and coming close to the walls, the sight of it was so unusual and unexpected that it prompted them to send envoys to Caesar to ask for peace. The envoys spoke to the effect that in their opinion the Romans had divine help in waging war, to enable them to move such tall structures forward so quickly. And so, they declared, they surrendered themselves and all their possessions to the Romans' control.[27]

Caesar demanded that the Aduatuci first handed in their weapons. Only then would there be a formal surrender. And so, as requested, "they threw a large number of weapons down from the wall into the ditch in front of the town", but during the night something went wrong when a group of Aduatuci broke out of the oppidum – at least, that was Caesar's version of this episode. The Romans drove their enemies back, killing 4,000 (it would seem), and sold the rest of the inhabitants as slaves the following day.

For Caesar's soldiers this was an occasion for celebration. Thousands of men, women and children were sold, and it was usual for a general to let his men have a share of the profits. Almost two centuries later, the looting was still remembered by the Roman biographer Suetonius:

In Gaul, Caesar pillaged shrines and temples of the gods filled with offerings. Very often, he sacked towns more for the sake of plunder than for anything they might have done wrong. Consequently, he had more gold than he knew what to do with, and offered it for sale throughout Italy and the provinces at the rate of three thousand sesterces a pound.[28]

Although this refers to Gaul in general, it is likely that the country of the Aduatuci was also looted on a massive scale. Archaeologists have established that there was a substantial amount of gold in circulation in the first half of the first century BC, which came to an abrupt end after the Roman conquest. Several gold treasure troves can be dated to the middle of the first century BC, suggesting that people hid their capital.[29]

In October, the legionaries marched about 500 kilometres to the southwest to set up their winter camp on the Loire, where grain was grown to feed the Roman troops. Caesar had now to set about the reorganization of the conquered territories and, to this end, he broke apart the patronage system. Before the Romans took power, the most powerful Gallic and Belgian tribes had been surrounded by smaller neighbouring tribes, their 'client tribes', who had to fight side-by-side with the more powerful tribe. In return, these powerful tribes had the duty of protecting their clients. Caesar put an end to this system by absorbing the small tribes into the Roman clientele. Among those who now acquired the Romans as protectors were the Eburones. They lived east of the Aduatuci, from whom they were now delivered. We will meet the Eburones again later in our story.

"The whole of Gaul was now peaceful", Caesar noted.[30] After all, virtually all the tribes had sent him envoys and pledged their loyalty. In Rome, the orator Cicero had more insight into the situation:

In Gaul, a very important war has been fought. Caesar has conquered powerful tribes, but they have not yet agreed to our laws, to mutual rights, or to a peace that can really be depended upon.[31]

• To the Edges of the Earth

Caesar needed a daily supply of around sixty tons of grain to feed his tens of thousands of soldiers, horses and pack animals. His requisitioning of this amount put so much strain on the Gallic tribes that, very soon, they began to regret pledging loyalty to the Romans. To temper the unrest, Caesar spread his troops around in 56 BC. In this way, the burden of providing supplies was more evenly distributed and revolts could be nipped in the bud, merely by the visible presence of the troops. Thus, a consolidation policy.

A section of the troops, commanded by Caesar, advanced into the territories of two Belgian tribes who had not submitted in the previous year: the Morini and the Menapii. The latter lived in what is now the Belgian and Dutch part of Flanders, the former in what is now French Flanders. For centuries, they would be seen as the "people at the end of the world", an expression coined by the poet Virgil,[32] that evoked the same associations as when Caesar said that the Belgae were "furthest away from the civilization and culture of the Province".

In the following fragment, the Greek historian Cassius Dio is speaking of the campaign on the Flemish coast. Although this writer lived three centuries after the events described in the *Gallic War*, his *Roman History* made use of older sources. Among these was presumably the historical work of Livy, who knew Caesar's propaganda and saw through it.

Then Caesar advanced against the Morini and their neighbours, the Menapii, in the hope that he could intimidate them and, because of his earlier military feats, could easily overpower them. However, he could not get the better of them because they did not have towns but lived in huts, had moved their most precious possessions to the most densely forested parts of the mountains, and caused the Roman assailants much more damage than they suffered themselves. It is true, Caesar tried to clear a way through the mountains by cutting down the trees, but he gave that up because of the magnitude of the enterprise and because winter had set in, and retreated.[33]

Perhaps we could identify the mountains that Dio writes about as the Kemmelberg near Ypres, where traces of habitation from the last centuries BC have been found. However, it is more likely that the mountains never existed beyond Dio's imagination, as it appears that he quite often coloured the facts to make them comply with contemporary ideas about the edge of the world. And yet, although his report is probably marred by erroneous geographical assumptions, Dio does not gloss over the fact that the Roman expedition to West-Flanders ended in a fiasco.

During this operation, the plan to cross over to Britannia must have taken root. Caesar had already seen all the things that the Britons exported to Gaul: tin, lead, copper, silver, hides, slaves, and hunting dogs. The notion that even pearls could be found there must have made the plan altogether irresistible. To be sure, there was no point in this action from a military perspective, but for a propagandist like Caesar, this did not constitute a problem.

It turned out differently. Unexpectedly, in the spring of 55 BC, two small tribes, the Usipetes and the Tencteri, crossed the Rhine. They had originally lived in the lands on the other side of the Rhine, which culturally had much in common with Gaul, and they also spoke the language of the Gauls. However, the German tribal federation of the Suebi had driven them out, so they eventually crossed into the northern areas of Gaul. They must have been a poverty-stricken group of refugees, driven on by hunger.

Their presence, somewhere in the southeast of what is now called the Netherlands, gave Caesar the opportunity, at a meeting of Gallic chieftains, to show that the Romans were just the right people to protect them from the barbarian hordes. In the meantime, the refugees had sent envoys who promised the Romans that, in exchange for land, they would become loyal allies. Caesar's only answer was that he did not need the support of people who could not defend their own lands. He then advanced along the Meuse, ready to play his role as protector of Gaul.

The Usipetes and Tencteri knew that this did not bode well for them, and so they sent new envoys, this time to inform Caesar of their intention of returning to their own lands. In this way, they hoped that the Romans would take no military action against them. During the truce which was observed during the negotiations, Caesar heard that the cavalry of the Usipetes and Tencteri had gone to collect grain somewhere and that only 800 young warriors had been left to guard the camp. He sent a small group of Roman cavalry to the camp with the task of provoking those left behind. And they, as expected, drew their weapons and rushed to protect their women and children. Cassius Dio goes on to say:

The older Usipetes and Tencteri condemned it (that the young warriors had allowed themselves to be provoked) and against the advice of the young ones went to Caesar to ask his forgiveness. They put the blame on a small group. He kept them in suspense, telling them that he would let them know shortly, and rushed to their fellow-tribesmen and attacked them while they were having a siesta in their tents, for, as long as their elders were with Caesar, they did not expect to be attacked. During this assault, Caesar killed numerous footsoldiers, who did not even have time to pick up their weapons since they were prevented from doing so by the wagons and the writhing of women and children. As soon as the cavalry, who were not present at that moment, heard what had happened, they left with the intention of fleeing to the Sugambri.[34]

Breaking a truce and an armed attack on a group of refugees were two violations of ancient international law, and the Roman Senate was quickly informed about it. This did not discourage Caesar. While the senators were discussing the (not very practical) proposal to redeem Rome's damaged reputation by handing over the unreliable commander of eight legions to the Usipetes and Tencteri, news came that Caesar had crossed the Rhine. He had demanded from the Sugambri, who lived in the Ruhr area, the extradition of the cavalry of the Usipetes and Tencteri. According to Cassius Dio, Caesar did so,

not because he expected that they would be handed over, but to have an excuse to cross the river. He was actually obsessed with the desire to do something that none of his peers had done, and hoped, furthermore, to keep the Germans far from Gaul by attacking them in their own country. When the cavalry were not handed over and the Ubii, who lived beside the Sugambri and were on a warlike footing with them, called in Caesar's help, he had a bridge built across the river and marched over. On the other side he found that the Sugambri had retreated into their forts. When the Suebi also began to quickly mobilize in order to come to the aid of the Sugambri, he withdrew within twenty days.[35]

In his own report, Caesar formulates it very differently. He claims that he had accomplished all his objectives for which he decided to take the army across: namely, to intimidate the Suebi, to wreak vengeance on the Sugambri, and to liberate the Ubii.[36]

The Senate, too, received an enthusiastic missive and forgot very quickly the way in which Caesar had treated the Usipetes and Tencteri. The members of that high college had not yet got over their amazement when they learned that Caesar had even crossed over the Channel. The campaign in Kent yielded just as little success militarily and politically as the expedition on the other side of the Rhine. The legions were more or less washed away, but again the Senate was deeply impressed. Cicero declared that Caesar's high command formed a more significant defence line for Italy against aggressive Gauls and Germans than the Alps and the Rhine.[37]

Meanwhile, the reality of the war was less elevating than Cicero's rhetoric. On returning from Britannia, Caesar settled his account with the Morini and the Menapii. He writes:

The following day, Caesar sent his legate Titus Labienus, with the legions he had brought back from Britannia, against the Morini, who had renewed hostilities. The marshes which they had used as a refuge in the previous year were too dry to offer a place of retreat, so almost all surrendered themselves to Labienus' control. The legates Quintus Titurius and Lucius Cotta, meanwhile, had led their legions into the territory of the Menapii. There they ravaged the fields, cut down the corn, and burned the buildings, because the Menapii had concealed themselves in the depths of the forest. Then they returned to Caesar.[38]

Although he does not say this in so many words, Caesar practically exterminated the Morini. In 57 BC they could put 25,000 warriors in the field, but by 52 BC only 5000.[39]

During the winter, the Romans assembled a fleet for a second invasion of Britannia. However, just before the crossing was to take place in the spring of 54 BC, Caesar learnt that the Treveri were planning to revolt, and he hastened to the valley of the Moselle. When it seemed that peace had been restored, he crossed over to Britannia with five legions and carried on an extremely successful campaign. At any rate, the Senate was deeply impressed and, after all, that was what it was all about.

A sherd from Vechten (Netherlands) with a depiction of a warship.

● Ambiorix

Only when he returned from Britannia did it become clear that it would have been better for Caesar to have remained on the Continent. During the absence of half of the occupation force, the social unrest which had been simmering for some time had burst to the surface and vented itself on the Roman troops dispersed across northern Gaul. The first target of the attack was the newly formed Fourteenth legion that was billeted on the Eburones, the tribe that Rome had taken over from the patronage of the Aduatuci.

The Romans were not aware that, in their absence, the Eburones had become dependent upon the Treveri, who first had their new clients rise in revolt. Only if the Eburones were successful would the Treveri show their true colours. If the Eburones were not successful, the Treveri would stay out the line of fire. Cassius Dio writes the following about this first major revolt against Roman authority.

This war was begun by the Eburones, under Ambiorix as chief. They claimed they had been roused to action because they were annoyed at the presence of the Romans, who were commanded by the legates Sabinus and Lucius Cotta. The truth was, however, that they scorned those officers, thinking they would not prove competent to defend their men and not expecting that Caesar would quickly make an expedition against their tribe. They accordingly came upon the soldiers unawares, expecting to take the camp without striking a blow, and, when they failed in this, resorted to deceit. For Ambiorix, after planting ambuscades in the most suitable spots, came to the Romans after sending an envoy to arrange for a parley, and represented that he had taken part in the war against his will and was himself sorry; but against the others he advised them to be on their guard, for his countrymen would not obey him and were intending to attack the garrison at night. Consequently, he made the suggestion to them that they should abandon Eburonia, since they would be in danger if they remained, and should move on as quickly as possible to some of their comrades who were wintering nearby.

Upon hearing this, the Romans believed him, especially as Ambiorix had received many favours from Caesar and seemed to be repaying his kindness in this way. They hastily packed up their belongings, and setting out just after nightfall, fell into the ambush, where they suf-

fered a terrible reverse. Cotta with many others perished immediately. Sabinus was sent for by Ambiorix under the pretext of saving him, for the Gallic leader was not present at the ambush and at that time was still thought to be trustworthy; on his arrival, however, Ambiorix seized him, stripped him of his arms and clothing, and then struck him down with his javelin, uttering boastful words over him, such as these: "How can such creatures as you wish to rule us who are so great?" This was the fate that these men suffered. The rest managed to break through to the camp from which they had set out, but when the barbarians assailed that, too, and they could neither repel them nor escape, they killed one another.

After this event, some others of the neighbouring tribes revolted, among them the Nervii, though Quintus Cicero, brother of Marcus Cicero and legate of Caesar, was wintering in their territory. Ambiorix added them to his force and engaged in battle with Cicero. The contest was close, and after capturing some prisoners alive, the chieftain tried to deceive him also in some manner, but, being unable to do so, besieged him. Thanks to his large force and the experience which he had gained from his service with the Romans, together with information that he obtained from the individual captives, he quickly managed to enclose him with a palisade and ditch.

There were numerous battles, as was natural in such a situation, and far larger numbers of the barbarians perished, because there were more of them. They, however, by reason of the multitude of their army, did not feel their loss at all, whereas the Romans, who were not numerous to begin with, continued to grow fewer and were hemmed in without difficulty. They were unable to care for their wounds through lack of the necessary appliances, and did not have a large supply of food, because they had been besieged unexpectedly. No one came to their aid, though many were wintering at no great distance; for the barbarians guarded the roads with care and caught all who were sent out and slaughtered them before the eyes of their friends. Now when they were in danger of being captured, one of the Nervii, who was friendly to them as the result of kindness shown him and was at this time besieged with Cicero, furnished a slave of his to send as a messenger through the lines. Because of his dress and his speech, which was that of the natives, he was able to mingle with the enemy as one of their number without attracting notice, and afterwards went his way.

In this way Caesar, who had not yet returned to Italy but was still on the way, learned of what was taking place, and turning back, he took with him the soldiers in the winter quarters through which he passed, and pressed rapidly on. Meanwhile, being afraid that Cicero, in despair of assistance, might suffer disaster or even capitulate, he sent a horseman on ahead. For he did not trust the Nervian servant, in spite of having received an actual proof of his good will, fearing that he might pity his countrymen and work the Romans some great evil; so he sent a horseman of the allies who knew the dialect of Eburones and was dressed in their garb. And in order that even he might not reveal anything, voluntarily or involuntarily, he gave him no verbal message and wrote to Cicero in Greek all that he wished to say, in order that even if the letter were captured, it should be meaningless to the barbarians and afford them no information. In fact, it was his usual practice, whenever he was sending a secret message to any one, to substitute in every case for the proper letter of the alphabet the fourth letter beyond, so that the writing might be unintelligible to most persons. Now the horseman reached the camp of the Romans, but not being able to come close up to it, he fastened the letter to a javelin, and acting as if he were hurling it against the enemy, fixed it purposely in a tower. Thus Cicero learned of the approach of Caesar, and so took courage and held out more zealously.

But the barbarians for a long time knew nothing of the assistance Caesar was bringing; for he journeyed by night, bivouacking by day in very obscure places, in order that he might fall upon them as unexpectedly as possible. But they finally grew suspicious because of the excessive cheerfulness of the besieged and sent out scouts; and learning from them that Caesar was already drawing near, they set out against him, thinking to attack him while off his guard. He learned of it in time and remained where he was that night, and just before dawn took up a strong position.

There he encamped seemingly in the utmost haste, for the purpose of appearing to have only a few followers, to have suffered from the journey, and to fear an attack from them, and so in this manner to draw them to the higher ground. And thus it turned out; for in their contempt of him because of this move they charged up the hill, and met with so severe a defeat that they carried on the war against him no longer.[41]

In the other camps, winter did not pass without incident, either. Titus Labienus, who was spending the winter in the area of what is now Luxembourg, discovered what Caesar himself should have actually discovered, if he had not been in such a hurry to leave for Britannia that spring: that the Treveri had been the real instigators of the revolt. Labienus' camp was also attacked, but he ousted his assailants and killed the organizer of the revolt. The Romans had repelled the attack.

• Genocide

The successes of 54 BC did not put an end to insurrection in the valley of the Meuse, and in the new year of 53 BC, the Romans took a dreadful revenge. In the meantime, Caesar had ten legions at his disposal, making more than 40,000 heavily-armed infantry, as well as an unknown number of cavalry recruited from allies in Gaul and the lands on the opposite side of the Rhine. In this year, a decision would be made about the future of the Low Countries: from then on, they would be Roman, purely and simply because the Romans could call up more and better-trained troops than the Belgae, who could only get support from some adventurers from the tribes on the opposite side of the Rhine.

Near the borders of the Eburones lived the Menapii, protected by their continuous stretches of marsh and woodland: of all the Gauls, only this people had never sent envoys to Caesar to negotiate peace. He knew that friendship existed between them and Ambiorix; he was also aware that, through the Treveri, they had formed an alliance of friendship with the Germans. He judged it essential to detach these sources of assistance from Ambiorix before launching a campaign against him. Otherwise Ambiorix might panic for his own safety and hide among the Menapii, or be forced to join up with the peoples over the Rhine.

This was the strategy Caesar adopted. He sent all the baggage of the army to Labienus among the Treveri and ordered two legions to set out and join him. Caesar himself set out for the territory of the Menapii, leading five legions now unencumbered by baggage. The Menapii did not muster a force, but relied on the protection offered by their geographical location: they fled into the woods and marshes and took their property with them.

Caesar divided his force with his legate Gaius Fabius and quaestor Marcus Crassus, quickly constructed causeways over the marshes, and advanced in three divisions, setting fire to buildings and settlements and seizing a large number of cattle and people. These actions compelled the Menapii to send him envoys to sue for peace. He accepted their hostages and insisted that he would count them among his enemies if they received Ambiorix or his legates within their borders. These matters settled, Caesar left Commius the Atrebatian (his Gallic ally) and some cavalry as a guard among the Menapii, and then set off against the Treveri.[42]

The Treveri had been brought under control by Labienus' winter campaign, but had received help from tribes from the other side of the Rhine, and that merited reprisals. Therefore, Caesar crossed the Rhine for the second time. In his own report, he holds forth for many chapters on the way of life of the Gauls and Germans and gives descriptions of curious animals such as the aurochs, the elk, and the unicorn. By this, he wanted to gloss over the fact that the campaign had been a failure. Cassius Dio is somewhat more succinct.

Once again, Caesar achieved nothing, and because he feared the Suebi, he soon withdrew.[43]

Yet, Caesar's campaign brought him more than simply the prestige of a second expedition into wild Germania: the Treveri no longer dared to trust the help of their eastern neighbours and kept the peace from then on, so that Caesar could now concentrate on the Eburones and their leader, Ambiorix. Caesar ordered his cavalry commander Lucius Minucius Basilus to carry out a surprise attack.

Basilus did as he was ordered. Contrary to everyone's expectation, the march was quickly completed and he caught many of the people off guard and still in the fields. Acting on their information he made straight for Ambiorix himself at the spot where he was said to be with a few of his cavalry. Fortune is indeed powerful in all things, and especially in military affairs: for it was by purest chance that he came upon Ambiorix while he was off guard and unprepared. The first people knew of Basilus' arrival was when they saw it – they heard no report or tidings of it. It was equally the operation of fortune that, after all his military equipment had been seized, and his horses and carriages captured, Ambiorix himself escaped death. This happened because the building was surrounded by trees (as are most Gallic dwellings – to avoid the heat they usually look for sites close to woods and rivers), and in such a confined space his friends and comrades held off the assault of our cavalry for a time. During the fight, one of his men set him on a horse, and the woods closed over the fugitive. In this way fortune played a part in bringing Ambiorix into danger, and in allowing him to escape.

It is a moot point whether it was deliberate that Ambiorix did not assemble his forces (because he decided not to give battle) or whether he was barred and prevented from doing so by lack of time and the unexpected arrival of our cavalry, and believed that the rest of our army was following behind. It is certain, however, that he sent messengers throughout the land, with orders that each man should look out for himself. Some of his men escaped into the Ar-

Hoard of coins found in Heers (Tongeren, Gallo-Romeins museum/ Gallo-Roman Museum); see also page 21.

dennes forest, others into the long stretches of marshland. Those who were close to the Ocean hid themselves in areas which the tides tend to turn into islands. Many left their own borders and entrusted themselves and their property to total strangers.[44]

Caesar was not a particularly devout man and his mention of the goddess Fortune as an excuse for Ambiorix' escape is just too thin. In order to further distract attention from the reversal, he refers to the geography of the country where he was fighting: he calls the islands that are thrown up by the tide one of the most curious phenomena on the edge of the world, and this fascinated his countrymen back home. The story is untrue: the Zeeland archipelago in the south-west of the Netherlands did not yet exist and the only islands that complied with his description, the Wadden Islands, were so far to the north that the inhabitants could not possibly have been involved in the events in the valley of the Meuse.[45]

During the weeks that followed, the Romans attacked the Eburones. Caesar does little to obscure the fact that in all directions, people were treated mercilessly. He himself proceeded

Pollen Studies

When archaeologists retrieve ancient pollen residues, they can judge what vegetation existed in a particular area in the past. Of course, it only has to do with plants that spread pollen, so trees cannot be registered. Yet, this disadvantage is relative, as some plants only grow in the vicinity of trees, and because their pollen is found, a conclusion can be drawn about the presence of trees.

By repeating the analysis for different periods, it is possible to ascertain what kind of development took place: deforestation, for example (a process that often goes hand in hand with population growth), or reduction in the area under cultivation (which points to a decrease in population). The geological and archaeological study of pollen is called palynology.

to the place where he believed that the Scheldt united itself with the Meuse.

In that area there was no distinct force, no stronghold, no garrison to defend itself in arms. Rather, the whole population was widely scattered. Each one of them had taken up position wherever some secluded valley, wooded location, or impenetrable marsh provided any hope of safety or defence. These places were familiar to the people living nearby. Thus it was a matter requiring considerable care, not so much to protect the army as a whole (for no danger could befall a united force at the hands of frightened and scattered men), but to keep the individual soldiers safe. This problem, however, did to some extent affect the safety of the whole army. For the desire for booty lured large numbers of them farther afield, while the woods with their strange and hidden tracks prevented them marching in close formation.

If Caesar wanted an end to the business, and the wiping out of a race of criminals, he must send out more groups of men and disperse the soldiers more widely. If, on the other hand, he wanted his maniples[46] to remain in formation, as the established and customary tactics of the Roman army required, the actual locality would act as protection for the barbarians – and certain individuals among them were daring enough to set up secret ambushes and encircle scattered Roman soldiers.

So far as was possible in such a difficult situation, what could be anticipated – with care – was anticipated. Caesar preferred to overlook a chance to inflict injury, even though everyone's heart was burning for revenge, rather than inflict it and at the same time do some harm to his soldiers in the process. He sent messengers to the neighbouring states and summoned them all to come in search of booty, and pillage the Eburones. In this way the lives of Gauls, rather than those of legionary soldiers, were put at risk in the woods. At the same time, once this multitude had surrounded them, the race and name of the Eburones would be wiped out as a punishment for their crime. A large number quickly assembled from every direction.[47]

Nothing more was heard of the Eburones. About three hundred days after they had defeated a Roman legion, they no longer existed as a political entity. Later, a tribe called the Tungri was living in the area. However, it remains to be seen whether the Eburones were all wiped out, as Caesar claims. From pollen findings in the area of Jülich in western Germany, it appears that the number of pastures and cornfields fell from the mid-first century BC and that forests were again growing there. On this land at least, there were no farmers any more. However, it is not clear if this is representative of the whole country of the Eburones.

Several treasure troves, like those of Heers (Belgium) and Amby (The Netherlands), are silent witnesses to the human drama that took place; people buried their coins for fear of Roman reprisals. Perhaps the owners were sold as slaves, or murdered; we will never know for sure. What we do know, however, is that they never again had the opportunity to recover their belongings. Only Ambiorix, who had managed to cause the destruction of his people in the blink of an eye, was able to escape to safety on the other side of the Rhine.[48]

For the Belgae – at least, for those who had survived – the war was over. However, in central Gaul, a revolt broke out that was even more widespread, but which had already been suppressed in the autumn of 52 BC. Clearing up the last vestiges of revolt took a further two years. Resistance had been broken. According to Caesar, a million Gauls were sold as slaves and about as many had been killed. Taken together, that is a third of the original population. How reliable these figures are is disputable, but it would seem that Gaul had indeed been made peaceful, as Caesar wrote: the peace of a cemetery.

Meanwhile, Caesar had other worries. It was inevitable that he and his rival Pompey would enter into a struggle for power over the Mediterranean world. The civil war broke out in January 49 BC, but did not last very long. Thanks to his trained legions, Caesar was the indisputable dictator of an empire that stretched from the Ocean to the Euphrates.

3 Romanization Begins

● **From Republic to Empire**

Caesar might have won the civil war, but this did not mean that his position was unassailable. Although many people were of the opinion that the Roman Empire had grown too unwieldy to be ruled by the centuries-old republican institutions, at the same time almost everyone was convinced that the administrative problems could not be solved by simply transferring power to the strongest general. Some senators wanted, at all costs, to prevent the installation of a military dictatorship, and murdered Caesar on 15 March 44 BC.

Immediately, a new civil war erupted between Caesar's murderers and his supporters. When his supporters won, they, in turn, began to quarrel among themselves. Finally, the only survivor was Caesar's grandnephew, Octavian. From 31 BC, he was the most powerful man in the Roman Empire. This time, there were very few who resisted a monarchy, as most senators had been persuaded by Octavian's propaganda that the only choice they had was between peace and freedom, between him and chaos.

It took Octavian a few years to find a way to present his absolute power so that it was acceptable. In 27 BC, he relinquished a number of special powers, brought in at the time of the civil war, saying that he was gratified that he had been able to restore the republic, and claiming to be happy with the honorary title Augustus ('the Exalted One'). This gave him enough prestige to be unbeatable in elections, and, from then on, he combined the authority of a number of different republican offices, including the governorship of the provinces where the legions were stationed. What was, in fact, a military dictatorship, was concealed behind a republican façade.

The sources we get our information from, with regard to this period, are mainly about the civil wars: the government of the provinces is only dealt with *en passant*. One exception is the Roman writer Varro, who quotes a visitor to the Low Countries, General Scrofa, who had seen how marl was spread on the soil. Marl is a soft rock consisting of clay and pulverized lime. It is used as fertilizer to counteract acidity in the soil. Readers of Varro at the time will involuntarily have thought of the fanciful stories told about the edge of the world.

When I was in command of the army in Gaul near the Rhine, I visited a number of spots where neither vines, olives nor fruit trees grew; where they fertilized the land with a white chalk which they dug out of the ground; where they had no salt, either mineral or marine, but instead of it used salty coals obtained by burning certain kinds of wood.[49]

There are no more sources available from the first years of the Roman conquest. Therefore, we can only surmise that the native populations suffered the same fate as those of other places in Gaul where there was unrest. In 46 BC, the occupying forces took action against Gallic rebels, and Roman victories over the Gauls are also recorded in the years 43, 42, 40, 39, 31, 29 and 26 BC. However, it is not known what actually took place. Were these revolts major or minor? Did they arise from frustrated pride, or had the Gauls resigned themselves to Roman rule and only rebelled because there was a question of failing government? We only know that we do not know.

Initially, the Romans did not go to much trouble setting up a civil government. Where this did take place, however, it had a military character whose function was to pacify the region so that troops could be withdrawn for the Roman civil wars. To this end, chieftains were forbidden to start a war against another tribe. Whoever was still eager to fight could indulge this urge to the full as a Roman ally. Lyon became capital of the conquered regions in 43 BC, in spite of the fact that it was then little more than a garrison town for Caesar's veterans. Evidently, in those years, economic and social development did not have any priority: each region was referred to as a *provincia*, a word that indicated an area ruled by a military commander and, as yet, did not have the meaning of the word 'province', as we know it.

Another military measure was to send out land surveyors to prepare the way for laying military roads. In the year of his death, Caesar had already ordered the whole Roman world to be mapped out, but it took until 27 BC before Agrippa, the Emperor Augustus' right-hand man, completed the world map. A fifth-century cartographer says:

From the time of the consulate of Julius Caesar and Marc Anthony the world was criss-crossed by four talented and excellent men: Nicodemus travelled through the east, Didymus through the west, Theodotus through the north, and Polycleitus through the south. Between the above-mentioned consulates and the tenth consulate of Augustus, the north was measured in twenty-nine years and eight months.[50]

In these years of geographic activity in the provinces, the Roman poet Virgil was composing his *Aeneid*. In it, he mentions the Rhine, which he calls *bicornis*, 'two-horned': a reference to the fact that the river divides itself into two branches, the Waal and the Lower Rhine, which empty themselves into the North Sea.[51] Another writer in those days was the Greek geographer Strabo, who was active in Rome. From his work we get the following description of the northern climates, possibly based on the observation of the already-mentioned Theodotus.

The weather over there is more rainy than snowy, and even when the sky is clear, fog can remain for so long a time that, during a full day, the sun can only be observed for some three or four hours about midday. This is also true for the land of the Morini, the Menapii, and their neighbours.[52]

Agrippa (Paris, Louvre).

With the aid of the geographical information collected, the governors began to construct roads. They first joined the Rhône with the Rhine: if the tribes east of the river should make incursions into the west, troops from the Province could advance quickly to the threatened zone. Around 39 BC, during a pause in the civil wars, Octavian and Agrippa visited Gaul, where they gave instructions for the construction of other roads. One of these was intended to open up the most northerly regions. It ran from Lyon northwards and forked at modern Langres into a northwestern branch, leading to Reims and Boulogne, and a northern branch, going to Trier and Cologne.

The army immediately put the military road to Cologne into service when Agrippa crossed the Rhine. Unfortunately, it is not clear who he intended to fight against there, but it seems likely that – just like Caesar in 55 BC – he had been called in to help the pro-Roman tribe of the Ubii, who lived on a warlike footing with their neighbours, the Suebi. Be that as it may, Agrippa invited the Ubii to settle on the west bank of the Rhine, where they were granted land that may once have belonged to the Eburones, the tribe that Caesar claims to have massacred. And so, the Ubii were to become the first inhabitants of the recently-founded town of Cologne. Another new settlement was Neuss, where a military base was founded that has recently been dated to 30 BC.

The Ubii were not the only migrants in those years. A group of Chatti, a tribe that was likewise at loggerheads with the Suebi, and amongst whom there was a lot of in-fighting, allowed the Romans to persuade them to move to the Betuwe, the country between the Lower Rhine and the Lower Meuse in present-day Netherlands. From the merging of the migrating Chatti and the original inhabitants, a new tribe would evolve that became known by the name of their land: Batavians, "the people from the fertile water land".

Of all these peoples, the Batavians are the most conspicuous for their courage. They do not hold a large piece of the bank of the Rhine, but do hold an island in the Rhine. At one time they belonged to the Chatti, but after an internal struggle they migrated to their present home, where they are now part of the Roman Empire. They still have the honour and distinction of an old alliance, evidenced by the fact that they are not humiliated by the obligation to pay tribute. No toll collector can milk them dry. Since they are free from paying taxes and special levies, they are ear-marked for battle, just like weapons and armour are marked, only to be used in war.[53]

The Roman historian Tacitus wrote these words at the end of the first century AD. What he really wanted to say, was that the Batavians paid their taxes in the form of military service, which illustrates that the Romans made clever use of the warlike character of the tribe, or indeed even helped to create it. Tacitus' casual mention of the migration of the tribe is not the only proof that this happened: archaeologists have ascertained that the coins the Chatti used in their original homeland are also found in the Lower Rhine-Meuse area in the Netherlands and very rarely beyond this.

Gaul remained a focus of interest for Augustus. When he was confirmed as dictator of the Roman world in 27 BC, he considered the organization of Gaul to be his first concern, and travelled there to improve local government. It was high time. Two years earlier the Morini had rebelled. Although this revolt had been bloodily suppressed, it worried the Romans that the rebels had been able to coordinate their actions with the incursion into Gaul of the German Suebi. It appeared that the enemies were beginning to organize. In response, the Romans decided to develop the lands of the long-haired Gauls. By integrating the Gallic and Belgian tribes more securely into the Roman world, these tribes would also experience the advantages to be gained from being part of the empire, and would not be so quick to take part in rebellions.

Augustus called a census to establish how many tax payers there were and how much taxable land each tribe owned. Then he divided the land into three parts, one of which was called Lugdunensis, another Aquitania, and the third Belgica. The latter province was larger than the area that Caesar had designated with the same name: the Moselle valley, the Vosges and parts of Switzerland were now included. We do not know exactly why Augustus changed the borders of Gaul, but it was not the only occasion on which he did this: re-drawing the provincial borders seems to have been very dear to the first Roman emperor.

• Urbanization

The ancient Greeks and Romans considered living in a city to be an expression of refinement. Anyone who was not urbanized was not really civilized. Therefore, Augustus' decision to give civil government to the Gallic regions went hand-in-hand with a policy of urbanization, and establishing veteran colonies was the simplest way of doing this. As it was, many former soldiers had lived in Mediterranean cities before they went into the army and were therefore accustomed to the urban way of life. Moreover, Rome could depend on these veterans whenever agitation threatened.

Other towns were established when the native population was given to understand that they had to evacuate their oppidum and build a town in the valley. The reason for this was that a legion could capture a town on a plain more easily than a fort on a hill. Knowing this, the inhabitants would think twice before rebelling. Yet, the natives also profited from the move: generally speaking, they came to live closer to a river, which offered advantages with regard to water supplies, sewerage, accessibility, and trade. An example is the hillfort of Kanne-Caestert in Belgium, which seems to have been abandoned in favour of the new town of Tongeren in the last quarter of the first century BC.

Bureaucratic rationality contributed to urbanization. The tribes often had different but equally important settlements. For example, the Nervii had at least four oppida, located in Asse, Elewijt, Binche and Bicquy. However, the Roman governors wanted that number to be reduced to only one administrative centre, in line with the system they were accustomed to in the Mediterranean coastal region, where each administrative unit consisted of a town surrounded by a handful of hamlets. Therefore, they chose a favourably situated settlement as the administrative centre of such a tribe, and made all the other settlements subordinate to it. If there was not a suitable candidate, then a centre was hastily created. Tongeren is an example of this, but also Bavay, which, from then on, was *the* town of the Nervii.[54]

Initially, such an administrative centre was not a town in a social-geographical sense. It is true that military land surveyors laid out the main streets in straight lines; but, along these streets, soldiers and veterans set up their homes, in the first place, in tents. This quickly changed. The tents were replaced by wooden houses with stone foundations – an architectural first for the Low Countries – and roofs of slate and tiles. At fixed times, the provincial governor came to administer justice in the town. The gods were given their temples. Merchants moved in, as they could depend on many potential customers with well-lined purses. For the same reasons, too, craftsmen settled in the towns: the growing population guaranteed them a sufficient turnover to be able to make a reasonable living. Finally, the native elite were very keen to be noticed by the Romans, and therefore they had their houses built in these 'boom towns'. It did not take long for the real town, in every sense, to evolve.

• The Native Elite

For the members of the native upper classes, there was an extra stimulus to settle in the new towns: the Romans were pleased to leave the administration to them. After all, they had been the authority in the tribe from time immemorial and traditionally enjoyed great prestige. By giving them the task of administering justice and taking decisions in other matters, the Romans increased the possibility that these would, in fact, be implemented. Moreover, the local elite had sufficient wealth to advance a part of the taxes, which simplified tax collection. Therefore, it was more practical for the Romans to leave the administration of the towns to the natives' own leaders than to build up a complicated and expensive civil service. The Roman governor limited himself to the tasks of higher jurisdiction and supervision.

In turn, the local elite had discovered that, although they had lost a part of their freedom (war with a neighbouring tribe was no longer permitted), they had managed to retain a large part of their traditional prestige by collaborating with the new masters. Whoever wanted to make a name for themselves on the battlefield joined the auxiliary units of the Roman army. An extract from Livy's historical work reports that two Nervian warriors, Chumstinctus and Avectius, played a major role in the war against the Sugambri in 10 BC.[55] Those who wanted to gain prestige in a peaceful way chose to become magistrate of a town. The Roman authorities granted protection under civil law to both its military allies and its administrative officials. Civil rights were a collection of personal privileges coveted by everyone.

Therefore, the members of the local upper classes were very pleased to cooperate with the Roman governor. As their own authority was underpinned by the power of Roman arms, they let their tribal brothers know, in no uncertain terms, who was behind them, and took to showing off with everything Roman. They wore Roman clothes, tried to speak Latin, sent their children to Latin schools: in short, they began to behave like Romans and, therefore, it was a natural progression for them to go and live in towns.

The elite gave the cue to the rest of the tribe. Very soon, those who were on a lower rung of the social ladder also went to settle in towns, wore tunics and togas, smattered their conversation with Latin words, and sent their children to school. Anyone who could not afford this, but still wanted to climb the social ladder, could join the army. When they were discharged, they would have the benefit of civil rights and could become members of the town council.

On 1 August 12 BC, the tribal chieftains from the Gallic provinces assembled in Lyon at the temple built that year to honour the goddess Roma and the Emperor Augustus. Those present offered sacrifices together for the welfare of the ruler, and discussed the most important administrative matters. This was to become a tradition: from that time on, they would travel to Lyon every year for a meeting with the provincial governors and other tribal chieftains.

The institution in Lyon of the imperial cult brings to an end the first phase of the transformation of Gaul and the southern Low Countries. In the regions to the north of the Alps, towns had grown up – even if they still appeared somewhat unsophisticated – and military roads had been constructed. Roman civil law had been introduced and the population was becoming more and more charmed with the Roman way of life. True, most native leaders and warriors would continue to call themselves 'Batavi', 'Ubii', or 'Menapii' for quite a long time; but, at the same time, they would increasingly consider themselves to be Roman citizens. Their grandfathers might have fought against the Romans, but they themselves were, as the geographer Strabo wrote, "at the present time in peace with the Romans." [56]

4 The Other Side of the Rhine

- **To War**

In the villa of Augustus' wife, Livia, at the foot of the Apennines, a strong earthquake was felt. A torch in the sky, which stretched from south to north, made the night as bright as day. A tower in the Garden of Caesar near the Colline Gate was struck by lightning. Under the leadership of governor Marcus Lollius, the Romans were caught in an ambush and suffered heavy losses.[57]

These words were written by one Julius Obsequens, the compiler of a catalogue of omens. Marcus Lollius, the governor of Belgica, should therefore have heeded this forewarning, when he learned that there were disturbances on the other side of the Rhine.

What had happened was that the Sugambri, Usipetes, and Tencteri had first taken some Romans in their lands prisoner and crucified them. Then they had crossed the Rhine to plunder the Rhine provinces and Gaul. From an ambush, they had attacked the Roman cavalry that had been sent to deal with them, and pursued the cavalry in retreat. In doing so, they unexpectedly ran into governor Lollius, but they also defeated him.

When Augustus heard of these events, he immediately marched against the barbarians. However, he did not get the chance to engage them in battle as, when they got to hear of his advance and of Lollius' war preparations, they returned to their homeland and concluded a treaty.[58]

It is not known where the invaders defeated Lollius. Nor is it very clear why the Sugambri and their allies became so aggressive. Raids certainly occurred quite often, but their only aim was to carry off booty. The fact that the raid of 17-16 BC was preceded by the execution of some Romans means that at least some Sugambri chiefs were in no mood for compromise and chose an all-out conflict.

What, in fact, were the Romans doing on that side of the Rhine in the first place? We can find a possible explanation in the events of 19 BC. In that year the Romans set up an army base on the Hunerberg at Nijmegen, making it abundantly clear that they were planning to advance to the north. In fact, it looked as if they intended to settle permanently in an area that the Sugambri considered as their hunting grounds. If, subsequently, soldiers such as foragers or envoys were arrested beyond the Rhine, it is quite likely that the tribes drew the conclusion that the Romans were up to no good. This is a possible explanation for the fact that trouble flared up when it did.

Lollius' defeat was a huge blow to Roman prestige. What was particularly mortifying was that one of the two legions involved, the Fifth Alaudae, had lost its 'eagle' standard. However, although it was deeply humiliating, it was no more than that. The unit went on operating, and the fact that Lollius was later appointed to important functions also leads us to conclude that the damage was well contained. Yet, the Romans had been given quite a scare. If Augustus had been under the delusion that he could develop Belgica without any interference from the tribes on the other side of the Rhine, then this was a wake-up call for him. That is why the Emperor decided to secure the area to be developed by carrying out a few punitive expeditions on the north bank.

However, it was not only revenge and shock effect the Romans were out to achieve. Just like all Roman leaders of his generation, Augustus conceived the *Imperium Romanum* (the regions dominated by the Romans) not as a sharply delineated whole, but rather as spheres of influence. In the centre was Italy, where the inhabitants had Roman civil rights. This nucleus was surrounded by an inner core of old provinces. They were reasonably civilized and the inhabitants could eventually acquire civil rights. An outer zone consisted of vassal kingdoms and tribes with which Rome had concluded treaties and where there were some Roman outposts. This layer was a buffer against absolute barbarism. Belgica, which had belonged to the periphery since Caesar's time, became part of the inner core once roads and towns were constructed there. Granted, the area was not yet Romanized, but it would be, sooner or later. That is why a new protective outer zone had to be created, where the tribal chiefs were made loyal to Rome by means of treaties. With this in mind, Augustus decided not only to carry out punitive expeditions, but also to incorporate the tribes across the Rhine in the outer layer of the Roman diplomatic system.

The Emperor whose motto had always been "hasten slowly" was certainly not about to rush into anything. Four long years the Romans took to prepare for war with Germania. To start with, Augustus annexed the La Tène states to the south of the Danube,[60] so that, when marching to the Rhineland, the legions would no longer have to take the route via the Province, but could use the Great Saint Bernard pass and the Saint Gotthard pass. Furthermore, he placed the part of Belgica situated on the Rhine under military rule: the region downriver he put under the authority of the newly assembled army of Germania Inferior, and upriver he stationed the likewise recently-formed army of Germania Superior. In order to be assured of divine support in the impending war, Augustus founded a temple in Cologne, which he dedicated to Mars, the god of war. Here was preserved the sword of Julius Caesar, who, in the meantime, had been deified. He was the first to have crossed the Rhine.[61] Finally, Augustus appointed his stepson Drusus as general of the five or six legions stationed there. At that time, the number of men in a legion was about 5,300.

In order to be able to move more easily from Nijmegen to northern Germania, Drusus had some canals dug out, which are known as the Drusus Ditches. Up to a short time ago, it was assumed that one of these was identical to the River IJssel, the watercourse running between Arnhem and Doesburg in Gelderland (Netherlands), but it has been established recently that this stretch of water was not dug out until the Middle Ages.[62] Another possible candidate is the River Vecht, north of Utrecht: an ancient river from which several meanders may have been cut off. If this is true, it would explain why our sources refer to 'canals' in the plural. Anyhow, it would seem that the water-ways dug by Drusus enabled people to sail from the Rhine to Lake Flevo, and from there – perhaps through another canal – to the Wadden Sea. There is also mention of a Drusus Dam, which was probably located at the Roman fort called Carvium near present-day Herwen and Lobith in Gelderland. Presumably,

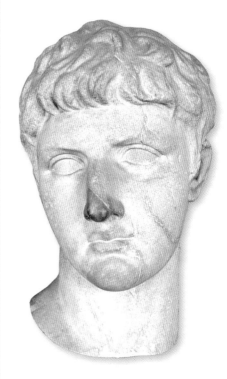

Drusus (Brussels, Koninklijke musea voor kunst en geschiedenis/ Royal Museums of Art and History).

Rome's first emperors (capitals letters), their wives (italics) and some other family members. The names underlined are those of the generals who undertook campaigns in Germania. Dotted lines are used for those adopted.

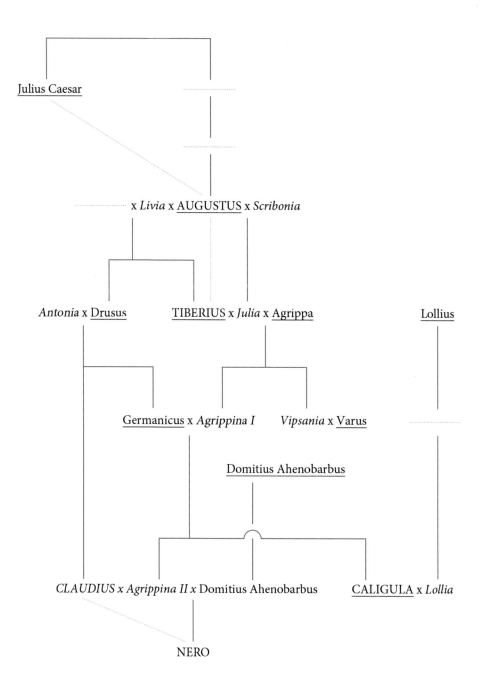

the function of the dam was to divert water into the Rhine that would otherwise have flowed into the Waal. Although nothing is very clear about these waterworks, it *is* clear that they were very impressive and changed the landscape drastically. No wonder the inhabitants of the Low Countries looked up to the Roman generals as gods.

Altering the landscape was not the only prerequisite for the Romans to move their armies to the Rhine. The economy of the Belgian interior had to undergo a metamorphosis as well. The practice of 'requisition in kind' was replaced by a tax payable in cash. Furthermore, this was not levied per tribe, but was calculated on the basis of rural estates, referred to as *fundi* in ancient fiscal jargon. These had names like Cortoriacum ('district of Koretoros', today's Kortrijk, Belgium), Feliciacum ('district of Felix', today's Velzeke, Belgium), and Tiberiacum ('district of Tiberius', today's Thorr, Germany). Here we see that the Roman tax services assumed duties which, up to then, had belonged to the tribes themselves. And so, the new rulers were also visible to those who lived outside the new towns.

In order to earn cash, the fundi had to produce goods for the market that, preferably, were commercially attractive. Consequently, in the last years before the beginning of our era, a Belgian pottery industry grew up. Along the banks of the Meuse and the Scheldt, red and black plates and drinking cups were produced by using the potter's wheel for the first time. The production of salt, iron, cattle, and cured Ardennes ham must have been set up as a commercial enterprise at this time, made possible by using German slave labour. However, the most important product was grain, bought principally by the army and the towns. When, in this period, the Romans constructed the military road connecting Boulogne and the principal towns of the Belgian tribes with the Roman military headquarters in Cologne (the Chaussée Brunehaut, see page 82), they did not choose the shortest route, but laid the road across the fertile loessial soil where there was extensive grain production.

In this way, a diverse and monetized market economy quickly developed. The speed at which this came about is evident from the fact that, in many settlements, coins have been found which had been chiselled in two to make small change. There was probably more demand for small change than the Roman mint masters had made available. That is not to say that the fast monetization was an indication that all transactions were done in cash: cash was probably only used for some payments, such as taxes and wages.

The consequences of this economic explosion were far-reaching. The region between Cologne and Boulogne became one of the most prosperous in western Europe; under the name of Austrasia, it was to play a major role in the early Middle Ages as well. The basis for this prosperity and power had been laid in the last decades BC, making this period one of the most crucial in the history of the Low Countries.

The last of the preparations for the German War was political in nature. As was mentioned at the end of the previous chapter, in August 12 BC, Roman administrators and Gallic leaders met in the temple of Roma and Augustus in Lyon. It is not known what they discussed, but doubtless Drusus explained Roman plans for the conquest of Germania and the Gallic chieftains informed him of how many troops they would contribute to the war.

• Drusus in Germania

Immediately after the conference ended, war broke out. Drusus' troops were ready for battle. The Sugambri hoped to avert the approaching disaster by a pre-emptive attack, but Drusus intercepted them as they crossed the Rhine. Cassius Dio describes what happened next:

Drusus crossed over to the country of the Usipetes from the island of the Batavians, and from there marched along the river to Sugambrian territory, leaving a trail of devastation along the way. He then sailed down the Rhine as far as the Ocean, concluded a treaty with the Frisians, crossed the lake, and invaded the land of the Chauki. There, he ran into danger when his ships were exposed to the Ocean tides. However, the Frisians, who had joined his expedition with their infantry, rescued him and enabled him to return when the winter set in.[63]

Relations between the Romans and the Frisians, the inhabitants of the present Dutch provinces of North Holland and Friesland, would remain friendly for a long time to come. The following year, Drusus was back on the Rhine after fulfilling an honorary post in Rome for a few weeks, as reward for what, after all, could only be considered as a punitive expedition. In 11 BC, however, it turned serious.

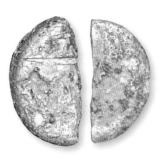

Coins from Velsen. The upper one is halved to make small change.

Early in the year, he set out again to make war, crossed the Rhine to subjugate the Usipetes, had the Lippe bridged in order to invade the country of the Sugambri, traversed this, and advanced into the country of the Cherusci on the Weser. This was made possible by the fact that the Sugambri had attacked the Chatti, angry at them for being the only tribe among their neighbours that had refused to join the alliance. Because of this stroke of luck, Drusus could traverse Sugambriland unnoticed. He would have crossed the Weser had he not run short of provisions, and had winter not set in. Besides, a swarm of bees had been seen in his camp.[64]

The last remark would have been incomprehensible, had it not been for the fact that the same story was passed down by Julius Obsequens, the compiler of the catalogue of omens. He wrote:

In Drusus' camp in Germania, a swarm of bees had nestled in such a way in the tent of the camp commandant, Hostilius Rufus, that they wrapped themselves around a guy rope and a javelin at the front of the tent.[65]

You did not need to be a soothsayer to understand that the bees stood for the Sugambri and that they would encircle a Roman army camp. And so, Obsequens goes on to say that "a great many Romans were killed in an ambush after this." Dio also reports that it would be a close call for Drusus:

He proceeded no further, and, on the way to seeking safety, encountered great danger. The enemies attacked him unexpectedly from ambushes. Once, they even trapped the Romans in a narrow ravine, almost annihilating them. The Roman army would have been completely destroyed if the attackers had not conceived a deep contempt for those they were surrounding, thinking that only the death blow was needed to finish them off. Consequently, the Germans in an undisciplined way got too close to the Romans. When they were defeated because of this, they no longer showed themselves to be so bold and were content to harass the Romans from a distance without getting very close. And now it was Drusus' turn to conceive a low opinion of the Germans, and so he built a fortified camp at the confluence of the Lippe and the Eliso, and another on the Rhine among the Chatti.[66]

We can possibly locate the 'narrow ravine' referred to, on the road from Paderborn to Bad Driburg, an age-old route from the Upper Lippe to the Weser. But this is not certain. What is definite, however, is that a fortified camp at the confluence of the Lippe and Eliso has been excavated at Oberaden, which, as the crow flies, is sixty kilometres east of the place where the Lippe flows into the Rhine. It was an immense complex where three legions and their auxiliaries could spend the winter in relative luxury, as appears from the discovery of Mediterranean products such as figs and olives, and even pepper from India. A little further up, there was a smaller camp at Beckinghausen, which seems to have served as a depot. Another camp, along the road from the Rhine to Oberaden, has recently been identified at Olfen. The military base on the Nijmegen Hunerberg would have been vacated at this time. However, the Romans retained a comfortable fort on the Kops Plateau, a hilltop. It was later to serve as a cavalry base.

With this, the war in the Low Countries came to an end. The only thing left for Drusus to do, in order to round off the enlargement of the outer layer of the Imperium Romanum, was to receive vassal monarchs and to accept their proofs of submission, about which Pliny the Elder wrote the following:

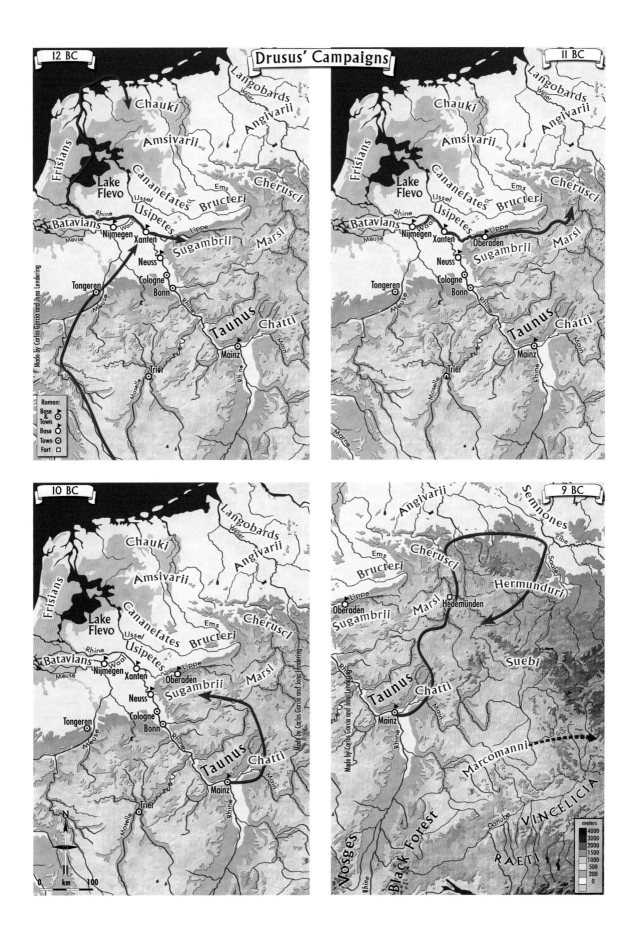

Drusus' Campaigns

12 BC

Chauki
Langobards
Weser
Angivarii
Amsivarii
Frisians
Lake Flevo
Cananefates
Ems
Cherusci
IJssel
Bructeri
Usipetes
Rhine
Batavians
Waal
Nijmegen
Xanten
Lippe
Meuse
Sugambrii
Marsi
Neuss
Tongeren
Cologne
Bonn
Rhine
Meuse
Taunus
Chatti
Mainz
Main
Trier
Moselle
Rhine

Made by Carlos García and Jona Lendering

Roman:
Base & Town
Base
Town
Fort

11 BC

Langobards
Weser
Chauki
Angivarii
Amsivarii
Frisians
Lake Flevo
Cananefates
Ems
Cherusci
IJssel
Bructeri
Usipetes
Rhine
Batavians
Waal
Nijmegen
Xanten
Lippe
Oberaden
Sugambrii
Marsi
Neuss
Cologne
Bonn
Tongeren
Rhine
Meuse
Taunus
Chatti
Mainz
Main
Trier
Rhine
Moselle
Marne

10 BC

Langobards
Weser
Chauki
Angivarii
Amsivarii
Frisians
Lake Flevo
Cananefates
Ems
Cherusci
IJssel
Bructeri
Usipetes
Rhine
Batavians
Waal
Nijmegen
Xanten
Lippe
Oberaden
Sugambrii
Marsi
Neuss
Cologne
Bonn
Tongeren
Rhine
Meuse
Taunus
Chatti
Mainz
Main
Trier
Moselle
Rhine

N

0   km   100

Made by Carlos García and Jona Lendering

9 BC

Angivarii
Semnones
Elbe
Bructeri
Cherusci
Saale
Ems
Hermunduri
Lippe
Oberaden
Marsi
Hedemünden
Sugambrii
Suebi
Rhine
Taunus
Chatti
Main
Mainz
Marcomanni
Rhine
Vosges
Black Forest
Danube
VINDELICIA
RAETI
Rhine

meters
4000
3000
2000
1500
1000
500
200
0

41

In the time of our ancestors, the most potent symbol of victory was that the defeated offered grass, an indication that they relinquished their land, and the soil that had nourished them and would be their grave. I know that this custom is still in use among the Germans.[67]

Immediately after this, Drusus travelled to Rome, where Augustus allowed him to hold a modest triumph. The following year, 10 BC, there was no fighting in northern Germania, but the Romans marched from Mainz across the Taunus Mountains to fight the Chatti. This done, they advanced to attack the Sugambri, yet again. During the fights, the Nervii Chumstinctus and Avectius distinguished themselves. The Roman supply base at Hedemünden probably belongs to this campaign.

The Sugambri seemed to be defeated at last. That is to say that, in 9 BC, Drusus left them alone. Instead, he led his soldiers into the valley of the Main against the Chatti, the Suebi and the Marcomanni. There was so much pressure put on the Marcomanni that their king, Maroboduus, decided to let his people migrate to Bohemia, where they would be safe from Roman weapons. In the summer, Drusus moved the war to the Cherusci on the Weser and explored the area along the Elbe. And that is where his career met a pathetic end: he fell from his horse, broke his leg, and died from the effects, while only twenty-nine years old.

● Tiberius in Germania

After the death of Drusus, his brother Tiberius was given supreme command. This experienced general trusted more to diplomacy than to violence. He demanded the tokens of submission that we are now familiar with.

A Roman helmet from Haltern (Haltern, Westfälisches Römermuseum/Roman Museum of Westphalia).

With the exception of the Sugambri, all the barbarians were sufficiently intimidated to send envoys for peace negotiations. These, however, achieved nothing: not at this time, because Augustus refused to conclude an armistice without the Sugambri, and not on a later occasion, when the Sugambri had sent envoys. These, however, had shown themselves to be so reluctant to compromise that they lost their lives because of it: Augustus had them arrested – they were both many and distinguished people – and deported to different towns where, feeling themselves to be deeply humiliated, they committed suicide.[68]

When the Sugambri had been deprived of their leaders in this way, Tiberius crossed the Rhine and would appear to have taken 40,000 people prisoner. However, they must have been amazed at the comparatively lenient treatment they were given, because they were not sold at the slave market, as was usually the case, but received orders to settle near Xanten, an army base on the other side of the Rhine. It was a compulsory version of the punishment the Ubii and the Batavi had received at an earlier date – migration to the Roman Rhineland – but, in this case, the deported people maintained a reasonable amount of freedom and stayed together as families. They merged with the original inhabitants to form a new tribe, the Cugerni.

Now that the Sugambri were living in secure detention at Xanten, the fortified camp at Oberaden may have been evacuated, and the camps at Haltern and Anreppen were possibly its replacements.[69] This signalled the end of the war and, to underline this fact, a temple was built for the imperial cult in Cologne, which was similar to the temple at Lyon. The Ubian settlement, whose original name we do not know, was renamed 'Altar of the Ubii'.

From this time, the countryside along the Lippe was cultivated using Roman agricultural techniques. This proves that the Romans settled farmers there – whether Roman veterans or allies – and this would suggest, again, that the development of Belgica was not sufficiently advanced to provision all the Rhine armies from the hinterland. Therefore, provisioning had to come from the fertile land near the rivers, in the same way that Caesar once exploited the Loire valley. Now that there were diplomatic bonds between all the tribes from the Rhine to the Weser, the region was secure. The cultivation of the valley of the Lippe also illustrates the self-confidence of the Romans, which was evident as well from the exploitation of lead mines in the Sauerland.

Yes, Rome had self-confidence in abundance; but, unfortunately, there were also limitations to it. That became obvious in the spring of AD 1, when a group of roaming Germani, the Hermunduri, arrived at the Danube. General Lucius Domitius Ahenobarbus assigned to them the region that the Marcomanni had evacuated a decade earlier, and accompanied them to their new lands. Now that he happened to be north of the Danube, he decided to undertake an exploration mission to the Elbe, where another group of Hermunduri still lived and he established friendly relations with the inhabitants of this region. After that, he advanced to the Rhine (see the map on page 58). By this time, it must have been summer. On the way, he was approached by a small number of expelled Cherusci, who wanted to return to their native lands on the Weser. Ahenobarbus sent a commander to meet them, but this meeting did nothing to appease the Cherusci and they revolted. In the course of suppressing the revolt, the Romans must have become aware that their road network was very inadequate, so they began the construction of new military roads, such as the *toghers* or plank roads across the marshy ground between the Rhine and the Ems.

The war lasted three long years, and, unfortunately, we know little more about it than that the Roman commander Marcus Vinicius was awarded an important distinction for his part.[70] But it is precisely our lack of information that is highly informative. The writer Gaius Velleius Paterculus, who makes a very brief mention of this major revolt, published his *Roman History* in AD 30 and dedicated it to Vinicius' grandson. The fact that Velleius, who served as an officer in the region across the Rhine from AD 5, does not report any glorious

Plank road (Oerlinghausen, Archäologisches Freilichtmuseum/ Archaeological Open Air Museum).

deeds in Vinicius' campaign suggests that it was a dirty war that his descendants preferred not to be reminded of.

When the revolt had been suppressed, Augustus decided to make an official province of the land between the Rhine and the Weser – in other words, incorporate it into the inner core of the empire. With hindsight, it can be said that he made this decision too hastily. The inhabitants of the lands on the other side of the Rhine had not yet been sufficiently integrated into the Roman economic world, and did not yet fully trust their new masters. However, after Vinicius' victory, the plan seemed feasible. For the second time, Augustus sent his stepson Tiberius to the north. His mission was, on the one hand, to demonstrate Roman power and mop up the last resistance, and on the other, to establish contacts with the tribes there, with a view to creating a new outer layer on the Elbe. In Tiberius' retinue was the twenty-four-year-old Velleius, who was later to praise his commander to the skies in his *Roman History*. It goes without saying that it would have been out of the question to voice criticism of the man who was emperor at the time of the publication of his work in AD 30; but, in Velleius' assessment of Tiberius, genuine sympathy seems also to be at play.

In the following fragment, he first describes a march through the Low Countries with the source of the Lippe as its destination. There is no mention of any battles. Then he writes about the campaign of AD 5, which began peacefully with the submission of the Chauki along the Wadden Sea, but deteriorated into a serious war against the Langobards in the area around modern Hamburg. Finally, he gives a report of a march along the Elbe, which demonstrates that, although Tiberius may not have been the first Roman general to reach the river, he was certainly the first to explore it over a very large distance.

I was sent with Tiberius to Germania as cavalry commander (in this function, I succeeded my father). Thus, for nine continuous years – first as cavalry commander and then as staff officer – I was witness to his superhuman achievements, in which I was allowed to assist to the extent of my modest ability.

I do not think that any mortal man will behold again a sight comparable to that which I enjoyed. In the most populous parts of Italy and throughout the length and breadth of Gaul, there were men who, when they saw their old commander again, were more joyful for themselves than for him. Truly, the tears of happiness which the sight of him drew from the soldiers, their passion, their unprecedented exuberant joy at being able to greet him again, their desire to shake his hand, unable to stop themselves from saying, "Is it really you, general? Are you safely back with us?" And then, "I fought under you in Armenia, general", "And I was in Raetia!" "You decorated me in Vindelicia!" "And me in Pannonia!" "And me in Germania!" … Words were inadequate. Yes, perhaps it is indeed difficult to credit.

He immediately invaded Germania, subdued the Cananefates, the Chattuari and the Bructeri, accepted the capitulation of the Cherusci, crossed the Weser, and penetrated into the regions beyond this river. For himself, he continuously demanded the most difficult and dangerous operations; he gave the command of the less hazardous actions to Sentius Saturninus. The fact that the summer campaign of that year lasted into December brought with it the advantage of tremendous successes, and we pitched our winter camp at the source of the Lippe, in the middle of the country.

Good grief, how many books could not be filled with all the operations we carried out under the command of Tiberius that summer! Our armies criss-crossed the whole of Germania; we were victorious over races whose names we hardly knew, and subjugated the Chauki, yet again. Their innumerable able-bodied men – huge in build and completely protected by the location of their homes – handed over their weapons and fell to their knees with their leaders before the raised seat of our commander, who was surrounded by a troop of our soldiers with their glittering weaponry. The Langobards, a race that even surpassed the Germans in fierceness, were also broken.

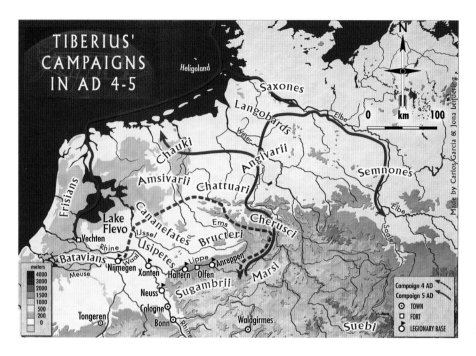

Tiberius' campaigns in AD 4 and 5.

Finally, something happened that nobody ever dared to hope would happen, let alone attempt to undertake: a regular Roman army was transported 600 kilometres from the Rhine to where the Elbe flows through the region of the Semnones and the Hermunduri. By an amazing combination of the good luck of the commander, his attention to detail, and perfect timing, the fleet linked up with Tiberius and his army at that point. It had sailed along the curved coast of the Ocean and up the Elbe from this unknown and uncharted stretch of water. Underway, it had subjugated many tribes and brought with it an abundance of supplies of all kinds.

I cannot refrain from inserting, in the middle of all these important events, the following incident, even if it is not so significant. We had set up camp on this side of the Elbe, while on the other side the weapons of the enemy warriors were gleaming. At each movement and every manoeuvre of our ships, they immediately slunk back. One of the barbarians – a man of advanced age with a remarkable build and, judging by his clothing, of high rank – embarked in a canoe (a hollowed-out tree trunk, as is customary there) and sailed it alone to the middle of the river.

There, he asked for permission to land unmolested on the bank that we were occupying, and to see Tiberius. Permission was granted. After he had moored his canoe, he gazed for a long time in silence at Tiberius and then exclaimed: "Our warriors are insane, for though they worship you as divine when you are absent, when you are present they fear your armies instead of trusting to your protection. But I, by your kind permission, Caesar, have today seen the gods of whom I merely used to hear; and in my life, I have never hoped for or experienced a happier day." After receiving permission to touch Caesar's hand, he again got into his canoe, and continued to gaze back upon him until he landed upon his own bank.

As victor of all the peoples and regions he had been to, Tiberius led his legions back to their winter quarters. His army had not suffered any losses and was completely intact; it had only been attacked once by means of an enemy ruse, with heavy losses on their side. There was nothing more to be conquered in Germania, except the tribe of the Marcomanni, who, under the leadership of Maroboduus, had left their lands and withdrawn to the interior, where they now lived on a plain surrounded by huge primeval forests.[71]

*Tiberius (Berlin, Altes Museum/
Old Museum).*

In this passage, there was mention of the Roman fleet. Some ships had sailed northwards along the coast of Jutland, eventually discovering the amber island that Pytheas had reached three centuries earlier. Still, it appears that the mystery had not yet been completely solved, as Heligoland could not have been the start of the trade route that ended at Bratislava. Therefore, there must have been another amber land. The Romans would continue to search for it.

For the time being, however, Augustus exploited the expedition along the coast of Jutland as propaganda. He bragged in his autobiography that his fleet had penetrated into the mother country of the once-fearsome Cimbri and Teutoni:

My fleet sailed east from the mouth of the Rhine over the Ocean to the end of the land of the Cimbri, where never before a Roman had dared to go, either by land or by sea. The Cimbri, the Charydes, the Semnones and other German peoples from that area sent envoys to request my friendship and that of the Roman people.[72]

It sounded so good. And it was true that the area between the Weser and the Elbe had now been incorporated into the outer layer of the global empire, while the regions between the Rhine and the Weser were ready to be transformed into tax-paying provinces. However, Augustus would quickly find himself forced to temper his optimism.

5 A Turning Point?

Coin with a portrait of Varus (Haltern, Westfälisches Römermuseum /Roman Museum of Westphalia). Before he became governor of Germania, he already had an imposing administrative career behind him. Two of his many posts had been commander of the Nineteenth Legion, during the conquest of the La Tène states south of the Danube, and the governorship of Syria.

• Varus' Defeat

From a military point of view, AD 5 marked the pinnacle of Augustus' reign. Germania had been completely subdued and Governor Publius Quinctilius Varus had begun the task of putting in place a civil authority. Meanwhile, the imperial troops were were making preparations to subdue the Marcomanni in Bohemia. An immense army was to be brought together at Bratislava on the Danube and at Marktbreit on the Main.

However, it never came to that. Just before Tiberius was to give the signal to attack, news reached him that there had been a rising in Pannonia (present-day Austria and Hungary) and Dalmatia (Croatia and Bosnia). The Romans were deeply shocked. In a hastily-convened meeting of the Senate, Augustus declared that the enemy could be at the gates of Rome within ten days. This prediction turned out to be too pessimistic, but the situation was indeed very worrying. It took until the summer of AD 9 for Tiberius to suppress the rebellion. And peace had barely been restored when the German Cherusci rose in revolt, annihilating the Seventeenth, Eighteenth and Nineteenth Legions.

Scarcely had Caesar put the finishing touch upon the Pannonian and Dalmatian war, when, within five days of the completion of this task, dispatches from Germany brought the baleful news of the death of Varus, and of the slaughter of three legions, of as many squadrons of cavalry, and of six cohorts – as though fortune were granting us this indulgence at least, that such a disaster should not be brought upon us when our commander was occupied by other wars. The cause of this defeat and the personality of the general require of me a brief digression.

Varus Quinctilius, descended from a famous rather than a high-born family, was a man of mild character and of a quiet disposition, somewhat slow in mind as he was in body, and more accustomed to the leisure of the camp than to actual service in war. That he was no despiser of money is demonstrated by his governorship of Syria: he entered the rich province a poor man, but left it a rich man and the province poor. When placed in charge of the army in Germania, he entertained the notion that the Germans, who are a people who are men only in limbs and voice, and cannot be subdued by the sword, could be soothed by the law. With this purpose in mind he entered the heart of Germania as though he were going among a people enjoying the blessings of peace, and sitting on his tribunal he wasted the time of a summer campaign in holding court and observing the proper details of legal procedure.

But the Germans, who with their great ferocity combine great craft, to an extent scarcely credible to one who has had no experience with them, and are a race to lying born, by trumping up a series of fictitious lawsuits, now provoking one another to disputes, and now expressing their gratitude that Roman justice was settling these disputes, that their own barbarous nature was being softened down by this new and hitherto unknown method, and that quarrels which were usually settled by arms were now being ended by law, brought Quinctilius to such a complete degree of negligence, that he came to look upon himself as a city praetor administering justice in the forum, and not a general in command of an army in the heart of Germania. Thereupon appeared a young man of noble birth, brave in action and alert in mind, possessing an intelligence quite beyond the ordinary barbarian; he was, namely, Arminius, the son of Sigimer, a prince of that nation, and he showed in his countenance and in his eyes the fire of

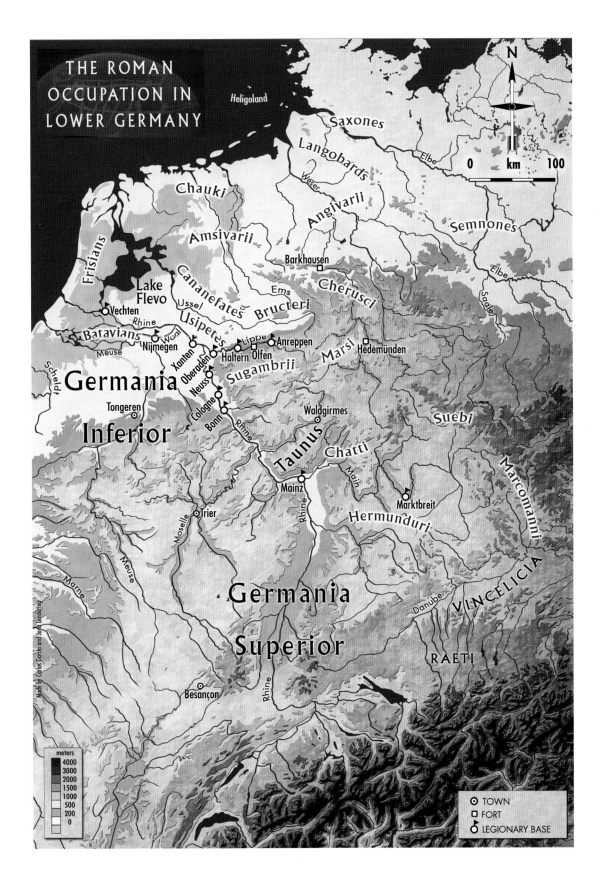

THE ROMAN
OCCUPATION IN
LOWER GERMANY

Heligoland

Saxones

Langobards

N

Elbe

0 km 100

Chauki

Angivarii

Weser

Semnones

Amsivarii

Frisians

Barkhausen

Elbe

Cananefates

Ems

Cherusci

Saale

Lake
Flevo

IJssel

Usipetes

Bructeri

Vechten

Rhine

Lippe

Anreppen

Marsi

Hedemünden

Batavians

Waal

Xanten

Haltern

Olfen

Nijmegen

Meuse

Oberaden

Sugambrii

Neuss

Scheldt

Germania

Cologne

Waldgirmes

Suebi

Tongeren

Bonn

Rhine

Marcomanni

Inferior

Taunus

Chatti

Mainz

Main

Marktbreit

Moselle

Trier

Rhine

Hermunduri

Meuse

VINCELICIA

Marne

Germania

Danube

Meuse

Superior

RAETI

Rhine

Besançon

Made by Carlos García and Jona Lendering

meters
4000
3000
2000
1500
1000
500
200
0

⊙ TOWN
□ FORT
⚲ LEGIONARY BASE

49

the mind within. He had been associated with us constantly on private campaigns, and had even attained the dignity of equestrian rank. This young man made use of the negligence of the general as an opportunity for treachery, sagaciously seeing that no one could be more quickly overpowered than the man who feared nothing, and that the most common beginning of disaster was a sense of security. At first, then, he admitted but a few, later a large number, to a share in his design; he told them, and convinced them too, that the Romans could be crushed, added execution to resolve, and named a day for carrying out the plot.

This was disclosed to Varus through Segestes, a loyal man of that race and of illustrious name, who also demanded that the conspirators be put in chains. But fate now dominated the plans of Varus and had blindfolded the eyes of his mind. Indeed, it is usually the case that heaven perverts the judgement of the man whose fortune it means to reverse, and brings it to pass – and this is the wretched part of it – that that which happens by chance seems to be deserved, and accident passes over into culpability. And so Varus refused to believe the story, and insisted upon judging the apparent friendship of the Germans toward him by the standard of his merit. And, after this first warning, there was no time left for a second.

The details of this terrible calamity, the heaviest that had befallen the Romans on foreign soil since the disaster of Crassus in Parthia, I shall endeavour to set forth, as others have done, in my larger work. Here I can merely lament the disaster as a whole. An army unexcelled in bravery, the first of Roman armies in discipline, in energy, and in experience in the field, through the negligence of its general, the perfidy of the enemy, and the unkindness of fortune was surrounded, nor was as much opportunity as they had wished given to the soldiers either of fighting or of extricating themselves, except against heavy odds; nay, some were even heavily chastised for using the arms and showing the spirit of Romans. Hemmed in by forests and marshes and ambuscades, it was exterminated almost to a man by the very enemy whom it had always slaughtered like cattle, whose life or death had depended solely upon the wrath or the pity of the Romans.

The general had more courage to die than to fight, for, following the example of his father and grandfather, he ran himself through with his sword. Of the two prefects of the camp, Lucius Eggius furnished a precedent as noble as that of Ceionius was base, who, after the greater part of the army had perished, proposed its surrender, preferring to die by torture at the hands of the enemy than in battle. Vala Numonius, lieutenant of Varus, who, in the rest of his life, had been an inoffensive and an honourable man, also set a fearful example in that he left the infantry unprotected by the cavalry and in flight tried to reach the Rhine with his squadrons of horse. But fortune avenged his act, for he did not survive those whom he had abandoned, but died in the act of deserting them. The body of Varus, partially burned, was mangled by the enemy in their barbarity; his head was cut off and taken to Maroboduus and was sent by him to Caesar; but in spite of the disaster it was honoured by burial in the tomb of his family.[73]

These events, which took place in September AD 9, have gone down in history as the Battle of the Teutoburg Forest. Its significance has been somewhat exaggerated, especially in the nineteenth century. Although it is true that the Romans never again attempted to dominate the lands beyond the Rhine in the way Drusus and Varus had attempted, they continued to control the region by means of a series of treaties, as Tiberius had done. This lowering of their sights was possible because there was no longer any necessity to rule the valleys of the Lippe and the Main: Belgian Gaul and the west bank of the Rhine were so well-developed by this time that sufficient grain could be grown to feed the legionaries and auxiliaries. However, according to Tacitus, the Romans did maintain positions on the other side of the Rhine and supervised the empire's outer zone efficiently enough to guarantee that the Gallic regions remained secure. It is true that there were a number of attempts to return to the strategy of Drusus and Varus, but after AD 41, the Emperor Claudius closed this chapter. We will return to this subject later.

Meanwhile, the larger work that Velleius Paterculus wanted to write, giving a fitting description of the events, either was never written or has been lost in the course of centuries. The only extensive account comes from the *Roman History* by Cassius Dio, which was written about two centuries after the battle.[74] He says that a report came first of a revolt by a tribe living far away, and that Varus went with his army to put it down. Dio's description of the place is very detailed … and very unreliable: the mountains, ravines, and impenetrably dense forests that he mentions belong to the stereotypical geography of every land on the edge of the world, while he ignores the most characteristic feature of the battlefield, namely the marshes. He describes how the army was hampered by the presence of wagons, pack animals, women, children and personnel, and consequently got separated. The chaos was exacerbated by heavy rains, wind, and falling trees. Now that the army was in disarray, the Germans seized their chance to harass them; but, despite heavy losses, the legions managed

Reconstruction of a German warrior (drawing by Johnny Shumate). The hairdo is based on the relief shown on page 137. Although he appears to be no match for his Roman opponent, light-armed men like these could swiftly hit and run, and might inflict great damage on their enemies. After the Battle in the Teutoburg Forest, swords became more fashionable, and over the decades, the Germans adapted to the legionaries. On the other hand, the shape of the German shield boss was to be copied by the Romans.

Reconstruction of a Roman legionary in the reign of Augustus (drawing by Johnny Shumate). The legionary is wearing a mail shirt and is carrying a light, oval shield. His main weapon is a sword, while he also carried a dagger. Not shown are the spears, which the soldiers used at the beginning of close combat.

to take a hilltop, where they spent the night. The next day, they reached open country and the situation seemed to improve, but when the troops marched into the woods again, the Germans resumed their attack.

Dio does not mention the setting-up of a second camp, but there must have been one, because it is mentioned by the historian Tacitus (see page 59). The Romans set off from this camp on the third day. That evening, they had no chance to build a camp, and when the fourth day dawned, Varus understood – again, according to Dio – that everything was lost and took his life.

The fight at Kalkriese
(drawing Graham Sumner).

The battlefield has been traced to a place called Kalkriese, about fifteen kilometres north-east of Osnabrück and quite a distance to the northwest of the range of hills which were christened 'Teutoburg Forest' in the nineteenth century. Besides weapons from diverse army units, the archaeologists have also found artefacts at Kalkriese that point to the presence of clerks, women, merchants, and other non-combatants. The conclusion is unavoidable: a Roman army together with a considerable number of private citizens died here. That it has to do with the defeat of AD 9 can be concluded from the coins found, which are all dated before that year.

The excavated battlefield is bordered on the north by an extensive bog and, in the south, by a range of hills where the archaeologists came across a long earthen wall. It is clear that the Romans were caught between the bog and a group of Germans who bombarded them from behind the wall. The skeleton of an ox tied to what was only a part of a wagon shaft is one of the most fascinating finds. The animal must have broken free when the wagon got stuck and the shaft broke, and the driver did not have the time to catch it and bring it back. That driver had stuck plants into the cowbell, as if he had wanted to dampen the sound. Some of the plants appear to have been in bloom, and thus the botanists could date the fighting at Kalkriese to the month of September.

Another silent witness to the Battle of the Teutoburg Forest – or better said, to the panic among the Romans in the days following – is Waldgirmes, a Roman town that is being excavated near Wetzlar on the River Lahn in Germany. The Romans had settled there at the beginning of our era, intending to stay for a long time. This is evident from the fact that they built the central meeting hall on stone foundations. However, the town was inhabited for less than ten years and was evacuated in great haste: a precious, gilded equestrian statue was left behind.

News of the defeat sent shock waves through Rome, where extra troops were put on guard to prevent disturbances. It is said that, for several months, Augustus did not cut his beard, and sometimes he would cry out to the deceased Varus to give him back his legions. Every year from then on, he observed the date of the disaster as a day of mourning.[75]

The unfortunate Varus had been a friend of the most illustrious Roman aristocrats and had married into the family of the emperor. After the death of Augustus in AD 14, Varus' family tried to clear his name and restore his damaged reputation. They put the blame on his legionaries, who, they said, had not fought bravely enough. Velleius, who had known some of those who had been killed, considered that to be defamation of character. Therefore, he petulantly rounded off his report of the event by giving a short list of their heroic deeds.

Tribute must be paid to Lucius Asprenas, the deputy of his uncle Varus. Supported by the two courageous and energetic legions under his command, he saved the non-active units [who had remained behind on the Rhine] from this great disaster. Quickly marching to the quarters in Germania Inferior, he strengthened the allegiance of the vacillating peoples on this side of the Rhine. (By the way, there are also those who believed that, although he brought the survivors to safety, he confiscated the possessions of the dead and gladly accepted the inheritances of those who had died with Varus.)

The heroism of Lucius Caedicius, prefect of the camp, was also very praiseworthy, and also the bravery of those who were besieged at Aliso by an overwhelming force of Germans. Although almost unequipped, they overcame almost unendurable difficulties, which were almost insurmountable because of the numbers of the enemy. With a well-worked-out plan and after short deliberation, they watched their chance, and with the sword they fought their way back to their comrades.

We can conclude that Varus, a sincere man of good intentions, lost his life and his splendid army more through his poor military judgement than through poor performance of his soldiers. When the Germans were venting their rage upon their captives, Caelius Caldus, a young man who was not inferior to his illustrious ancestors, acted as befitted him: he took a part of the chain with which he was bound, and brought it down upon his head with such force that both his brains and his blood gushed from the wound and he died immediately.[76]

Three legions (XVII, XVIII, XIX) were wiped out during the battle and with them went their eagle standards. Publius Annius Florus – who lived a century after these events, but who cites an almost contemporary report – tells what happened to one of the eagles and, furthermore, recalls the fate of the lawyers who were employed at Varus' court.

Nothing could be bloodier than the defeat that took place in the marshes and woods. Nothing could be more intolerable than the cruelties perpetrated by barbarians, especially on the captured lawyers. They put out the eyes of some of them and cut off the hands of others; they sewed up the mouth of one of them after first cutting out his tongue, which one of the barbarians held in his hand, exclaiming: "At last, you viper, you have ceased to hiss."

The body, too, of the commander himself, which some soldiers with a sense of decorum had buried, was disinterred. As for the standards and two of the eagles: they are still in the possession of the barbarians. The third eagle was wrenched from its pole by a standard bearer, before it could fall into the hands of the enemy. He carried it concealed in the folds around his belt and hid himself with it in the blood-stained marsh. The consequence of this disaster was that the empire, which had not stopped on the shores of the Ocean, was checked on the banks of the Rhine.[77]

The cenotaph of Marcus Caelius of the Eighteenth Legion. He was fifty-three-and-a-half years old when he fell in the Battle of the Teutoburg Forest (Bonn, Rheinisches Landesmuseum/State Museum of the Rhineland).

Hiding the eagle did not help very much. It must have been retrieved from the bog by the victors. We are quite sure about this, because the Romans were to recover all three eagles from German tribes. It seems that Florus uses a very old, or an unreliable, source.

• Tiberius' Punitive Expeditions

After his victory, Arminius created a new tribal coalition that, besides his own tribe, included the Bructeri, Marsi, Angivarii, Langobards, Chatti, Semnones, and probably the Chauki. The Frisians remained loyal to Rome, but even without them, in the view of many Romans, Arminius' tribal coalition constituted a real threat. Although Lucius Asprenas had made the Rhine border secure, it was evident that more than that was needed in order to stabilize the situation. In the spring of AD 10, Tiberius marched with reinforcements to the north, an event which Velleius seizes on to sound the trumpet of praise once again.

When Tiberius had heard the news, he hurried back to Augustus and assumed again his usual task of protector of the Roman Empire. Dispatched to the German front, he first secured the provinces of Gaul, reorganized the armies, reinforced the garrisons, and crossed the Rhine with his troops to the lands on the other side. Although his father Augustus and his fatherland would have been quite satisfied with only a defensive campaign, Tiberius measured himself by the standard of his own greatness and proceeded to launch an offensive action against the tribes there. He marched to the heart of the country, opened the frontier roads, devastated fields, burned houses, routed anyone who dared to resist him, and returned, without any losses among the troops. Covered with glory, he took up winter quarters.[78]

In AD 11 and 12, the Romans also fought on the east bank of the Rhine; but, as the historian Tacitus expresses it, that campaign had more to do with obliterating the shame of the Teutoburg Forest than with a lust for booty or the acquisition of new territory.[79] Tiberius' biographer, Suetonius, tells the following about this campaign:

He demanded even stricter security measures than usual. At the crossing of the Rhine, he only gave permission for the whole army train to be transported, after he, standing on the bank, had first inspected the contents of every transport wagon himself, to make sure that nothing was carried across for which he had not given permission and which was not strictly necessary. Once on the other side, he imposed on himself the following rules of behaviour. He ate his meals sitting on the bare ground, slept in the open, and passed on to his officers all his orders for the next day in writing, even when an unexpected command had to be given. To these measures, he added the regulation that any officer who had doubts about a particular point had to consult him personally at any hour of the day or night.

He imposed iron discipline on his men, and carried out all sorts of punishments and humiliations that had become obsolete. He even demoted a legionary commander because he had sent a few soldiers to escort a freedman who had gone across the river to hunt. Although he left very little to chance and seldom took risks, at one time, after a victory, he narrowly escaped with his life when a Bructerian penetrated his inner circle. Fortunately, this man betrayed himself by his nervousness.[80]

In the summer of AD 12, Augustus considered the dishonour to have been sufficiently wiped out. Tiberius made peace and held a triumph in Rome. The following year was peaceful. No fewer than eight legions were garrisoned along the Rhine, considerably more than the five or six that had previously been stationed there. The commander of the Rhine army was the nephew of Tiberius and a son of Drusus.

• Germanicus in Germania

On 19 August AD 14, the Emperor Augustus died. He was succeeded by Tiberius. In Rome, the succession went without incident, but in Cologne and Xanten the legions mutinied. Germanicus paid off the mutineers, but when peace was restored, he thought it a good idea to focus the attention of his soldiers elsewhere. Nothing seemed more appropriate for this than an attack on the peoples on the other side of the Rhine. At that moment, these tribes were celebrating a festival and, after two years of peace, nothing could be further from their minds than an attack by Rome.

The historian Tacitus writes about the event. The Caesian Forest he mentions lies in the

Germanicus (Stuttgart, Altes Schloß/Old Castle).

56

present-day Ruhr area and the Marsi lived east of this. After attacking this tribe, the Romans proceeded to focus their aggression on those who had in the meantime settled in the lands along the Lippe, and finally invaded the eastern part of what is now the Netherlands.

The Germans lived at a short distance, unconcerned as long as we were occupied with the public mourning because of the death of Augustus, and then by our dissensions. But now the Roman general, in a forced march, cut through the Caesian Forest and advanced along the road that Tiberius had starting laying, pitching his camp there. The front and rear of the camp were protected by an entrenchment, the flanks by timber barricades. From this point the legionaries marched on through dark forests. They deliberated if they should take the shortest and more usual of two roads or another where there were more obstacles. This second road was less trav-elled and therefore not guarded by the enemy. The longer road was chosen but the pace was increased. His scouts had brought word that there were going to be festivities for the Germans that night, a feast that was to be celebrated with public entertainment and an official banquet.

[The commander of the army of Germania Inferior] Caecina had orders to advance with some unencumbered legionaries, and to clear away any obstructions from the woods. The le-gions followed at a moderate interval. They were helped by a bright starlit night. When they reached the villages of the Marsi, they threw a cordon of soldiers round the enemy. The inhabit-ants were still lying scattered around in their sleeping area and at tables, without the least sense of fear. They had not even stationed sentries in front of their camp. Everything was in complete disarray; nobody was in the least bit worried. But, although there was no air of fear, it could not be said that the inhabitants were at peace either: this was just the languid and heedless ease of half-intoxicated people.

To extend the scope of the raid, Germanicus divided up his revenge-hungry legions into four groups. Over an area of seventy-five kilometres, they wasted the country with sword and flame. Neither the women and children nor indeed the old people could hope for mercy. Houses and sacred places were razed indifferently to the ground, among them, the most noted religious centre of these tribes, known as the forest of Tanfana. None of our soldiers were wounded as the people they had been cutting down did not resist, they being half-asleep, unarmed and stum-bling around separated from each other.

The Bructeri, Tubantes, and Usipetes were alerted by the carnage. They dug in along the forest passes through which the army would have to return. This came to the commander's ear, and he prepared himself for the march and for the fight. A detachment of cavalry and a number of auxiliary cohorts led the way, followed by the First Legion. The baggage-train was in the mid-dle, guarded on the left flank by the Twenty-First Legion and on the right flank by the Fifth. The Twentieth Legion formed the rearguard and was followed by the rest of the allies.

The enemy, however, made no move until the whole line was filing through the woods. Then they began to provoke small skirmishes at the front and the flanks, while they threw their full weight at the rear. The lightly-armed cohorts were hemmed in by the closely-packed Germans. Then Germanicus rode up to the men of the Twenty-First on the left flank, and, raising his voice, he called out to them repeatedly that now was the moment for them to efface the memory of the mutiny. They should rush forward and attack the enemy and in this way turn disgrace into glory. Flushed with enthusiasm, they charged against the enemy, broke through their lines and drove them into the open where they cut them down. At the same time, the troops who made up the vanguard emerged from the forest and began the construction of a fortified camp. From this time on, the campaign went without incident, and the soldiers moved into their winter quarters. Thanks to their recent success their self-confidence had returned, and they put behind them the events of the past.[81]

This is Tacitus' version, to which he adds the remark that the operation worried Tiberius. The historian is insinuating that this was because the Emperor was jealous of Germanicus'

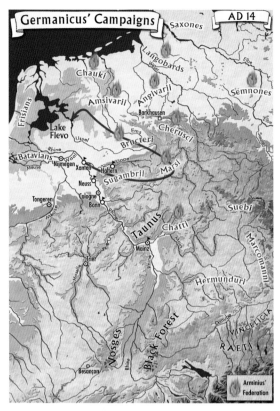

military prestige, but the real reason could well have been that he had his doubts about the resumption of the German War.

In the following summer, various expeditions took place. Germanicus attacked the Chatti in the Taunus Mountains; the commander of the army on the Lower Rhine, Caecina, advanced to the upper reaches of the Ems; a certain Pedo advanced with some cavalry (perhaps Batavian?) through the lands of the Frisians and the Chauki to the mouth of the Ems, proceeding upstream from there. When the two last-mentioned armies met on the Upper Ems, Germanicus ordered the fleet to transport his own soldiers to the north, so that

the infantry, the cavalry and the fleet met at the same time on the river mentioned. A unit, promised by the Chauki, was given a place in the Roman army. Lucius Stertinius, who had been sent out on the orders of Germanicus with a unit of lightly-armed soldiers, drove the Bructeri to flight, while they were in the act of burning and devastating their own possessions. While murdering and plundering, Germanicus found the eagle standard of the Nineteenth Legion, which had been lost with Varus.

From there, the army marched on to the very extremity of the lands of the Bructeri, razing the whole area between the Ems and the Lippe on the way. They were now not very far away from the Teutoburg Forest, where it was said the remains of Varus and his legions still lay unburied.

Consequently, Germanicus was seized by a longing to pay a last tribute to the fallen legionaries and their leader. The soldiers that were present were moved by pity at the thought of their kindred and their friends who had lost their lives, ruminating on what can happen in war and what can overtake a man. After Caecina had been sent ahead to explore the obscure forest area, and to build bridges and dams across the marshes and the treacherous terrain, they advanced into the sombre tract of land that was just as dire to see now as it was in their memory.

Varus' first camp with its broad sweep and measured spaces for the command centre, showed clearly that it was the work of three legions. At the second camp, it was obvious by the half-ruined wall and shallow ditch that here the remains of the already depleted army had bedded down. In the area between the two camps were layers of bleached bones, scattered here and there in little heaps, depending on whether the men had been fleeing or had been standing fast. Broken spears and carcasses of horses were lying nearby, and human skulls were nailed to tree trunks. In the open spaces of this area, they found the macabre altars on which the tribunes and centurions of the first rank had been slaughtered.

Survivors of the bloodbath, who had managed to get away from the battle or had escaped after being taken prisoner, gave a running commentary: here is where the commanders died, there is where the eagle standards were taken; on this spot, Varus was hit for the first time, and on that spot, he had run himself through in his misery. They pointed out the podium where Arminius had addressed the army; they told how many crosses had been erected for the prisoners, how many torture pits had been dug out, and how, in his arrogance, Arminius had mocked the standards and eagles.

Therefore, the Roman army that was there six years after the disaster, buried the bones of the three legions. Nobody knew whether he was consigning to earth the remains of a kinsman or of a stranger. They were all kinsmen to them as they were all bound together with bonds of blood. While they were working, the soldiers grew increasingly bitter about the enemy, alternately experiencing emotions of great sorrow and intense hatred.

Germanicus laid the first sod for the erection of the funeral mound. It was a gesture of deep tribute to the deceased and of intimate union with the grief of those present. [82]

Following this, Germanicus left for the Ems, and his army and the fleet returned to their winter camps. One of these camps must have been the fleet base at Velsen; we will refer to this later.

A lead bar, now in Tongeren's Gallo-Roman Museum, with an inscription that is not fully comprehensible. It is certain that the first words translate as 'From the Emperor Tiberius Caesar Augustus,' but the meaning of the two last words is not very clear. What we can glean from it, however, is that the material originated in Germania, and if we take the text at its face value, it would suggest that the Romans still exploited the lands on the opposite bank of the Rhine during the reign of Tiberius (AD 14-37). However, another interpretation could be that the bar came from the land of the tribes who had emigrated to the west bank of the Rhine, which was called Germania *in the second half of the first century. That this name was customary during the reign of Tiberius, however, remains to be proven. The isotopic examination did not supply any clues: the metal could have originated either in Sauerland (on the right bank of the Rhine) or in the Eifel mountains (on the left bank).[83]*

Caecina returned overland to the Rhine and suffered heavy losses on the way when he marched through the bogs by using the plank roads that Ahenobarbus had laid. That must have set the Emperor Tiberius thinking even harder about the wisdom of engaging in warfare there. Now that Belgica was producing sufficient grain, there was no longer any necessity for Roman troops to continue to occupy the valleys of the Lippe and the Main. Would it not be better to reach a peace agreement, as had been done in 8 BC and in the autumn of AD 12? Naturally, Caecina's losses would have to be avenged by carrying out one more punitive raid through free Germania; but after that, it seemed to be more sensible to station the legions along the Rhine again, and to keep the German tribes in check by means of diplomacy.

Therefore, in AD 16, the last Roman campaign east of the Rhine took place. On the other side of the Weser, in the area of Minden, it came to a battle between Germanicus' legions and Arminius' tribes. The Romans triumphed and, in the aftermath, they recovered the second of the three lost eagles.

From then on, the Romans refrained from punitive raids, so the inhabitants of the area no longer needed to submit to the authority of one leader. Arminius was killed three years later by one of his own family. His tribal confederation disintegrated. Tiberius turned out to have correctly interpreted the situation when he had ordered the end of the German War: the independent tribes seldom collaborated and thus no longer posed a threat to the Empire.

• A Turning Point?

Was the fight in the Teutoburg Forest decisive? The question is important, as, in the nineteenth century, the battle grew into a decisive conflict in the European imagination, the result of which would have been that the Rhine became a sort of absolute border which initially separated the Romans from the Germans, then the Romance people from the Germans, and finally France from Germany. In other words, there seemed to be a direct line running from AD 9 to 1870, 1914–1918, and 1939–1945.

The only ancient writer who talked about the decisive character of the battle was Florus, who was of the opinion that "the Empire which had not stopped on the shores of the Ocean, was checked on the banks of the Rhine". However, he wrote these words 120 years after the event and almost 90 years after the reorganization of the army by the Emperor Claudius. Claudius decided to give up direct control of the lands on the opposite bank of the Rhine and it seems that, at the same time, he gave orders to redeploy Roman troops to man the permanent reinforcement of the border itself (the *limes*). It is conceivable that this reorganization of the army was, in fact, the true cause of the schism in Roman policy, and that Florus has superimposed a situation which prevailed at a later date onto the events of September AD 9. Therefore, there is no need to give any credence to his report.

This is a point on which archaeology should help ancient history further; but, alas, the archaeologists have dated all the Roman finds along the Lippe and the Main, almost as a matter of course, to before AD 9. Therefore, potentially conflicting information has been ignored and, at the moment, we have no clear picture of the Roman presence in the lands

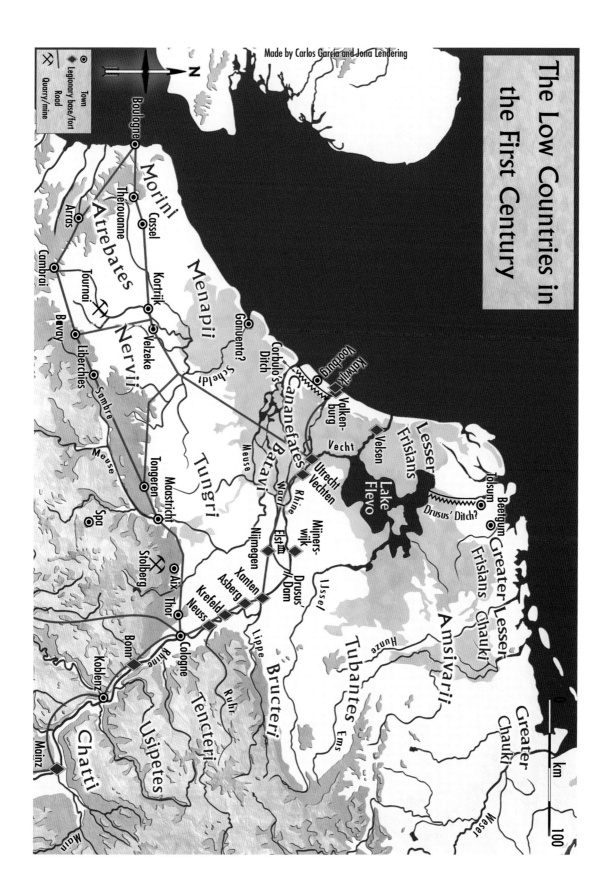

The Low Countries in the First Century

Made by Carlos García and Jona Lendering

across the Rhine. This means that the significance of the Battle of the Teutoburg Forest is, in fact, an open question and a weak point in our knowledge of the ancient world.

Be that as it may, obvious changes were taking place. Before the arrival of the Romans, the region between the Somme and the Weser was a cultural and linguistic continuum in which the Lower Rhine did not mark the border. The Middle Rhine was also insignificant as a border because, on both sides, the La Tène cultures were dominant and the people spoke related languages. In the centuries that followed, the lands on the west bank of the Rhine would increasingly assume a Roman character, while the lands in the east would become more Germanized. Newer, bigger and more aggressive coalitions of German warriors were to arise, creating significant problems for the Romans in the third century.

Long before the German wars began, Caesar had written that the Rhine constituted the border between the Germans and the Gauls. This was a ridiculous thing to say at that time, but from the moment the Romans gave up the occupation of the east bank of the Rhine, whether that was after the Battle of the Teutoburg Forest or after the Claudian reorganization of the army, reality began to adapt itself to Caesar's assertion.

6 Chauki and Frisians

• Life on the Edge of the World

In Roman eyes, the most valiant barbarians lived farthest from civilization. Of all the Gauls, Caesar regarded the Belgians as the most valiant, and he typified the Nervii "considered particularly fierce by the Gauls themselves". Virgil called the Morini the "people at the end of the world", and Tacitus confined himself to saying that, of all the Germans, the Batavi were the most intrepid. There was another tribe, however, that lived even further from the Mediterranean world: the Frisians. That they are not mentioned anywhere as being the bravest of the brave is due to the fact that, as a rule, their relationship with Rome was harmonious.

The Frisians had concluded a treaty with Drusus in 12 BC. That same autumn, they

The naval base at Velsen (drawing Graham Sumner).

saved his fleet when it got into difficulties in the Wadden Sea. From that time on, it is very likely that there was a small Roman garrison in Friesland, although it is not known where this could have been located. Winsum, in the Dutch province still called Friesland, has been mentioned as a possibility. There, typical Roman artifacts, such as amphora fragments, have been excavated, but there are no traces of a fort and the finds are also a bit too young. Something similar can be said of the Roman camp of Bentumersiel in northwestern Germany, in Chaukian lands, where Roman artifacts have also been dug up, but where no traces of habitation have been found. We have more information about the Roman fort at Velsen, North Holland, which was in use from AD 15. As we will see on page 74, we are almost certain that this fort was called Flevum in Latin.

The Frisians paid an annual tribute of a number of ox hides to the tax collector, more as an acknowledgement of the emperor's authority than as a substantial contribution to his coffers. The Frisians living around Velsen probably paid less in tribute than they earned on supplying food to the fort: the soldiers, numbering about thousand, ate more than 350 tons of grain annually, which must (partly) have been bought from the neighbours. The Romans also bought cattle and other products. The Frisians' relations with the Romans were lucrative in every respect, and they continued to be loyal to them after the Battle of the Teutoburg Forest.

There were four races living in the northern coastal region. The Lesser Frisians lived to the west of Lake Flevo in what is now called North Holland, and the Greater Frisians inhabited present-day Friesland. Further east, the Romans differentiated between the Lesser and Greater Chauki: the former tribe lived in the provinces of Groningen and Ostfriesland (in Germany), the latter between the mouths of the Weser and the Elbe. In spite of this variation in names, these tribes had a lot in common. They shared the same economy, characterized by a system of mixed agriculture and trading along far-flung coastal regions. They also had more or less the same manner of living, determined by their similar coastal habitats.

This coastal habitat particularly intrigued Roman writers. That the Chauki lived on the very edge of the world was already evident from their habitat: it belonged neither to the sea nor to the land, and the elements there behaved in quite a remarkable way. Travelling across Lake Flevo, people had to be on the alert for drifting pieces of peat, as described by Pliny the Elder.

Oak trees grow there in abundance, right up to the water's edge. When the trees are undermined and torn loose by floods, they sail upright through the water, with huge islands of soil trapped between their roots. Our crews were often terrified by the riggings of their numerous wide branches when, as if intentionally, the current drove them straight at the ships riding at anchor for the night. Consequently, our ships had no other option but to fight a naval battle ... with trees! [84]

Pliny was a no-nonsense man, but a superstitious visitor would surely have concluded that the edges of the world had begun to erode in these regions. There, primordial chaos constantly threatened. The place where the Oer-IJ estuary broke through the dunes, somewhere near present-day Castricum in North Holland, was given a nickname by the Romans: "the Pillars of Hercules",[85] an ironic reference to the boundary posts that the demigod had erected at Gibraltar to keep monstrous creatures out of the civilized world.

• The Terrors of the Wadden Sea

For the Greeks and Romans, the most striking thing about the Ocean was the phenomenon of ebb and flow, a spectacle that is almost unnoticeable in the Mediterranean Sea. The turn of the tides of the northern seas sometimes caused problems: for instance, when Drusus realized that his ships had suddenly run aground. Of course, it could also happen the other way around, as when a Roman fleet got into difficulties because the tide suddenly turned and the flow unexpectedly surged. The following excerpt from Tacitus' *Annals* describes how something very much like this happened in AD 15, when the Roman army was marching back after burying the dead in the Teutoburg Forest.

In the meantime, Germanicus had handed over the Second and Fourth Legions, which he had transported by ship, to Publius Vitellius, who would lead them overland from there. In this way, the ships would not be so heavily laden should the water become too shallow or the ships strand because of the ebbing tide. For Vitellius, the beginning of the march went without incident: the ground was dry and the flood was not very deep. However, it was not long before a strong north wind began to blow. It was the time of the equinox, during which the Ocean is at its wildest, and the marching columns began to get into great difficulties.

The area became flooded: the sea, the beach, the countryside, it looked the same all around, and one could not see where it was dangerous or safe, where it was deep or shallow. The men were tossed about by the waves, sucked into whirlpools; pack animals, baggage, dead bodies, all drifted around and crashed into each other. The different units got completely mixed up; one moment, the water came up to their armpits, and the next, it was up to their mouths; sometimes, too, they lost their footing and were torn apart or swallowed up by the water. They could shout and call encouragement to each other, but that was no help whatsoever if the water surged at them. It made absolutely no difference whether they fought for all they were worth, or just gave up; whether they were very alert, or paid no attention; whether they were calculating, or left it all to chance: everything and everyone was equally overwhelmed by the violence of the weather.

Finally, Vitellius managed to reach higher ground and succeeded in bringing the columns to safety there. They spent the night without food or fire; many soldiers had lost all their clothes or were physically battered. They were no less pitiable than the soldiers who had been caught in an ambush by the enemy. But at least, in the latter circumstances, one could die with honour while, in this situation, there was only an inglorious end.

Day came and there was land again. They pushed on towards the river, which Germanicus had set course to reach. The legions embarked. A story had gone around that they were all drowned. Nobody believed that they were alive until they saw, with their own eyes, that Germanicus and his army were back.[86]

It was never far from Roman minds that there were sea monsters and mountains at the periphery of the world. This is evidenced by the following fragment, in which Tacitus casually mentions the rocky islands, capes and cliffs that, according to the Romans, must have been part of the coast of Groningen, although it is in fact a vast plain. There, even without all these reputed horrors, it can be pretty rough, as Germanicus experienced when he returned from his last campaign in Germania in AD 16.

At first, the sea was calm and the only thing that could be heard was the sound of the oars of a thousand ships and the wind in their sails. But very soon, dark clouds packed together and hailstones clattered down. Because the strong wind blew this way and that, the men's vision was marred by treacherous waves that made steering the ships very difficult. In their panic and unfamiliarity with this sea and its vagaries, the soldiers distracted the crew or tried to help them in the wrong way, by which they seriously hampered the work of the professional sailors who, after all, were the only ones with the necessary experience.

Then all heaven and the expanse of the sea came into the clutches of the south wind. This wind drew its strength from the high degree of moisture in the countryside of Germania, the

A Roman helmet from the first half of the first century AD found on a beach on the island of Texel, Netherlands, which can perhaps be linked to the Germanicus expeditions (Leiden, Rijksmuseum van oudheden/National Museum of Antiquities).

deep rivers and infinite banks of clouds. It was made more devastating by the bitter cold caused by the region's proximity to the north. It dragged the ships with it and scattered them here and there over the Ocean, or sent them scurrying in the direction of islands with steep rocks or hidden shallows. After they had escaped with much difficulty and had a short respite, the tide turned and went in the same direction as the wind, so that they could not hold anchor or bail out the inrushing flood of water. Horses, pack animals, pieces of luggage and even weapons were jettisoned to lighten the holds, which were taking in water directly through the sides or indirectly through enormous waves that washed over the ship.

The Ocean is wilder than any other sea, and such extreme weather conditions can only be found in Germania. The extent of the disaster was therefore consistent with the awful weather, and surpassed everything imaginable. Besides, no one had ever before experienced anything like this: surrounding them were hostile shores on all sides, or a sea so ubiquitous that they believed themselves to be at the very edge of the world. A number of ships were engulfed in the waves; more were stranded on remote islands. Because of the lack of human habitation there, the soldiers died of hunger, except for those who kept themselves alive by eating the flesh of the horse cadavers washed up on the same shore. Germanicus' trireme was the only ship that eventually landed on the coast of the Chaukian lands. Days and nights he spent on the cliffs and promontories, exclaiming that the disaster was his fault, and his friends had trouble preventing him from throwing himself into the sea as well.

When the level of the water eventually dropped and the wind was favourable, the heavily listing ships turned back, with the help of whatever oars were still functioning and with clothing stretched across the rigging for sails. Some were taken in tow by other ships that were in somewhat better condition.

They were hurriedly refitted and sent out again to search the islands. During the rescue operation, a very large number of those stranded were picked up. Many returned after they had been ransomed by the Angivarii [a German tribe on the Weser] – who, shortly before, had submitted to us – from tribes who lived deeper in the interior. Some of them had even been swept as far as Britannia and had been sent back by the local chieftains. Everyone who came back from distant regions told the most amazing stories: enormous tornadoes, birds that nobody had ever heard of before, sea monsters, and enigmatic forms that were half man and half beast: they had seen or imagined them in their terror.[87]

The same event has been described by the poet Albinovanus Pedo, who is presumably the cavalry commander we met on page 59. In the following exuberant poem, he reports on the fears which his men were met with:

They have already left the sun and the daylight far behind them.
Now they find themselves, they notice, beyond the part of the

world familiar to them, and fully determined, they go on
through the shadow land forbidden to man,
towards the edge of the world and to the furthest coast,
located in the west. And they see the world sea swell
and tilt ships up – while all around under the slow waves
huge monsters, the dogs of the sea, and tempestuous freaks
are carried along. Powerful thunder heightens their intense fear.
They see it all for themselves: Favourable winds forget to blow,
so that, drawn into quicksand, they are stuck, left to die a slow death,
horribly rent by the jaws of sea monsters. Someone high
in the forecastle, who, with a sharp eye was trying unsuccessfully
to pierce the dark night to catch a glimpse of the world
that was hidden from him and did not succeed,
relieved his frustrated feelings with words like these:
"Where are we racing to, now that daylight itself is fleeing from us?
The most remote edge of the world shuts us off
with eternal darkness from the earth disc we have left.
Are we looking for people who live under another heaven
in a realm where wind is unknown? The gods forbid people
to see the borders of their creation with their human eyes.
Turn around! On this strange sea we are violating
with our oars the sacred waters, and we are disturbing
the quiet peace of the divine dwelling place.[88]

In short, the Wadden Sea was terrifying, and it was vital to know which islands really existed and which were, in fact, sand-banks that would be covered by water at high tide. The Roman officer Pliny the Elder reports:

Reconstruction of a farm-house on the terp of Ezinge in the Dutch province of Groningen (Alphen aan de Rijn, Archeon).

Model of the terp at Feddersen Wierde (at Cuxhaven), Germany. Such large settlements are only known from the lands of the Chauki, who lived along the Wadden Sea in the area of modern Groningen and Emden.

There are twenty-three islands known to the Roman armies. The most important of these are Burcana, called the Bean Island by our boys because wild pigeon beans grow there in abundance, and the island that the soldiers call Amber Island because of the amber there, although the barbarians call it Austeravia, and finally Actania.[89]

A very strange coast, indeed, where strange products originated. But there were more unusual things, such as the terps (or mounds) on which Frisians and Chauki lived. (By the way, Chauki is probably a corruption of *Hauhae*, a word meaning something like 'high homes'.) The following description also comes from Pliny, who visited the area during the military operations that took place there in AD 47.

I have observed the lives of those who survive without trees or crops. My admiration impels me to say something about their way of living. In the north, I have seen, for example, the Greater and Lesser Chauki. There, the Ocean in its awesome expanse floods over an immense plain twice a day with long intervals, so that you wonder whether this secret, constantly-disputed region is now actually land or sea.

In this place, a poverty-stricken tribe lives on high terps and hand-built platforms, which raise their homes above the known high-water mark. When the waves wash over the surrounding land, the inhabitants look like seafarers, but when the water subsides, they have the appearance of shipwrecked people. Then, around their huts, they try to catch the fish that escape with the seawater. Because they cannot keep cattle, they do not nourish themselves with milk, in contrast to their neighbours who do; and because the vegetation in the surrounding countryside is regularly washed away, they cannot hunt for game. They plait rope from reeds and rushes, from which they, in turn, make nets for fishing. They dig out mud with their hands and dry it more in the wind than in the sun. This turf they then use to heat up their food, but also their bodies, frozen by the north wind. They have no other drink than rainwater, which they catch in holes in the forecourt of their houses. And these people actually have the gall to declare – now that they have been subjugated by the Romans – that they have lost their freedom! And that is just possible, as Fate often punishes people by letting them live.[90]

In the eyes of Pliny, accustomed to the towns of Italy and the comfortable military base at Xanten, the terp-people lived in abject poverty. However, his observations are biased, and, in his efforts to adequately illustrate the misery of their conditions, his description is inconsistent. After all, if the land was so poor that not even trees could grow there, then where did the people get the wood to build the stilts under their huts and cottages that Pliny had seen? In fact, it was not nearly as bad as he paints it, and the terp-dwellers' economy was quite varied.

Where Pliny was right, however, was in his description of the landscape. The coastal area did indeed lie open to the sea and was flooded twice a day. On this coastal plain, different-

The Tolsum writing tablet was excavated in 1914 and was considered for a long time to be a contract for the sale of an ox. Renewed research has shown that it is probably a debt note to a slave, which can be dated to 23 February AD 29. How the tablet came to be in Friesland is a mystery.

sized terps arose on which sometimes single farm-houses, or sometimes several, were erected. The inhabitants did not sit down to meals of wild game, but their diet was more varied than Pliny reports. They collected eggs and hunted birds and seals. Furthermore, they had at their disposal vast stretches of pastureland on the mud flats, where cattle and, especially, sheep grazed. Sometimes they engaged in farming behind low dykes. And although the soil was saline, it was still possible to grow barley, flax, and pigeon beans on it.

As the Roman writers were fixated by the idea that those living on the edge of the world were barbarians, they failed systematically to see that, in the lands around the Wadden Sea, barter was a very important part of the economy. The Frisians and Chauki not only exported cheese, salt, wool, leather, and sheep, but they were also a link in the transit chain for slaves, hides, and amber. The Roman troops on the Rhine were among their most important customers; therefore, it is not so odd that, in the terps, glass, pottery, jewellery, and statuettes of gods were found that had originated in southern regions. (So many Roman coins have been found that it is assumed that they played a role in economic exchange, though more for hoarding than as a means of payment.)

Furthermore, the Chauki and Frisians sailed up the coasts of the lands that are now called England, Flanders, and Denmark. As we shall see in the next chapter, Chaukian pirates harassed the Romans in the North Sea. Other seafarers had more peaceful intentions

A dugout canoe with raised boards from Zwammerdam.

Velsen

In Velsen, between Amsterdam and the North Sea, archaeologists have found the remains of two Roman forts. Velsen 1 was constructed in AD 15, during Germanicus' retaliatory campaigns, and appears to have been abandoned not so long after a fierce battle. As indicated in the main text, this could have had something to do with the Frisian Revolt in AD 28. Velsen 2 was occupied in the forties.

Velsen 1 was a naval base, controlling the main outlet from Lake Flevo, a water course referred to as the Oer-IJ. The original triangular fort was surrounded by a ditch and a single wall that graduated into a quay with a pier. Further up, it became a platform and two piers. At least thirteen ships could moor at the same time, while further downstream ships could be hauled onto dry land. A structure outside the fort, whose function initially baffled the archaeologists, has been identified as a bathhouse.

After AD 21, the fort was enlarged and took on a trapezoidal form. No fewer than three defensive ditches were dug, which suggests that an attack was expected. Over the inner ditch a drawbridge was build, the harbour was enlarged, and a strikingly heavy structure found there, has been identified as a beacon. The piers were partly replaced by open jetties, allowing the water to flow more freely. It looks as if the Romans were beginning to be troubled by the silting up of the Oer-IJ.

In the third phase of Velsen 1, a second trapezoidal fort was built on to the original. The garrison increased from five hundred to a thousand men. This extension, which lay downstream, was surrounded by two ditches. A remarkable find was an unusually large well, which was connected to the harbour via an aqueduct: it looks as if the rowers of the ships were supplied with fresh water from this well. This double fort was attacked around AD 28 and, shortly afterwards, it was abandoned.

Because of an extreme marine flood or transgression in medieval times, the top layers of Velsen 1 have been washed away. Only the deepest parts, such as the bottoms of the timber piles, have survived. Consequently, we cannot form a good picture of the buildings within the walls. However, the finding of tent pegs indicates that the soldiers, at least initially, lived in tents. Whether more permanent military quarters with shallow foundations were built at a later date, cannot be established, as their remains have long since disappeared. Several lumps of wattle and daub, found in a well, have a herring-bone structure, suggesting that they belonged to a monumental, decorated wall, such as the headquarters or the home of the commander.

An examination of traces of restoration work carried out on the large well shows that the base was again, albeit briefly, in use in the spring of AD 38. Velsen 2 must have been built immediately after that, a little further downstream. From the few excavations carried out there, it is certain that the fort was surrounded by different ditches, which were re-routed several times. The conclusion can therefore be drawn that the fort, which was almost certainly a naval base, was functional for quite some time. The discovery of coins minted by the emperors Caligula and Claudius, verifies this conclusion. The silting up of the Oer-IJ-estuary north of Velsen seems to have been the reason why the base was eventually abandoned, making the Rhine the northern border of the Roman Empire.

Many Frisian peasants lived in the countryside around the two bases, and the presence of unusually large quantities of locally-produced pottery in the forts, shows that the Romans used to obtain their supplies locally.

Close to the two forts is the village of Velserbroek. It has been established that this was a sanctuary, and the many silver artefacts found there are evidence that it did not have purely local significance but was possibly a central sanctuary for the Frisians. The Romans, therefore, had an additional reason for settling in Velsen: they not only controlled the Oer-IJ, but they also controlled an important ritual centre, the focal point of the Frisian tribe.

Votive inscription for Hludana (Leeuwarden, Fries museum/ Frisian Museum).

and engaged in trade. Consequently, the German cultures along the Wadden Sea began to influence each other – one can speak of a 'North Sea culture' – and this culture would spread to England in the fifth century. The oh-so-miserable way of life of the Frisians and Chauki, as described by Pliny, most definitely had a future.

The ships in which the Frisians and Chauki sailed to the south are described by Pliny:

The German pirates sail in ships that are made from dug-out tree trunks. Some of them can carry as many as thirty people.[91]

Incidentally, when speaking of dugout vessels, we should not only think of dugout canoes, although these have indeed been found. But the ships seen by Pliny were dug out of trees, whose sides were sometimes raised with planks. However, if the oak tree was large enough, real sea-going sailing ships could be built from them, which might be used for piracy, trade, and fishing.

An indicator of the economic contacts between the Greater Frisians and the Romans has been found in the Beetgum terp, just north of Leeuwarden. It is a votive stone: a stele which believers placed in honour of the deity in gratitude for services rendered. From the Beetgum inscription, we can gather that a group of Romans had leased fishing rights in the Frisian waters from a local chieftain. The goddess mentioned, Hludana, was worshipped by the Batavi and Cugerni around Xanten. That the catch was possibly sold to these peoples can be deduced from the bones of saltwater fish found in Nijmegen, in Batavian lands.

To the goddess Hludana,
the fishing contractors,
when Quintus Valerius Secundus acted as tenant,
fulfilled their vow,
willingly and deservedly.[92]

The harmonious collaboration between Romans and Frisians was not confined to trade and fishing, as is evident from the following story told by Pliny:

When Germanicus built a camp on the other side of the Rhine in a part of Germania located on the sea, it turned out that there was only one freshwater source. Whoever drank from it found that his teeth fell out within two years and his knee-caps loosened. The doctors called this disorder scurvy and paralysis.

They found the remedy in a herb that was called Britannica. This herb turned out to be good not only for conditions of the nerves and for mouth disorders, but also for throat infections and snake-bites. It has dark, elongated leaves and a dark root; juice is also tapped from the root. The flower is called vibones, and whoever plucks it and swallows it before he hears the thunder, does not need to worry about throat disorders for a whole year. This plant was shown to us by the Frisians, the people where we built our camp and who were loyal to us at that time.

I wonder why the plant is so called. Perhaps it is because the Frisians, who live on the coast, have called it after their British neighbours across the sea. In any case, it is not called by this name because it abounds on that island, as, in those days, the island was independent [and practically unknown].[93]

Unfortunately, we do not know which plant had these miraculous properties and we are just as much in the dark about where the fort stood, although Velsen in North Holland is an attractive candidate.

• The Frisian Revolt

In 12 BC, Drusus had stationed an occupation force in the coastal region, and our sources do not report any irregularities in the thirty-nine years that followed. In AD 28, however, the Frisians revolted. The only report we have of this is in Tacitus' *Annals*. The aurochs in this text probably refers to a large cow, as the aurochs had already disappeared from the Low Countries by that time. The remark is in itself somewhat odd, as the Frisian economy was certainly doing quite well and we would have expected the Frisians to be well able to pay the taxes demanded by the Romans.

In the same year, the Frisians, a people on the other side of the Rhine, broke the bonds of peace, not so much because they did not want to be subservient to us any longer but because they had had enough of our rapaciousness. Drusus had imposed a moderate tribute on them, suitable to their limited resources. They had to supply ox hides for military purposes. Nobody had really paid much attention to how strong and large the hides should be, until Olennius, a senior centurion appointed to govern the Frisians, had selected hides of an aurochs as the standard they had to apply. This demand that would have been steep enough for other tribes was even more difficult for the Germans to meet, as, although they do have some forests on their lands where very large beasts abound, the cattle on their farms are undersized.

First they handed over their cattle, then their fields and finally they even gave up the persons of their wives and children to bondage. That led to remonstrations and complaints and, since there was no offer of tax relief, they sought redress in war. The soldiers that were charged with collecting the tribute were seized and crucified. Olennius managed to escape their fury by fleeing as fast as he could, and he found refuge in a fort called Flevum. There, a considerable military force of Romans and inhabitants of the province kept guard on the shores of the Ocean.

As soon as this was reported to Lucius Apronius, the governor of Germania Inferior, he called up detachments of from the legions of Germania Superior and a selection of auxiliaries comprised of infantry and cavalry. He conveyed both armies down the Rhine and marched against the Frisians. The siege of the fort had been abandoned and the rebels had withdrawn to defend their own lands. And so he started to lay dams and footbridges over the bogs in the estuary, to facilitate the passage of the heavier army units into the area.

Meanwhile, after they had found places that could be forded, he issued orders to a squadron of the Cananefates, and all the German infantry that served with us, to attack the enemy from the rear with an encircling movement. The enemy was already drawn up in battle order and routed the squadrons of the auxiliaries, as well as the cavalry of the legions who had come to their aid. After this, three lightly-armoured cohorts were sent against them, and then, after some time, two more, as well as the cavalry of the auxiliaries. They would have been strong enough if they had all charged at the same time, but coming up as they did at intervals, they failed to stem the flight of the units that were already in disarray and instead found themselves dragged along by the panic of the fleeing soldiers.

Thereupon he entrusted the rest of the auxiliaries to Cethegus Labeo, commander of the Fifth Legion. But he, too, finding his men's position critical and being in extreme peril himself, dispatched messengers urgently requesting that all the legions be sent into action. The soldiers of the Fifth Legion rushed forward and, after a fierce encounter, put the enemy to flight and saved our cohorts and cavalry, who were seriously weakened due to the great numbers that had been wounded.

But the Roman commander did not take any retaliatory action, or even bury the dead, although a large number of tribunes and prefects and some first-rate centurions had been killed. Soon afterwards, it was learned from deserters that nine hundred Romans who had fought on until the next day, had been cut to pieces in what they called the sacred forest of

Two graffiti from Velsen. One of them shows a Roman name (Lucius Cominius), the other the name of someone who wanted to remember his native origins (Batavus).

Once again it is not possible to say exactly where this event took place, but it is very likely that the besieged Flevum is identical to the naval base at Velsen, which was stormed by enemies in about AD 28. As explained on page 71, the fort had been doubled in size some years earlier, and the garrison comprised as many as a thousand soldiers. Five-hundred-and-twenty lead sling-bullets (known as *glandes* to the Romans) make it even possible to reconstruct the course of the battle in quite some detail and to be able to conclude that the Frisians were very close to winning it. That was mainly possible because they could mobilise a large number of men, a fact which again proves that the revolt had been well prepared and, in spite of Tacitus' words, was probably not a tax protest that had got out of hand.

Five different kinds of sling-bullets have been found. To start with, the ordinary ones weighed about fifty grams and were cast in a mould. A second type of bullet was similar to the first one, except that these were beaten with hammers to make them more pointed, so that they could inflict nastier wounds. The third category was identical to the second, although only one half was worked with hammers: perhaps they were made during the last hours before the attack. The final two sorts consisted of bullets that had been cast in a great hurry by sticking either a stick or a thumb in the ground and pouring lead into the hole. These stick and thumb *glandes* weigh about fifteen grams, but the penetration of such a lightweight projectile can also inflict deep wounds. When we plot the find-spots of these five types of bullet on a map, we can see how the battle went, even if we must consider that besides slings, spears and swords were also being used. However, battles where a mix of weapons was used are not traceable archaeologically. Even the broken sword hilt and a couple of spearheads cannot be linked with certainty to the battle.

The sling-bullets of the first and second types have been dug up in the northwest and southeast of the site, which proves that at that point two groups of Frisians launched the attack at the same time. That the attack in the southeast was repelled, can be deduced from the fact that only these high-quality bullets were found. We may assume that the triple ditches and the earthen rampart broke the attack. The Frisians who attacked the recently added part, with only two ditches, had more success. They forced their way into the fort and held on for so long that the Romans ran out of first-class sling-bullets. Using unhammered bullets and of course other weapons, the besieged finally drove the Frisians out of this part of the fort as well.

The battle could not have lasted very long as the Romans did not have to break into their last supplies. They would have been at work mending the breach in the wall when the third attack began: a new group of Frisians came across the water and were welcomed with a hail of second-class sling-bullets. When these were exhausted, the worst bullets had to be used: the fifteen-gram *glandes* made by sticking a stick or a thumb in the ground and pouring lead into the hole. Using these missiles, the Frisians were finally repulsed.

Some artifacts illustrate what happened during the evacuation of the fort. To guarantee that the Frisians would not occupy the abandoned fort, the Romans poisoned the ground water; they threw dead bodies into two wells and half a horse cadaver into another water source. We are certain that this was done by the defenders, because one of these hastily buried soldiers still had his dagger, with a richly decorated scabbard. If the Frisians had thrown him into the well, they would, presumably, have seized these objects. A coin in the wallet of another soldier offers a valuable clue to the date of his death: it was minted between AD 22 and AD 30, and because it shows no traces of wear, it is compatible with his being killed in action during the Frisian Revolt.

The evacuation of the fort must have been done in a great hurry as, in the harbour, pieces of human bone have been discovered on top of the refuse that found its way into the water in Roman times. The only interpretation archaeologists can give is that these bones are the remains of the floating bodies of those killed, which were left behind and slowly disintegrated.

It is uncertain whether the battlefield excavated at Velsen is identical to the Flevum Tacitus describes. This will remain so until an inscription is found that confirms the name. For the moment, however, what has been dug up does not contradict what Tacitus wrote.

He suggests that the Roman government of the northern tribes came to an abrupt end. He rounds off his report by saying: "From then on, the Germans had a high opinion of the Frisians." Oddly enough, the Romans were back in Velsen shortly afterwards: dendrochronological analysis of a piece of wood that was used to repair the well, shows that the tree was felled in the thirties AD. Therefore, it would appear that Roman dominion was suspended for only a short time. It is extremely frustrating that Tacitus' *Annals*, our main source for the years 37-47, contains a gap at this point. We know that in this missing piece it was reported that Caligula visited the Rhineland and that subsequently Claudius reformed the army and gave orders to evacuate all the military installations on the right bank of the Rhine. Both these events had consequences for Velsen, as we shall see in the next chapter.

Remains of a Roman soldier killed in Velsen. His skeleton was found in one of the wells (photo courtesy of the National Museum of Antiquities, Leiden).

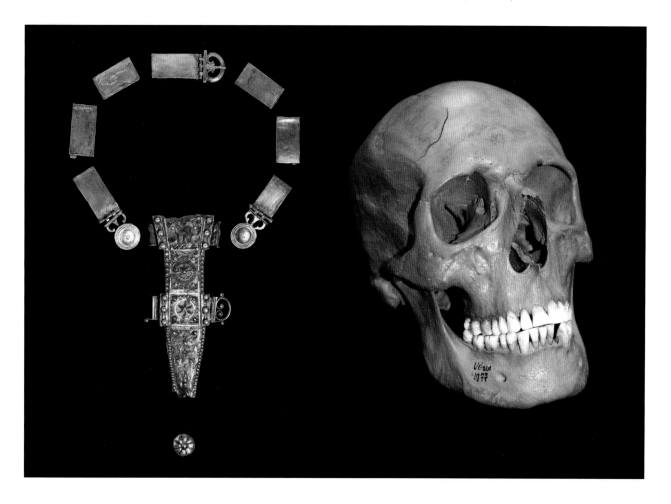

Early Nijmegen

The settlement at Nijmegen is made up of different parts. In the east, there is the Kops Plateau, where Drusus once had his headquarters. This later became a cavalry fort. Then there is the Hunerberg, which was a legionary base. Next, there is the settlement around the Valkhof hill. This was occupied up to AD 70, and, in Late Antiquity, was given a second lease on life. Finally, located over to the west, there is the second-century town of Ulpia Noviomagus.

Of these, the early settlement around the Valkhof is the most interesting. The town was created by the Roman authorities for the Batavi, just as Xanten had been created for the Cugerni, Tongeren for the Tungri, and Cologne for the Ubii. Not one of these towns was built on the site of an earlier, native settlement and, by the middle of the first century AD, all of them had taken on a certain urban glamour. However, that does not mean that they did not have a military function. There are indications that the first inhabitants were veterans. The discovery of a particular style of Italian pottery that is easy to put a date on, suggests that the civil settlement was founded around 10 BC, some ten years after the construction of the military base on the Hunerberg.

Nijmegen was called an *oppidum* and was surrounded by a ditch. It appears to have had an east-west orientation, probably along the road running parallel to the River Waal, which linked the military base to the residential areas in the west inhabited by the Batavians. It has been established that the Batavian leaders maintained villas in the country, but that does not say that they did not also own town houses. They would have used these when they had to do business with the military command. The other inhabitants were immigrants from Gaul (they probably worked as peasants or in urban industry) and veterans. The cremation graves to the east of the town suggest that the citizens did not put much store by the traditional Batavian burial rituals, and, therefore, they did not belong to this tribe.

That Nijmegen was meant to be a symbol of Roman power is evidenced by the discovery of an enormous stone monument in honour of Tiberius (see page 78). The construction of such a monument in the river region, where stone is not found, was very rare. A portrait of Caesar (see page 10) also found in Nijmegen, further illustrates the bond between the town and the imperial court. In short, here, on the road from the military base to the tribal lands, Rome presented itself to the Batavians.

Although the houses of old Nijmegen have only been examined in some places, the plots they stood on must have been systematically planned. It is true that these were not all the same size, but they do show that Roman surveyors had been at work. Nowhere is there evidence of native building methods. In Nijmegen, long, single-nave buildings ('strip houses') were built. Facing the street, there was a veranda, and behind that there could be a shop. Behind the shop, a series of rooms began, which were connected by a corridor. The houses were a little shorter than 50 metres and the walls were plastered and covered with paint. As these long houses resembled each other, it is conceivable that they were all built at the same time by a (military) 'property developer'. Around the middle of the first century AD, the houses were further extended to a length of 200 Roman feet, 59.4 metres. The addition of cellars also dates from this time.

In the aftermath of the Batavian Revolt, the rebels set fire to Nijmegen. The traces of this fire are very evident. Some inhabitants foresaw the destruction and evacuated their houses. Others were taken by surprise. The archaeologists found a precious bronze cauldron in one cellar, which the residents would surely have taken with them if they had had the chance. In another house, they found a spearhead, an axe, and the mask from a Batavian warrior's helmet. A wine merchant or innkeeper could not save his stores from the fire-raisers, who took the trouble to smash the amphorae before they torched the house. Perhaps the looters associated wine with the Roman way of life. What has been established is that before AD 70, Nijmegen was a town for the Batavians, but the inhabitants did not act like Batavians. In fact, it never did become a Batavian town.

7 Romanization

Column erected for Tiberius (Nijmegen, Valkhof museum).

• Armed Peace

At the beginning of our era, a six-metre high square column was erected in the oppidum that the Romans had allocated to the Batavi. On the front face of the stone monument, you could see the goddess Victoria crowning a man who was making an offering to the emperor; on the other three sides, there were representations of, respectively, the Roman gods of grain, hunting and the arts. The message was clear: thanks to the emperor's reign, the Empire experienced the blessings of peace. The Roman historian Tacitus expressed the same sentiment when he typified the period with the laconic word *otium*, "peace".[95]

Although Tacitus' description refers to the period of AD 41 to 68, it is very likely that AD 16 actually marked the beginning of the era of relative peace. That is to say, we are not aware of any serious disturbances after the suspension of hostilities that marked the end of the German War, although this could be due to the incompleteness of our sources. The fact that the Emperor Tiberius did not undertake wide-scale reprisals after the Frisians revolted in AD 28 appears to indicate an atmosphere of détente. It was in nobody's interests to enter into armed conflict. Besides, if we are to believe Tacitus, the Romans were well aware that the rebellion had been provoked by the unreasonably high tax demands which Olennius had imposed on their Frisian allies, a tribe which the Romans held in high regard. From a strategic point of view, putting down the revolt was of major importance, but Roman losses remained contained and the Frisians had possibly promised to keep the peace in the future. There was ample room for a peaceful compromise, which made it possible for the Romans to concentrate on the more important southern regions of Gallia Belgica.

The Romans went on exploiting the north and east, at any rate indirectly, via diplomatic contacts. The tribes on the other side of the Rhine, where warriors, true to form, dreamed of accumulating booty and fame, were taught the lesson, time and time again, that raids on the Empire were punished mercilessly. They channelled their energy now into warring against other tribes, and Rome did not need to use force to keep the situation under control.

In order to ensure that the tribes maintained a healthy respect for them, the Romans stationed four legions in Germania Inferior. In Bonn, there was the First Legion, with the epithet Germanica. Further downstream in Neuss, there was the Twentieth, known as the Valeria Victrix, 'Victorious Black Eagle'. Opposite the mouth of the Lippe, the enormous military base of Xanten was erected, where a further two legions were garrisoned: the Twenty-First Rapax, 'Predator', and the Fifth Alaudae, 'Larks'. In between these bases lay the smaller camps of the auxiliaries, such as Castra Herculis (Meinerswijk, opposite Arnhem) and Fectio (Vechten, near Utrecht), which guarded the fork of the Old Rhine and the Vecht.

The auxiliary troops, the non-citizen corps of the Roman army, played a significant role in binding the native populations to Roman authority. The Batavian squadrons are the best-known example. These cavalry troops were able to ride through the widest rivers, an act of daring which few could imitate. Other Batavi formed the backbone of the imperial guard. But although these units appeal to the imagination, they were not representative of Roman auxiliaries. The Batavi exclusively contributed military specialists, and, beyond that, they were exempt from paying taxes.[96] A Batavian felt himself to be more an ally of the Romans

*Batavian cavalrymen
(Nijmegen, Valkhof museum).*

than an inhabitant of the Roman Empire.

More representative of the auxiliaries were the Tungri, who actually *did* pay taxes. This tribe was a fusion of immigrants from Gaul, the regions across the Rhine, and Italy as well, who had settled among those Eburones who had survived Caesar's genocidal operations. Their newly constructed capital city, modern Tongeren, dominated the eastern part of present-day Belgium. The inhabitants were long-standing supporters of the Roman armies and, when the legions were transferred to the Rhine between 19 BC and 12 BC, Tongeren became an important logistics base in the hinterland. In the first half of the first century AD, the Tungri supplied two squadrons of cavalry and four cohorts of infantry for the Roman army. (In comparison, the Morini, Menapii, and Frisiavones contributed only one cohort each, the Ubii three, and the Batavi no fewer than nine cohorts and one cavalry squadron.) The Tungrian units were stationed in Germania Inferior. Thus, at the beginning of the forties of the first century AD, their first squadron of auxiliaries – known as "the squadron of Fronto" – was garrisoned at Bonn and then in Moers-Asberg, opposite the place where the River Ruhr flows into the Rhine.

*Treveran cavalrymen (Arlon, Musée
archéologique/Archaeological museum).*

Romanization

The term 'Romanization' is both clarifying and problematic. Originally, scholars meant by it that the native culture began to display Roman characteristics. But it was not just one-way traffic: the Roman rulers, for their part, adopted elements from the culture of those they had subjugated. The most striking example of this is that a sect from Judaea, Christianity, developed into a Roman state religion.

The way in which this mutual influencing took place differed from place to place and from time to time, and our view of the process changes likewise. In the first half of the twentieth century, people looked particularly at the way the Romans imposed their will on their subjects. However, since the decolonization process in the twentieth century, emphasis has been put more on the way in which native populations selected what they wanted to adopt, and could even manipulate the suppressors into dancing to their tune.

Some experts hold the view that it would be better to avoid the terms 'Romanized' and 'indigenous' altogether, and that, instead, we should highlight the processes of globalization, which had begun long before the Roman era. In this view, the world was becoming more and more of a unit. The campaigns of Alexander the Great had prevented this unit from assuming the veneer of Persian culture, and the successes of the Romans saw to it that the unit displayed distinctly Roman characteristics. Here, we reach a level of abstraction that can no longer be tested with the tools historians and archaeologists have at their disposal.

The auxiliaries from the north were held in high regard. Caesar already had an elite squadron that accompanied him on all his campaigns. The fact that these were barbarians alone made them highly recommendable. After all, they were very good warriors. Strabo remarks about these troops:

Although they are all warriors by nature, they make better cavalry than infantry. The best Roman cavalry troops come from their midst. Incidentally, those who live in the most northerly regions and on the Ocean shore are the most warlike.[97]

• The First Romanized Belgians

It is difficult to overestimate the significance of the auxiliaries. The men who served in the auxiliary cohorts began to behave like real Romans as the years passed, adopting Roman-sounding names and acquiring Roman citizenship. From the time of Claudius' remodelling of the army, veterans received a copy of their certificate of discharge, neatly etched in bronze: a *diploma*, as it would be called today. On their inscriptions, this first generation of Romanized Gauls are easily recognizable because they took on the surname of the emperor and thus were all called Julius. Likewise, later 'new' Romans would bear the names of Claudius or Flavius for life.

Julii who returned to their fatherland were rich enough to acquire large estates and retire to them for a life of leisure. Not only were they the new Romans, but also the new rich. Consequently, they belonged to the most prominent and influential citizens of their tribe. It followed on that they began to play a role in public administration. As members of city councils, they defended the Roman point of view whenever anyone objected to a regulation

introduced by the governor. Alternatively, they could present a credible argument to the governor on behalf of the council, whenever they found one of his ordinances impossible to execute. Consequently, the Julii became important political allies of the central government.

Moreover, they had developed Roman tastes. It is likely that they were the inhabitants of the town houses with a distinct Mediterranean appearance that began to replace the old farmhouses in Tongeren from AD 40 (these were the first houses in the Low Countries with ornamental gardens). In order to keep up their Roman status, they continued to use products that they had been introduced to in the military barracks: olive oil from Andalusia, fish-sauce from Catalonia, wine from Provence, thrushes from the Ardennes, or eels from Lake Flevo, and every now and then, Egyptian dates or Greek wine. Furthermore, they gave commissions to travelling fresco-painters. Their houses must have been palaces in the eyes of their fellow citizens; showcases of Roman culture. Their presence contributed to the growth of places like Tongeren, which, at the beginning of our era, was only an administrative centre but quickly developed into city in the socio-geographic sense of the word.

Another factor that went hand in hand with urbanization was the execution of public works. It is quite possible that the council financed the paving of important roads, but private citizens paid for almost all public buildings. You see, it was usual in ancient times for well-heeled people to make donations to their native towns in return for political influence. This could take the form of sponsored food distribution, but anyone who was really well-off might donate a concert hall, a theatre, a temple, a library, a water system, or a bathhouse. This custom is well documented in the Mediterranean world, where generous donors made a public display of their generosity in sometimes endless inscriptions. The inhabitants of the Low Countries were a little more modest, although political influence was also bought with gifts. A lovely illustration of this is an inscription in the baths at Heerlen, which had been improved by a certain Marcus Sattonius, a municipal administrator from Xanten, with thanks to the local goddess Fortuna Redux.

To have a better understanding of what follows, it is perhaps useful to point out that such a gift usually consisted of two parts. On the one hand, there was a sum for the execution of the work itself; on the other hand, the interest on an additional fund was reserved for its maintenance. It would be two centuries before it turned out that this system was not foolproof.

• Gallia Belgica and Germania Inferior

Of course, Tongeren was not the only town that began to grow after the German War had ended. A road that is still quite straight nowadays connected the capital of the Tungri with Bavay, the town of the Nervii of East Flanders and Henegouwen. The Morini lived close to the Straits of Dover – as had been the case in Caesar's day. The port of Boulogne, where merchants would cross the Channel to Britannia, rivalled their official capital, Thérouanne. Cassel (France) was the administrative centre of the Menapii, who lived in Flanders and the south of the Dutch province of Zeeland.[98]

All these towns were part of the province of Gallia Belgica, to which places such as Arras, Amiens, Reims (the seat of the governor), Metz, and Trier also belonged.

If the letter of the law were applied, then the regions along the Rhine also belonged to this province; but, in fact, it was the legionary commanders who held sway here. It would take until the eighties of the first century AD before the military zones of Germania Inferior and Germania Superior were officially separated from Belgica as independent provinces. However, in practice, these had already been independent for almost a century. Urbaniza-

The Chaussée Brunehaut

The road from Cologne to Boulogne was the economic axis of northern Gaul. It was not a Roman creation. In some places, it still runs parallel to rows of burial mounds from the Bronze and Iron Ages, which proves that, in pre-Roman times, there was a road already there. Caesar took this road when he attacked the Nervii, and Agrippa improved the road's surface. (This explains the German name *Agrippa-Strasse*.) After that, the road became more important because it ran across the loess land, where large estates were located.

The prosperity that this road created survived the Roman Empire and the area formed the nucleus of the mighty Frankish kingdom of Austrasia. It is no coincidence that the repair of the road was, in a fourteenth-century legend, attributed to a Frankish queen named Brunhilda. In France and Wallonia, the road is still known as *Chaussée Brunehaut*. The ancient name is not known, but one thing is certain: the name *Via Belgica*, used today by tourist organizations, is pertinently wrong, as that would have indicated a road that ran *to* Belgica and not *through* Belgica.[99]

tion took off much later in these regions, although under Tiberius they already had administrative centres: for the Ubii, that was Cologne; for the Batavi, an oppidum on the Valkhof at Nijmegen; for the Cananefates, who lived in the area occupied nowadays by The Hague, it would have been Voorburg.

Gallia Belgica and the more militarized Germania Inferior formed one economic unit.

Ancient Place Names

How do we know the names of places in ancient times? Sometimes, there is a recognizable continuity in the name: thus, Bavay is a contraction of *Bagacum*, and Tongeren comes from the tribal name *Tungri*. Etymologies are, however, notoriously unreliable. For example, since the time of the Renaissance until quite recently, the ancient town of *Lugdunum* had been identified with Leiden (cp. page 113). We now know that the ancient name for Leiden was, in fact, *Matilo*. It turns out that the real Lugdunum was at the mouth of the Rhine. Therefore, as a rule, etymology is only used if all other options have been exhausted.

We can only be absolutely sure that a place name is correct when an inscription has been found to confirm it. Thus, there is no doubt that the Romans referred to Xanten as *Colonia Ulpia Traiana*.

A second aid is the so-called Peutinger Map, a medieval copy of an ancient road map, which was once in the possession of the Augsburg scholar Konrad Peutinger (1465-1547) and which is now kept in Vienna, in the Austrian National Library. On this map the distances are given between different places. Thus, we know that there must have been a place called *Pernacum* west of Tongeren. Roman remains have been found at present-day Braives in the province of Liege that point to this town's existence. Incidentally, the map contains numerous spelling mistakes: *Pernacum*, for example, should actually be *Perniciacum*, and it has been suggested that the incomprehensible name *Levefanum* is a corruption of *Haevae fanum*, i.e. the sanctuary of the Batavian goddess Haeva.

The Belgian peasants in the valleys of the Meuse and the Sambre, and the craftsmen in the towns, sold their products to the army of Germania Inferior. However, there were two significant differences. The urbanization of the north began a century after this transformation had begun in the south. Moreover, the taxes collected by the Roman government from the inhabitants of Belgica were spent outside their province; that is to say, on the Rhine, where the troops received wages. Consequently, Germania Inferior was, in modern terms, an economic stimulation area, while Belgica was expected to financially support other regions.

• Caligula in Katwijk

Roman historians preferred to write about events that enhanced the honour of a statesman or soldier. Consequently, the time of peace between the rebellion of the Frisians in AD 28 and the outbreak of the Batavian revolt in AD 69 is poorly documented. However, we read that the Emperor Caligula visited Katwijk in AD 40, that the Chauki were practising piracy, and that a Frisian delegation visited Rome. That is all.

Let us talk about the emperor's visit first. In AD 37, Tiberius was succeeded by his grandnephew, Caligula. The ancient authors describe him as a bloodthirsty maniac, who would have been got rid of immediately, if it were not for the fact that he was constantly surrounded by his Batavian bodyguard. A more realistic view would probably be that his power as emperor went to his head, as very few Roman princes had such illustrious ancestors: son of Germanicus, grandson of both Drusus and Agrippa, great-grandson of Augustus. Through adoption, he had become the son of Tiberius and the great-grandson of Julius Caesar. All these men had fought against the tribes on the opposite side of the Rhine, and therefore Caligula was honour-bound to wage war against them as well. The campaign took place in the spring of AD 40. Suetonius records, in his *Life of Caligula*, the pretext Caligula used.

Only once in his life did he get involved in military service and affairs of war, and this happened on a sudden impulse. When he went to Mevania to view the grove and river of Clitumnus, while he was there, it was suggested that he should increase the unit of Batavians he surrounded himself with. This suggestion gave him a sudden desire to undertake an expedition to Germania. Without more ado, he called up legions and auxiliaries from all corners of the Empire, troops were levied from all quarters without any consideration, and incredible amounts of all sorts of supplies were collected. Thereupon, he started his advance: sometimes he travelled so fast and feverishly, that, contrary to custom, the Praetorian cohorts were forced to load their standards onto packhorses and so to follow him. At other times, he advanced so slowly and comfortably that he had himself transported in a litter carried by eight men and along the way he demanded that the people of the neighbouring towns should sweep the roads in front of him and sprinkle them with water to settle the dust.[100]

From Mainz, Caligula led the attack on the Chatti. Suetonius claims that it was a farce, but that mainly shows gross insensitivity on his part, as many soldiers died during this campaign. (Their gravestones are on view in the museum of Mainz.) Near Wiesbaden, the remains have been found of a fort built in these years. Even so, the expedition was short, since, in the autumn, Caligula set off again and travelled downstream.

At last, he positioned his army for battle on the shore of the Ocean, as if he wanted to bring the war to a definite conclusion. His ballistae and other engines of war were drawn up, and nobody knew or could even conceive of what he was going to do. All of a sudden, he gave the order to collect sea shells, which he called "war spoils which the Ocean owed to Rome" and to fill their

Caligula (Paris, Louvre).

helmets and folds of their tunics with them. As a monument to this victory, he erected a very
high tower from where light signals were to be sent at night to guide ships, as from the light-
house of Alexandria. And after he had promised the soldiers a gift of a hundred denarii a man,
he said, as if he had outdone his predecessors in generosity: "Go from here, merry and rich."[101]

Suetonius again presents this operation as a farce, but it is more likely that it was a large-scale military exercise where Caligula tested the possibility of organizing the quick transport of large numbers of troops by ship down the Rhine. The construction of a military base at Valkenburg in South Holland, in the winter of AD 39/40, suggests that the goal of the operation was the nearby beach at Katwijk. The Valkenburg complex was called *Praetorium Agrippinae*, the first word meaning 'headquarters' and the second the name of Caligula's mother. That the Emperor made a state visit to the Dutch coastal area at the mouth of the Rhine has been proven by the recovery in Vechten and Valkenburg of wine barrels which once contained wine from the Emperor's private vineyard. The lighthouse memorial mentioned by Suetonius may have been conserved for a long time: as late as the sixteenth century, the fishermen from Katwijk in the Netherlands called a ruin off the coast the 'tower of Kalla'.[102]

As it happens, the imperial building activities were not just confined to Katwijk. It looks as if the fort at Laurum, present-day Woerden in the Netherlands, was also constructed at this time. There was also building activity at Vechten, and we know that, a little further north, the marine base at Velsen was in use by Caligula's fleet.[103] There is evidence, too, for construction in Alphen aan den Rijn, and Vleuten. It is possible that the Rhine was being brought under tighter Roman control as a preliminary to the intended invasion of Britannia. However, it is also possible that these forts were to be used for launching a number of operations further to the north. These took place in the summer of AD 41, and Cassius Dio says the following:

In this year, Sulpicius Galba defeated the Chatti and Publius Gabinius distinguished himself by
defeating the Chauki, but also especially by recovering the last eagle standard, which they had
had in their possession since Varus' defeat.[104]

• Chaukian Pirates

However, there was absolutely no question of the Chauki being defeated. During the following years, they plundered the unprotected coast of Gallia Belgica, and even dared to carry out an attack on Germania Inferior. Tacitus gives us a report:

In that same time, the Chauki raided Germania Inferior. Their leader was Gannascus, a
Cananefate by birth. He had served in the Roman auxiliaries, had subsequently deserted, and
undertook plundering raids with a number of light ships, mainly harassing the Gallic coastal
area. He knew very well that the Gauls were rich and had no stomach for war.[105]

The passage is especially interesting because of the last line, in which it appears that the source Tacitus uses was of the opinion that, at that time, the Belgians were a cultured people and therefore not very interested in waging war. It also illustrates that an unbiased observer could establish that Belgica was well on the way to becoming a prosperous land.

The raids by the Chauki came at quite an unfortunate moment for the Romans, because the Emperor Claudius, who had succeeded Caligula to the imperial throne in AD 41, had just launched his conquest of Britannia. The last thing he needed was a run-in with pirates in the Channel, even if they only used dugout canoes. As far as the Chauki were concerned, they were very quickly aware that the commander of the army of Germania Inferior was not someone you trifled with. His name was Corbulo, and he would prove himself to be one of the most important Roman generals of his time. In his company was a young officer named Pliny, who saw the Chaukian terps during this operation (cf. page 69).

As soon as he arrived in his province, Corbulo sent the triremes down the Rhine while he led the remaining ships – insofar as they were suitable – via the Wadden Sea and the canals. After he had scuttled the ships of the enemy and driven Gannascus to flee, he had the situation sufficiently under control, if only for a short time. For the legions that showed very little commitment when performing strenuous tasks and were drunk on plundering raids, he reinstated the old rule that no one could break ranks, and he forbade men to fight without orders. Soldiers were to be armed when on patrol, standing watch or performing any other task, either by day or by night. It is on record that one soldier was given the death sentence because he did not have his sword on while digging soil for the ramparts and another for doing the same job armed only with his dagger.[106]

With the words "it is on record that", Tacitus distances himself from the last story. And with justification, as this sort of anecdote was told about every Roman general.[107]

Even the Frisians, who had become hostile or, in any case, untrustworthy since their rebellion, capitulated and settled in the area that Corbulo allocated to them. He imposed on them a senate, magistrates and laws. To see to it that they would not evade executing his orders, he built a fort where he garrisoned troops.

At the same time, he sent a mission to the Greater Chauki with the task of persuading them to submit, and to put in motion a plot against Gannascus. The attack was successful and, at the same time, it was not dishonourable either; after all, Gannascus was both a deserter and a traitor. And yet his death caused great emotion among the Chauki, while, at the same time, Corbulo was trying to sow the seeds of a rebellion. Most people approved, but some considered it bad news. Why was it so important for him to provoke the enemy? If it were to turn out badly, would that not be damaging to the state, and if it were successful, would he as a man of name and fame not become a threat to peace, considered a threat by a nervous emperor?

Claudius exercised his veto on new, violent actions against the German regions, going so far as to give orders to withdraw the occupying forces to the west bank of the Rhine.[108]

Again, it is possible that Corbulo's fort was identical to Velsen, where the wood used was felled in the winter of AD 42/43. Be that as it may, the general halted the construction, having remarked, it is said, that the life of a commander was easier in the past.

To avoid idleness taking root among his soldiers, he ordered them to dig a canal between the Meuse and the Rhine over a length of thirty-eight kilometres, which spared people the hazards of a journey across the Ocean.[109]

The 'Corbulo canal' is still in use: it is more or less identical to the Vliet between Leiden and The Hague. The course of the canal passes by Voorburg, the capital of the Cananefates, which no doubt profited from this link with the Rhine and the Meuse.

As has been noted above, work had already begun on the construction of a series of fortifications along the Lower Rhine, commissioned by Caligula: Velsen, Valkenburg, Alphen aan den Rijn, Woerden, Vleuten and Vechten. Nigrum Pullum ('black hen', Zwammerdam) appears to date from AD 57, while Traiectum ('ford', near Utrecht cathedral) is as yet undated. All in all, about two dozen auxiliary forts must have arisen between Katwijk and Xanten. These would continue to be functional until AD 240.

In order to be able to transport troops rapidly up- or down-river, a Rhine fleet was also

Corbulo (Paris, Louvre).

set up, which had its headquarters a little to the south of Cologne. At least one watchtower, excavated west of Utrecht, dates from the forties AD,[110] but this was probably an isolated case. The long line of watchtowers, built to be used for passing on light and smoke signals, appears to have been constructed a little later. However, even one excavation can radically change this view.

The whole system is known as the *limes*, an expression from Latin surveyors' jargon. The word actually refers to the path between two fields, but as early as Velleius Paterculus' time it could mean 'frontier road'.[111] Modern archaeologists use the term to refer to the whole border of the Roman Empire in all its facets.

Claudius' decision to keep the Rhine and the Danube as the borders of the Roman Empire probably had more to do with logistics than with tactics. After all, water transport was cheaper than transport over land, and patrols could be carried out much faster by boat than on foot. Another motive for drawing the border at a river had a religious background: the river gods would support the legions in protecting the empire. Which of these motives carried most weight is difficult to say.

The significance of Claudius' decision to make the Rhine border a permanent fixture is all too often disregarded. The Romans chose a defensive strategy and abandoned any idea of further expansion. Up until then, the term *Imperium Romanum* had to do with a sphere of influence that was difficult to define; but, from this time on, we can speak of a well-defined territorial unit. Because, by coincidence, there are many sources that report on the Battle of the Teutoburg Forest, this is often referred to as being decisive for the independence of the lands on the east bank of the Rhine. However, it is possible that this is not the case, and that the defining occasion was the construction of the limes more than thirty years later.

At this time, the combination of legions that constituted the army of Germania Inferior also changed. At Neuss, the Twentieth Legion was replaced by the Sixteenth Gallica, and at Xanten, the Twenty-First made way for the Fifteenth Primigenia (the nickname is a title of honour from the Goddess of Fortune). Together with the First and the Fifth Legions, they would guard the border river for another quarter of a century. In the framework of this reorganization of Germania Inferior, Cologne was given the rank of *colonia* in AD 50, which meant that all the inhabitants were given Roman citizenship. This proved that the Emperor Claudius considered the Ubii who were living there as real Romans.

The Claudian Army Reforms

At the beginning of the reign of the Emperor Claudius (AD 41-54), a number of army reforms were put through that have no equal in the history of ancient times. To start with, the Romans set out to make their borders simpler to define and more permanent. Simpler: they annexed several regions to shorten the border. An example is present-day Bulgaria, where the legions advanced to the Danube. The conquest of much of mainland Britannia fits into this pattern, although Claudius never completed the conquest, which would have simplified the borders there. Permanent: up until then, most forts had been built of wood; but, from this time on, the foundations were built of stone (as at Xanten). Later, the buildings themselves would also be built from stone. With the construction of forts along the Lower Rhine, the border was also fixed permanently there.

Other changes had to do with the careers of the officers, the equipment of the soldiers, the organization of the auxiliaries, and the layout of the camps. What is most striking is the custom that auxiliaries, on being discharged, received a *diploma*, where it was recorded that they had acquired Roman citizenship.

Replica of a Roman watch-tower, similar to the type Corbulo ordered to be built (Vechten, photograph by Robert Vermaat).

• Frisians in Rome

To the north of the Rhineland border lived several more tribes. The Frisians and Chauki have already been dealt with in some detail. Although they were independent in name, they were very much part of the Roman world: the Frisians supplied a unit of auxiliaries to the Roman army. Amongst the other tribes, the Chamavi are usually located along the IJssel in the eastern Netherlands, while the Tubantes could possibly have given their name to Twente, the easternmost part of the Netherlands. A little more to the east, in Germany, lived the Amsivarii (literally 'the people of the Ems'), and the Bructeri (northwest of the Lippe valley).

None of these tribes lived close to the Rhine, as the Romans did not allow anyone to settle there. The Usipetes, who originally lived east of Arnhem, seem to have been driven south, as, in AD 69, it is mentioned that they lived opposite Mainz.[112] However, many peasants wanted to establish their farms on the fertile banks of the Rhine. That appeared to be the case in 58, when a delegation of Frisians turned to Nero, who had become emperor four years earlier.

But from the continued inaction of our armies, there was a rumour that the commanders had been deprived of the right to start military operations against the enemy. Because of this, the Frisians moved up to the bank of the Rhine – the fighting men via the forests and swamps, and the non-fighting population over the lakes – and settled on the uninhabited arable land which was reserved for the use of our soldiers. They did this on the initiative of Verritus and Malorix, the kings of the tribe, insofar as the Germans accept kings.

They had already built houses and sown seed in the fields, and they behaved as though the land had been in their possession for generations, when [General] Dubius Avitus threatened to send in Roman troops if the Frisians did not return to their original lands. Alternatively, they could turn to the emperor to be given a new place to settle. Avitus was able to motivate Verritus and Malorix to take the latter option and they set out for Rome.

While waiting to be received by Nero, who was occupied with other engagements, they visited Pompey's theatre, one of the sights that are always shown to visiting barbarians to impress them with the majesty of the Roman people. As they were idly hanging around there (you see, in their ignorance, they did not find the entertainment interesting), they asked all sorts of questions about the crowd on the benches, what the difference was between the various classes, who were the knights and who belonged to the senatorial class. They saw a few people in foreign dress sitting among the senators, and asked who those people were.

When they were told that this honour was granted to envoys from those nations which distinguished themselves by their military prowess and their close ties with Rome, they exclaimed loudly that there was no tribe on earth that could fight as well as the Germans. Then, they walked down and took their seats among the senators. The spectators reacted good-naturedly; it was seen as an act of primitive impulsivity, as well as a healthy form of rivalry.[113]

Although the two Frisian kings received Roman citizenship for themselves, they achieved nothing for their subjects, who were driven out of the borderlands by the Roman auxiliaries. Not long afterwards, other tribes on the other side of the Rhine displayed interest in the uncultivated lands and it cost General Avitus all his diplomatic and military skills to keep them away from the border zone.

In spite of this incident, relations between the Romans and the tribes beyond the Rhine remained harmonious during Nero's reign. In fact, they were so harmonious that a Roman knight (who has remained anonymous) could travel unimpeded right through Germania to the mouth of the Vistula. And there, he found, at last, what had been sought in vain by the

Greeks and the Carthaginians, long before his time: beaches of amber. Laden down with this precious ware, he returned. It was the end of a quest that had gone on for almost four centuries and which, for many ancient writers, had been an obsession. In the meantime, however, it is questionable if the discovery of amber was really so important; when our sources talk of barter, they only mention trade in meat, hides, and salt.

The exploration of regions deep in Germania was only possible because of the peace that reigned in the border areas under Tiberius, Claudius, and Nero. The provinces prospered, the tax system was improved,[114] and there was peaceful commercial traffic with the tribes on the other side of the Rhine. Very few people could have suspected how this peace would be rudely shattered in AD 69.

8 The Batavian Revolt

• The Year of the Four Emperors

In the century that had passed since Augustus established the monarchy, the inhabitants of the Roman Empire had become accustomed to one-man rule. In exchange for peace, they had given up any say in the government. As long as the emperor was someone as capable as Augustus, Tiberius, or Claudius, there was no objection to this lack of influence. But when the ruler turned out to be less talented, problems were bound to arise.

Under Nero, the Roman Empire continued to flourish, but when he started to display despotic tendencies, the Senate, comprising the administrative class of the Roman Empire, began to suffer. Gaius Julius Vindex was one of the group that believed that Nero had to be stopped. Coming from a leading Gallic family, he had risen to the rank of senator and governor of one of the Gallic provinces. Evidently, he thought more like a Roman senator than a native aristocrat, as he set about trying to replace the despot in the most constitutional way possible. In April AD 68, he believed he had found a worthy successor to Nero in the person of one of the successful commanders mentioned on page 85: Servius Sulpicius Galba.

Vindex' revolt proceeded disastrously. The Rhine armies, fearing a nationalist Gallic rebellion like that of Ambiorix or Vercingetorix, marched with great speed against Vindex. He had not been very effective in putting across his true motives for rebelling, and, having lost the propaganda war, he was then defeated on the battlefield and eventually lost his life. In the meantime, Nero had played out his role in Rome. The Senate declared him a public enemy and decided to recognize Galba as emperor, after all. Nero committed suicide on 9 June AD 68.

Germania Superior and Germania Inferior were two of the regions that did not join in the general joy at Nero's defeat. The soldiers there had thought they were doing effective work by nipping a Gallic rebellion in the bud, but they now had to accept that their action was interpreted as an attempt to prevent Galba's accession. The native population of the Rhineland, who had prudently backed the same party as the legions stationed nearby, discovered that they were distrusted by the new emperor. Thus, Galba dismissed his Batavian bodyguard without a decent financial reward.

The dissatisfaction came to a head in January AD 69, when the army of Germania Inferior proclaimed their general, Vitellius, emperor. When Galba heard of this, he flew into a panic, affronted many very important people, made an enemy of the Praetorian Guard, and ended up being lynched. His successor, Otho, was no match for Vitellius, who, in the meantime, had also won the support of the legions from Germania Superior and Britannia. After a victory in the Po valley and the suicide of Otho, Vitellius was lord and master of the world empire. It was the first time that the enormous potential of the economies of Belgica and the Rhine legions was transformed into political power.

In order to have the command of a large army when invading Italy, Vitellius had withdrawn a considerable number of soldiers from the legions serving on the Rhine border, leaving the garrisons there with only a quarter of their original military strength. To rectify this situation as quickly as possible after his victory in Italy, he sent troops to the north, including eight Batavian cohorts that had displayed exceptional courage in the battle in the

Vitellius (Nijmegen, Valkhof museum).

Po valley. These legions had reached Mainz when they received the order to turn around and march back to Italy. Once again, they had to assist Vitellius, this time in his struggle against Vespasian, a new pretender to the imperial throne. Vespasian was commander of an army that had been involved in an attempt to put down a revolt by the Jews in the East. He used these troops now for a coup d'état. For the second time in AD 69, the Mediterranean regions were the theatre of a civil war.

• Batavian Discontent

Vitellius now requested further reinforcements from Hordeonius Flaccus, the commander of the troops that had remained behind on the Rhine border. Tacitus, our most important source of information about the events of these months, has almost nothing positive to say about this man. In his biased report of the Batavian Revolt, he continually emphasizes the familiar contrasts between barbarism and civilization, valour and decadence, vitality and defeatism. These opposing qualities are represented in the flesh, on the one hand, by Julius Civilis, the Batavian general and a noble savage, and on the other hand, by Hordeonius Flaccus, the Roman general with all the character flaws of cultivation. All things considered, these are no more than stereotypes.

It is possible that Hordeonius was not up to the task of putting down the impending revolt, but it is questionable whether another general would have fared any better, with only a quarter of his troops at his disposal. Be that as it may, Hordeonius certainly foresaw the problems that would arise. Considering it irresponsible to further deplete the legions on the Rhine border, he refused to supply the reinforcements Vitellius had requested. Thereupon, the Emperor gave orders to levy fresh troops. This was the final provocation for the Batavian leader Civilis, and he rose in revolt. Tacitus writes:

On the orders of Vitellius, a levy was held among the Batavi. This in itself was a burden for the natives, but was made heavier by the corruption and perversion of those carrying it out: they selected the old and the weak so that they could demand a ransom for letting them go again, while, on the other hand, they dragged away the most beautiful youths to satisfy their lust – and, generally speaking, the Batavian children are developed beyond their years. This aroused resentment, and a revolt was set in motion: those responsible advocated refusal to serve.

Civilis called the leaders of his tribe and the boldest of the common men into a sacred grove under the pretext of giving a banquet. When he saw that the night and revelry had fired their spirits, he began to speak of the honour and glory of their tribe, then went on to recount all the wrongs, the extortion and all the rest of the misfortunes of slavery imposed on them. "For", he declared, "we are no longer regarded as allies, as we once were, but as slaves."[115]

Julius Civilis, Roman citizen, was descended from the royal family that, at one time, had ruled the Batavi, but had, by now, been replaced by a 'highest magistrate'. However, although he was not actually a king, Civilis was still a very prominent man, if only because he had served in the auxiliaries for twenty-five years. (He would have been nearly fifty at this time.) Tacitus reports that the Batavian "was more intelligent than most barbarians", a platitude that writers in Antiquity pulled out of the hat for every barbarian who had defeated a Roman army. The fact is, however, that Civilis knew how to deal with the Romans and certainly understood how to thwart them.

He was ruled in his decision by personal motives. In Nero's last year as emperor, shortly before Civilis had completed his service in the Batavian auxiliaries in Britannia, he and his brother Paulus had been arrested on suspicion of planning a rebellion. Paulus was immediately executed and Civilis was put on a transport to Rome to answer to the emperor. However, when he arrived in the capital, Galba who had by now assumed power, pardoned him. Civilis was then sent back to Germania Inferior, again arrested, and released for the second time – this time by Vitellius, who had hoped, in this way, to win the sympathy of the eight Batavian cohorts. As already mentioned, these units were later incorporated into Vitellius' army.

The ceremonial feast in the sacred grove (described above) illustrates that the Batavi were only partly Romanized – or that Tacitus wants to create that impression. Otherwise, Civilis would have summoned the meeting in a council hall. It reflects what Tacitus says in his monograph about the Germans:

They generally deliberate on war and peace during feasts, in the conviction that people are never as open to sincere council or enthusiastically embrace elevated thoughts as then. These people, naturally void of artifice or disguise, always disclose the most secret emotions of their hearts in the freedom of festivity. Their thoughts are then open to everyone. The following day [when they are sober] everything is again considered. Each of these occasions has its advantages: they hold council when they cannot dissemble and take decisions when they cannot make a mistake.[116]

It is possible that Tacitus is the inventor of the idea that the Batavi made decisions when drunk. In his *Germania*, he wants to hold up a mirror to his contemporaries and, therefore, he compares the decadence he observes in Roman society with the noble savagery of the Rhine delta tribes. More than once, he attributes characteristics to them that every tribe living on the edge of the world was supposed to have, and perhaps that is what he is doing here. In any case, his story about the German assembly culture resembles Herodotus' story about the Persians, who also made decisions in both inebriated and sober circumstances.

• Causes of the Batavian Revolt

Civilis, twice arrested but never condemned, therefore had a very good personal reason for organizing a revolt against the Romans: he wanted to avenge his brother's death. Furthermore, it is plausible that he played – even for a short time – with the idea of restoring the royal power that his family had once had. Be that as it may, Civilis' motivation does not explain why others were willing to join him. As we shall see below, they had their own private reasons.

Tacitus attributes a speech to Civilis in which he presents the corrupt practices of the recruiting officers as evidence that the Romans did not look on the Batavi as allies, but as subjects. It is questionable if Tacitus faithfully conveys here the thrust of the argument Civilis used to win his fellow tribesmen to his cause, as the corruption of the Roman imperialists is one of Tacitus' own hobbyhorses. Whether the press-gangs were really as heavy-handed and perverted as Tacitus wants us to believe, remains to be seen. The fact that he mentions the recruitment of old and weak men as well as youths suggests something other than corruption; i.e. that the press-gangs went beyond what was possible. From almost every Batavian family, there was already a son doing military service in the auxiliaries, and more than that was demanding too much. Most probably, the revolt was indeed a reaction to Vitellius' strong-arm recruiting methods. However, these had less to do with corruption than with a lack of a realistic sense of what could possibly be demanded of the Batavi.

Sometimes, Tacitus puts words into the mouth of the Batavian leader in which he defends the freedom of the Batavi. Alas, in ancient texts, the barbarians *always* fight for freedom, so this is quite possibly a cliché. Besides, Tacitus claims somewhere else that, for the Batavi, glory and not freedom was the spur.[117]

There is an extra complication here, as it is unclear what is meant by freedom in this context: the independence of the tribe, or the autonomy of the elite. This last could be historically true, as Roman citizenship was no longer confined to the Julii. Since the reign of Claudius, a second generation of 'new Romans' had evolved all over Gaul, who were all called Claudii, after the man who had enfranchised them. From this time on, the old Batavian elite had to share their privileges with others and may have longed for the reinstatement of their former authority. This is not to say that there may not also have been Batavians who dreamed of real political independence. After all, the Frisians had set the example.

To sum up: we can think of various reasons for the Batavian Revolt. Civilis had personal motives; the old tribal elite did not want to share power; the tribe as a whole may have wanted independence and, in any case, was deeply offended by the dismissal of the imperial guard. For everyone, the strong-arm method of recruiting was a reason to take up arms.

• First Skirmishes

Just as the Treveri had once started a rebellion by getting the Eburones to do the dirty work, Civilis now, too, got a client tribe to rebel first: the Cananefates, living in the far West.

One of the Cananefates was Brinno, a man of brute courage, who was of particularly illustrious descent. His father had dared to commit many hostile acts and, with impunity, had displayed contempt for Caligula's absurd expedition. The very mention of the name of his rebellious family made Brinno a favourite. In accordance with their tribal custom, he was put on a shield and shaken back and forth on the shoulders of the shield-bearers, the ritual by which the Cananefates chose him as leader. He, at once, called on the Frisians (a tribe living across the Rhine) to join him, and attacked two forts very close to the North Sea.[118]

Aquillius' medallion. The inscription reads "Possession of Gaius Aquillius Proculus, centurion of the Eighth Legion Augusta" (Nijmegen, Valkhof museum).

One of the devastated camps is Valkenburg, where a thick charred layer bears witness to Brinno's success. It was not long before other forts, such as Utrecht, also went up in flames. At Utrecht, archaeologists found 50 gold pieces under the burn layer. This fortune must have been buried before the attack, and the owner was never again in a position to come and collect his savings.

Tacitus mentions a certain Aquilius who collected the soldiers from the devastated forts and led them to safety. It is conceivable that he was the owner of a silver medallion that was found in the cavalry fort on the Kops Plateau at Nijmegen. If this is so – and the name is rare enough for it to be likely – then a number of things become immediately clear, because the medallion mentions that the officer was part of the Eighth Legion Augusta. This is an interesting fact. This unit was stationed in Svishtov in Bulgaria in AD 69. If it is true that soldiers from the Balkans were transferred to Nijmegen, then Hordeonius Flaccus, whom Tacitus called incompetent, had at least seen what was coming. He asked Vitellius for reinforcements and received them. This silver artefact amounts to nothing less than the rehabilitation of the governor.

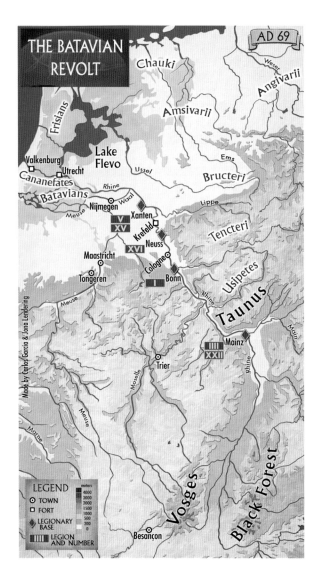

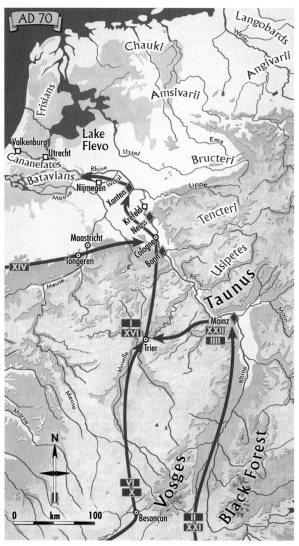

While Aquilius tried to save whatever was possible, Civilis made an offer to the Romans to put down the insurrection of the Cananefates with his Batavi. The legionaries and auxiliaries could rest in Xanten. However, the Romans saw through his ruse and, somewhere around Nijmegen, it came to an engagement between the two armies.

Civilis now turned to force. He organized the Cananefates, Frisians, and Batavi into different troop units. The Romans were drawn up in a wide battle-line opposite, not far from the River Waal, with their ships turned towards the enemy.

The battle had not been going on for long when a cohort of the Tungri defected to Civilis. Thrown into confusion by this unpredicted treachery, the Roman soldiers were cut down by allies and enemy alike. There was the same lack of loyalty on the part of the fleet: some of the crew were Batavi, who, feigning a lack of skill, hampered the rowers and combatants in their work, so that presently these began to row in the wrong direction towards the enemy bank. Finally, the helmsmen and centurions who did not want to defect to the enemy were slaughtered, so that the ships of the entire fleet of twenty-four vessels either went over to the enemy or were captured.

That enemy victory was glorious for the moment and useful for the future, as the Batavi had got hold of all the weapons and ships they needed. All over Germania and Gaul, they were extensively hailed as 'champions of freedom'. The German regions immediately sent delegations offering help, while Civilis, using diplomacy and bribery, pressed for an alliance with the Gauls. And so, he allowed all the commanders of the cohorts who had been taken prisoner to return to their tribes and gave the cohorts the choice of leaving or staying. Those who stayed were given honourable positions in his army, those who left were given spoils from the Romans.[119]

The Romans were now driven out of the Dutch river area, and it became abundantly clear that the Batavi were deadly serious in their revolt. In order to get to grips with the situation, Hordeonius Flaccus ordered the Fifth Legion Alaudae and the Fifteenth Primigenia from Xanten to march to meet the Batavi. Because these units were not complete, he added the Ubian and Treveran auxiliaries, as well as a Batavian squadron. The latter was to turn out to be a mistake.

Civilis surrounded himself with the standards of the defeated cohorts, to remind his soldiers of their newly-won glorious victory and to put the fear of God in the enemy by reminding them of their recent defeat. His mother and sisters, together with all the women and children of his men, were ordered to range themselves behind the troops, so as to encourage them to victory or to shame them if they should be defeated.

Singing from the enemy soldiers, loud cries from their women, the din echoed down the lines. The clamour from our legions and cohorts could not rise above it. Our left flank had become exposed because of the Batavian squadron that had deserted, and this immediately made us vulnerable. The legionaries managed to hold on to their weapons and keep in rank, despite the alarming situation. But the Ubian and Treveran auxiliaries turned tail and fled in a shameful way, fanning out over the battlefield, where the Germani rushed forward to attack them. Meanwhile, the legions made use of the diversion to escape, and they reached the safety of the camp at Xanten.[120]

In all probability, this battle took place east of Nijmegen: the presence of women on the battlefield leads us to suspect that there was a town nearby. The deserting Batavian squadron could have been billeted on the Kops Plateau.

After the victory, Civilis did not demonstrate very noble behaviour by handing over the squadron commander, who had contributed so much to his victory, to the Frisians as a prisoner. This Claudius Labeo was one of the Claudii, the 'new Romans' who threatened the position of the Julii.

Whatever the aims of the rebellion may have been, they had now been achieved. The presence of hundreds of Roman dead proved that the Batavian prince had avenged his brother's death, while his tribe had taken revenge for the dishonourable discharge of the imperial guard and the recruiting methods of the Romans. For Civilis, absolute sovereignty was within reach, should he wish it: anyone who defeated Roman legionaries gained an unassailable position within his tribe.

Furthermore, they did not need to fear Roman reprisals. Civilis could always claim that he had acted on the orders of Vespasian, who, as we have already seen, was threatening Vitellius' throne from Judaea. In the past, the Batavi and the Romans had fought side by side in Britannia, and Vespasian had recently written a letter to Civilis in which he had requested his former brother-in-arms to start a revolt and tie up Vitellius' troops in Germania Inferior. There had, indeed, been casualties, but the Batavi had not really caused the Romans any lasting damage. Thus, Civilis could now count on Vespasian being well disposed towards the Batavi.

• The Attack on Xanten

The stupidest action that Civilis could now take would be to carry out an attack on the legionary base at Xanten. No Roman emperor could let such a humiliation go unpunished. As soon as even one spear was cast at the walls, an invincibly large Roman army would inevitably march northwards to avenge the shame. The conflict between Vitellius and Vespasian would first have to be resolved, of course, but, irrespective of who should win, once there was only one emperor at the helm, he would be duty-bound to punish such an attack. The Batavi knew enough about the Roman army to know this; and Civilis, who enjoyed Roman citizenship and had served for twenty-five years in the auxiliaries, knew the consequences more than anyone else. And yet, the Batavi resolved to destroy Xanten, and Civilis swore that he would let his hair hang loose and paint it red for as long as it took to reduce Xanten to ashes.

Whatever pushed the Batavi into undertaking this apparently reckless action remains a mystery. They were certainly well prepared, as the eight Batavian cohorts had joined them by now. As we have seen, these troops had learnt, in Mainz, that Vitellius needed their assistance in the war against Vespasian. They had only just set out for the south, when they received a summons from Civilis to join him. The First Legion from Bonn had tried to stop the defectors but was numerically incapable of holding back the 4000 Batavi.

The arrival of the veteran cohorts meant that Civilis now commanded a real army. But he still hesitated on which course of action to take, reflecting that Rome was strong. So he made all the men he had under him swear allegiance to Vespasian, and sent an appeal to the two legions that had been beaten in the previous engagement and had retired to the camp at Xanten, asking them to accept the same oath. Back came the reply: they were not in the habit of taking advice from those who were both traitors and enemies. They already had an emperor, Vitellius, and in his defence they would maintain their loyalty and arms to their dying breath. Therefore, that Batavian turncoat should not have the arrogance to determine Roman policy and could expect the punishment he deserved.

When this reply reached Civilis, he flew into a rage, and hurried the whole Batavian nation into arms. They were joined by the Bructeri and Tencteri, and as the news spread, Germania awoke to the call of spoil and glory.[121]

Thus began the siege of Xanten at the end of September AD 69. Only some 5000 Romans, who belonged to the Fifth and Fifteenth Legions and their auxiliaries, were defending the

camp. Despite the fact that they had already been defeated once, they were sufficiently mo-
tivated to drive back an initial Batavian attack and Civilis' attempt to take the camp with a
siege tower did not have the projected results. And so, the Batavi tried to starve the Romans
out. They may have been under the misapprehension that Xanten did not have large supplies
in store and would run out quickly. In any case, that is what Tacitus states, and perhaps he
is right, although it is certainly quite remarkable, as the harvest had just been saved. As it
turned out, Xanten was to hold out for many weeks.

Civilis' superfluous troops had, meanwhile, begun to plunder Belgica. Perhaps the treas-
ure-trove of 65 silver and six gold coins from Montfort in Dutch Limburg dates from this
time. The plunderers even reached the towns situated on the Channel. In his description of
this pillaging spree, Tacitus does not forget to allude to Virgil's words that the Morini are the
"people living on the edge of the world", once again underlining, for those who were not yet
aware of it, that the Batavian Revolt had taken place on the edge of the world.

● Counterattack

Hordeonius – again, not nearly as indolent as Tacitus would give us to understand – had,
meanwhile, taken counter-measures: leaving the Fourth Legion Macedonica behind to
guard Mainz, he sent the Twenty-second Primigenia to the north, under the command of
Gaius Dillius Vocula, while he himself sailed down the Rhine to Bonn, to assume command
of the First Gemanica. The troops came together at Cologne, and at Neuss units of the Sixteenth Legion Gallica joined them. Together, they marched to present-day Krefeld.

And here, the advance came to a halt. Tacitus gives all sorts of reasons for this. He suggests that the men – the very ones who had defeated Vindex in a lightning campaign the
previous year! – needed to be given extra training. Another reason he offers is that the land
to the southwest of Xanten had to be plundered; and, then again, that the legionaries had to
fight to requisition a grain vessel … The true reason was most probably that there had been
reports from the south that the Danube legions had joined Vespasian and were now on their
way to Italy. As the legions from the Rhine army had placed Vitellius on the throne, and the
Batavi had written proof that they were fighting in the name of Vespasian, Hordeonius and
Vocula wanted, at all costs, to prevent the two forces from coming to blows. In AD 68, the
Rhine armies had fought for an emperor who had lost a civil war, and the commanders were
anxious to avoid a repetition of this.

At the beginning of November, the soldiers in Krefeld received the bad news that Vitellius had been defeated. Needless to say, that did not improve their morale, and they swore
allegiance to Vespasian without much conviction. Moreover, their generals, Hordeonius and
Vocula, now had no idea what they should do. The initiative lay with Civilis. The war could
now be suspended, if it was true that he had been fighting for Vespasian; but, if that had only
been a masquerade, then the Romans would have to fight against the most daunting of all
local tribes. The fact that the Batavi did not try to contact them after hearing the news of
Vitellius' defeat was evidence that they intended to continue the war.

As far as the Batavi were concerned, Civilis knew that he had to destroy the army at
Krefeld before it joined the besieged legionaries in Xanten. After that, he could capture the
Xanten military base. As it would take at least half a year for the Romans to send fresh
troops, Civilis would have plenty of time to extend his power to other regions. Negotiations were already underway with the inhabitants of Trier; they would certainly turn against
Rome if the Roman forces north of the Alps were reduced to the military base at Mainz
alone. The big problem for Civilis now was that the army of Hordeonius and Vocula was too
large for him to meet on a regular battlefield, even though it consisted of units that were not
up to full military strength.

The Romans did not need to be mind readers to know that Civilis would try to take them by surprise. Furthermore, they had a very good idea that they should be especially on their guard during the moonless nights at the beginning of December. Therefore, contrary to what Tacitus insinuates, it was probably no coincidence that when the Batavi attacked Krefeld, the Roman garrison was relieved by Basque troops sent by Hordeonius from Neuss. This resulted in an important Roman victory, even though the auxiliaries suffered shocking losses, as it appears from the archaeological discovery that the dead, both men and horses, could not be given a decent cremation and had to be buried hurriedly.

The most valiant of the Batavian fighters – that is to say, of their infantry – lay dead. Their cavalry managed to get away with our standards and with the prisoners they took in the first phase of the engagement. That day, the casualties on our side were heavier; but those who were killed were the poorer fighters, whereas the Batavians lost the pick of their men.[122]

With "the pick of their men", Tacitus is referring to the eight Batavian cohorts, of which we will hear only one more time. Nothing now stood in the way of the Romans, who continued their advance and proceeded to relieve Xanten. However, they only managed to fortify the walls of the barracks, replenish the stores, and bring the wounded to a safe place, when news reached them that the civilian settlement in Mainz had been attacked by tribes from the opposite bank of the Rhine, who were after easy spoils. As soon as the Roman relief army had left to deal with this emergency, Civilis resumed the siege of Xanten with the remainder of his men. He knew that he now had a chance to take the camp while the main Roman forces were occupied elsewhere.

The Roman legionaries had marked up a significant victory at Krefeld and, when they arrived at Neuss in the last days of AD 69, they received money to celebrate Vespasian's accession as emperor. As loyal supporters of Vitellius, this was more than they had ever dared to hope for. However, the festivities, which may have coincided with the Roman carnival celebrations in honour of the god Saturn, were rudely disrupted by the murder of Hordeonius by his own men. Vocula would have suffered the same fate, if he had not left the camp by night, dressed as a slave.

The attack on the generals – just at the moment that the tide was turning for the Romans – is one of the inexplicable events of these months. We can only speculate about the circumstances. Tacitus writes that Vocula had brought the wounded at Xanten to safety and, moreover, had increased the strength of his own army by a thousand men. This means that the garrison at Xanten had been reduced to about 3500 men. Tacitus reports that those left behind had complained that they had been deserted. All things considered, they were right, because these troops mainly served to keep Civilis at bay, while the bulk of the Roman forces were occupied elsewhere. Could it be that Hordeonius' murderers were not acting in drunken hysteria, but that this killing was, in fact, an act of fragging?

• The Gallic Empire

In Italy, AD 70 began promisingly. The civil war was over, Vespasian's rule was uncontested, and there were plans to strengthen the Rhine armies. The question was now whether these reinforcements could cross the wintry Alps quickly enough to put an end to the revolt. It was soon apparent that they were too late.

In January, the inhabitants of Trier and Langres joined the revolt. It is true that the victories at Krefeld and Xanten had somewhat restored the prestige of the Romans, but Civilis was still laying siege to Xanten, Hordeonius had been murdered, and the Batavi had plundered large parts of Belgica. For the people of Trier and Langres, breaking the bonds with Rome was a way of preventing the pillaging of their own land. That was not to say that they chose to side with the Batavi. The inhabitants of the two cities were completely Romanized and had their own candidate, Julius Sabinus, for the imperial throne. Sabinus declared himself to be the great-grandson of Caesar: you could not get any more Roman than that! His lieutenant commanders, Julius Classicus and Julius Tutor, carried Roman insignia and spoke proudly of their 'Gallic Empire'. While the Batavian revolt had to do with pride in a non-Roman identity, the very opposite was true of the new rebels.

One last Roman success was the driving out of the pillaging tribes from the area around Mainz. From then on, both the Twenty-Second Legion and the Fourth Legion defended this area. When Vocula again marched northwards with the First and the Sixteenth Legions to bolster the Roman defence at Xanten, his auxiliaries began to desert him and, after a few days, one of his officers murdered him: an unworthy end for a brave man, who, over the course of a few months, had managed to save all that he could, namely the military base of Mainz. The two incomplete legions that had been under his command now pledged their allegiance to the Gallic Empire and Sabinus. As former supporters of Vitellius, they would not have had many qualms about breaking their oath to Vespasian. However, the Emperor Sabinus ordered them to leave the battle-zone, as he did not wholly trust them.

• The Fall of Xanten

After the murder of Vocula and the capitulation of his army, the defenders surrendered in February or March AD 70.

For the besieged, it was a matter of loyalty or starvation, a difficult choice between honour and dishonour. While they hesitated, all normal and emergency rations ran out. They had already consumed the mules, horses, and other animals, as well as other impure and dirty animals, which served to relieve their desperate plight. Finally, they were reduced to tearing up plants and roots, as well as the weeds growing between the stones, thereby creating an example of patient endurance of privation. But then, at long last, they spoiled their splendid record with a dishonourable conclusion: they sent envoys to Civilis to plead for their lives. He accepted their pleas only when they had taken an oath of allegiance to the Gallic Empire.

Then Civilis took over the camp as plunder and sent out guards, some to get hold of all the money, sutlers and baggage, and others to escort the soldiers when they marched out of their camp, destitute. Almost eight kilometers from Xanten, the unsuspecting Roman column was ambushed by the Germans. The toughest fighters fell in their tracks, many others were killed in scattered flight, and the rest made good their retreat to the camp.

It is true that Civilis protested, and loudly blamed the Germans for what he described as a criminal breach of faith. But our sources do not make it clear whether this was mere hypocrisy, or whether Civilis was really incapable of restraining his ferocious allies.[123]

After the military base had been gutted, the last defenders had been burnt alive, and Civilis had restyled his hair, he gave a few prisoners of war to his son as a present to use for target practice. Tacitus does imply that he has his doubts about this story, but it fits well into what we know about the native religion: prisoners of war were put to death.

After that, Civilis marched to Cologne, to move into his headquarters there. The Batavi were now the most powerful tribe in northwestern Europe and, in the following months, their leader would attempt to make allies of the inhabitants of the local communities in Belgica. (How he intended to govern the region is unknown. Tacitus seems to have thought that the Batavi wanted to set up a sort of tribal federation, but that, again, could be stereotyping.) One of the reasons for changing the focus of attention to the valley of the Meuse was the presence of Claudius Labeo, the cavalry general treated so roughly by Civilis. Labeo had, meanwhile, escaped from his Frisian guards and, with soldiers from Bavay and Tongeren, was carrying on a civil war against the Batavi. At Maastricht, it came to an engagement, which Tacitus describes as if it were a tribal war.

Labeo was confident of his position: he had meanwhile secured the bridge over the River Meuse. The battle fought in this confined space gave neither side the advantage, until the Batavi swam across the river and attacked Labeo from behind. At the same time, whether out of daring or by prior arrangement, Civilis pushed through up to the Tungrian front lines and addressed them loudly: "We have not started a war so that we, the Batavi and Treveri, should have power over all the tribes. We are not interested in such pretensions. Let us be allies. I am coming over to your side, whether you want me as leader or follower." This made a great impression on the ordinary soldiers and they sheathed their swords, after which two of the Tungrian nobles, Campanus and Juvenalis, offered him the surrender of the whole tribe. Labeo got away before he could be rounded up.[124]

The words that are translated here as "in this confined space", *in angustiis*, are often (although not exclusively) used in Latin to refer to mountain passes, which, in turn, brings to mind that a man like Tacitus expected inhospitable, high mountains at the edges of the world – somewhat different from the gentle hills east of Maastricht.

After the battle, Civilis must have left for Tongeren. In spite of a defensive earth wall quickly erected around Tongeren (excavated by archaeologists), the town was devastated. We do not have to be philosophers to realize that the support the town would give to Civilis after that was not very wholehearted.

• The Empire Strikes Back

As was only to be expected, from the moment Civilis attacked Xanten, it was but a question of time before Rome mobilized an immense army. The general was called Cerialis. He was not only a relation of Vespasian's, but had also served in Britannia, in the same army in which both the new emperor and Julius Civilis had served. Tacitus portrays Cerialis as a somewhat eccentric but efficient fire-eater. He had, under his command, the Twenty-First Legion Rapax, units of the Rhine legions that had gone to Italy with Vitellius, and the Second Legion Adiutrix ('assistant'). At the head of this large force, Cerialis marched on Mainz.

His arrival was enough to turn the tide. Without meeting much resistance, the Romans could proceed to Trier, which they reached in June of AD 70. The Gallic Emperor, Julius Sabinus, was in hiding at this time, and, as there was no Gallic commander for the legionaries that had sworn allegiance to the Gallic Empire a few months earlier, these men no longer felt bound by their pledge. Once again, they changed their allegiance, crossing back to the side of the Romans, and joined up with the units returning from the south.

From then on, the Romans were both qualitatively and numerically superior to their opponents. The Second, Fourth and Twenty-Second Legions guarded Mainz; the Twenty-First, First and Sixteenth were stationed in Trier. Besides these units, there were reinforcements on the way from Spain: the Sixth Victrix ('triumphant') and the Tenth Gemina ('twins'). Civilis and the Gallic leaders Classicus and Tutor had, at all costs, to prevent these three armies from joining up. Therefore, they carried out a pre-emptive attack on Trier. Tacitus' story is more exciting than the battle by night could possibly have been. The combined forces of the rebels were no match for the Romans.

Tutor and Classicus spurred on the different groups to battle, urging the Gauls to fight for liberty, the Batavi for glory, and the Germans for booty. Everything favoured the enemy until the Twenty-First Legion, having more room than the rest, concentrated its entire strength and so resisted the enemy's attack, and presently drove him back.[125]

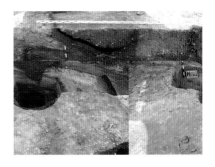

A burn layer from Cologne (Breslauer Platz) from the time of the Batavian Revolt, recognizable as a black line in the excavation trench.

Elsewhere in his report of this battle, Tacitus mentions the Batavian cohorts for the last time. He was probably referring to the eight cohorts that had formed the nucleus of Civilis' army, but no longer had the same fighting power.

Civilis was now forced to return to the north to defend the lands of the Batavi, but at this point everything began to go awry. The people of Cologne rose in rebellion against the Batavi; those holding the garrison were murdered. (A burn layer on the north side of the ancient town, is a witness to this event.) The Batavian leader wanted to retake the town with a cohort of Frisians and Chauki based in Zülpich, which he had recently recruited, but that turned out differently.

The cohort was destroyed by a ruse of the inhabitants of Cologne. The Germans had first been stupefied by elaborate dinners and lots of wine, then the doors were closed on them and everything set alight, burning them all alive. At the same time, Cerialis advanced quickly by making long daily marches. And, in addition, there was something else worrying Civilis: what would happen if the Fourteenth Legion, with the aid of the fleet from Britannia, were to launch an attack against the Batavi on the North Sea coast?

This did not happen. Instead, the legion was led overland by their commander Fabius Priscus to attack the Nervii and the Tungri, causing both tribes to surrender. The fleet fell victim to the Cananefates, who sank or captured most of the ships. The same group of Cananefates made short work of a multitude of Nervii who had come to fight for the Romans. Classicus, too, was successful when he engaged with a group of cavalry that Cerialis had dispatched to Neuss.[126]

Once again, Tacitus' use of tribal names is misleading. The Nervii and Tungri lived in towns and were, by Roman definition, civilized people. Only the Cananefates had no known developed urban centres at that time.

Meanwhile, in spite of the successes of the Cananefates, Cerialis' attack on the Batavian homeland along the rivers Meuse, Waal, and Rhine could not fail. Civilis' last hope was that the invasion of this area, nowadays called the Betuwe, would not have priority for the Romans, and that the recovery of the Rhine border and the recapture of the road overland via Bavay and Tongeren would take precedence.

Because the attention of the Romans was focused elsewhere, Civilis almost managed to defeat Cerialis at Xanten. The Batavian leader erected a dyke, flooding parts of the land and causing mobility problems for the heavily armed legionaries. Notwithstanding, the Romans held their ground and, the next day, Cerialis outflanked Civilis' soldiers and attacked them from behind. Once again, the water proved to be an ally of the Batavi, as a summer thunderstorm put an end to the battle before the Romans had won the day. In spite of this, Civilis was forced to retreat and the Sixth Legion had good reason to erect a victory monument there.

Civilis received reinforcements from the Chauki. Nevertheless, he did not dare mount an armed defence of Nijmegen, but seizing everything that was portable, he burned the rest and withdrew into the Betuwe. He realized very well that there were no boats to build a pontoon bridge, which was the only way to get the Roman army across the River Waal. He even dismantled the dam Drusus had built, and, as he had demolished the barriers that checked it, the Waal could take its natural course in the direction of Gaul. After the river had been diverted in this way, the

Victory monument of the Sixth Legion Victrix, found at Xanten. The text says that the commander of the legion, Sextus Caelius Tuscus, dedicated the victory to the Emperor Vespasian and his son Titus (Bonn, Rheinisches Landesmuseum / Rhineland Regional Museum).

Betuwe and Germania were only separated by a narrow channel and it looked like one uninterrupted stretch of land.[127]

Tacitus probably means to say here that, by demolishing the dam, Civilis succeeded in lowering the level of the Lower Rhine and, consequently, widening the Waal. Cerialis was realistic, as he understood that he had to be satisfied with the Waal as the northern border, as long as he did not have a large fleet at his disposal. Therefore, he concentrated on reorganizing the Middle Rhine frontier. To keep the Batavians in check, he took up defensive positions in Nijmegen, where the Second Legion Adiutrix built its fortress on top of the burned city. The Tenth was stationed a bit more to the east, while auxiliary units were placed in two forts downstream.

• Order Restored

Meanwhile, Civilis believed that the absence of the Roman general presented a chance for a simultaneous attack on the four garrisons, but he appears to have underestimated Cerialis' quick reactions. Although the attacks failed, the Romans could not avenge them as long as their fleet was below its full strength. Nevertheless, Cerialis determined to invade the Betuwe as soon as possible, and was strengthened in his resolve when he miraculously escaped falling victim to Civilis' last scheme.

Cerialis had gone to Neuss and Bonn to inspect the winter camps that were being built for the legions, and was now returning with the fleet. However, his escort became scattered and the night watch was not on the alert. The Germans got to know of this and planned an ambush.

On a dark, overcast night, they slipped downstream and got inside the garrison walls without meeting any opposition. The onslaught was initially helped by cunning: they cut the guy ropes, burying the soldiers under their own tents and making it easy to finish them off. Another group bombarded the ships, threw grappling irons in the afterdeck, and towed them away. And, as quiet as they had been in the beginning, in order not to raise the alarm, after the murders, they shouted for all they were worth, in order to increase the confusion and fear.

Roused by their wounds, the Romans searched for their weapons and ran up and down the streets, only a few in military garb, most with clothing around their arms and with swords drawn. The general, half-awake and almost naked, was saved only by the enemy's mistake: the Germans dragged away his flagship, recognizable by his standard, thinking the general was on board. However, the Roman general had spent the night elsewhere, and it was generally thought that he had been enjoying a sexual escapade with Claudia Sacrata, a Ubian woman.[128]

After this humiliation, Cerialis decided to invade the Betuwe, even though, as we have seen, his fleet was not yet fully operational. His aim was to demoralize the Batavians by a big demonstration of power.

Cerialis relentlessly plundered the Betuwe, but, adopting a familiar device of generals, he left Civilis' farmlands and houses intact. In the meantime, it was getting on for autumn. Because of the torrential autumnal rains, the river overflowed its banks and spilled into the marshy, low-lying Betuwe, turning it into a lake. There was nothing to be seen – neither the fleet nor the supplies – and the camp on the flats was washed away by the river.

At that moment, the legions could have been crushed, and that was what the Germans wanted to do, but Civilis craftily dissuaded them, or so he claimed later. That was not far from the truth, as a few days later he surrendered.[129]

The effects of Cerialis' show of force surpassed all expectations: confronted by Roman troops in their own country, the Batavi gave up even before the battle had really been fought. Tacitus' report breaks off with the negotiations between Cerialis and Civilis on a bridge in the Betuwe: the medieval manuscript of the *Histories* does not go any further. Because of this, it is not known what was discussed, although it appears from a quote in Tacitus' *Germania*, already given on page 32, that the "former alliance" was renewed. In other words, the Batavi again had to supply troops and were exempt from paying taxes.

That is not to say that they did well out of it. They had paid an enormous price for their support of Civilis. Their capital city had been destroyed and had to be rebuilt a little further downstream. Moreover, from then on, there was a legion stationed nearby. That was not very difficult to live with, but the grief for those who had lost their lives was less easy to accept. As has already been said, every family had at least one son in the Roman army. Many of these soldiers had perished, which plunged their families into deep mourning.

Civilis' final fate has not been passed down to us, but he would not have made old bones. Yes, he had been promised impunity, but Cerialis was surely not the first or, indeed, the last Roman general who felt no obligation to honour the promise made to someone who was himself a word-breaker. Civilis had done this twice: in the first place, he had committed high treason, and in the second, he was responsible for the murder of the garrison at Xanten that had surrendered to him in good faith. Perhaps the "Batavian turncoat" was arrested shortly after his surrender and got "the punishment he deserved", as predicted the first time he besieged Xanten (i.e. crucifixion). But perhaps that was not even necessary. Civilis may have been murdered by an angry tribal brother, just like Arminius and Gannascus. As is often the case, we simply do not know.

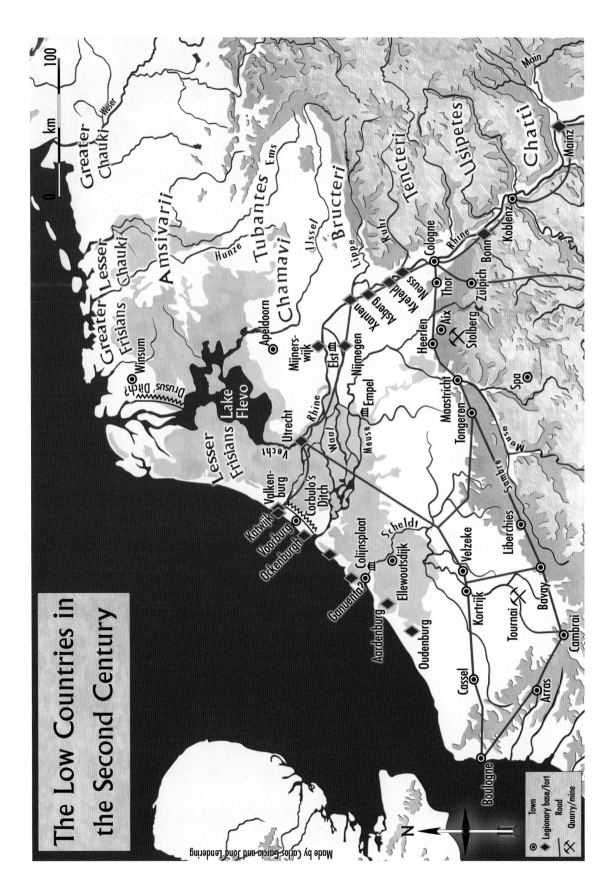

The Low Countries in the Second Century

Made by Carlos Garcia and Jono Lendering

Town
Legionary base/fort
Road
Quarry/mine

N

Greater Chauki
Weser
Lesser Chauki
Greater Frisians
Lesser Frisians
Winsum
Drusus' Ditch?
Lesser Frisians
Lake Flevo
Amsivarii
Hunze
Ems
Tubantes
Chamavi
IJssel
Apeldoorn
Mijners-wijk
Elst
Nijmegen
Empel
Utrecht
Vecht
Rhine
Waal
Meuse
Bructeri
Lippe
Ruhr
Tencteri
Usipetes
Chatti
Main
Mainz
Koblenz
Bonn
Zülpich
Cologne
Rhine
Neuss
Thor
Krefeld
Asberg
Xanten
Aix
Stolberg
Heerlen
Spa
Maastricht
Tongeren
Sambre
Meuse
Scheldt
Liberchies
Velzeke
Kortrijk
Bavay
Tournai
Cambrai
Arras
Cassel
Oudenburg
Aardenburg
Ellewoutsdijk
Colijnsplaat
Ganuenta?
Ockenburgh
Voorburg
Katwijk
Valken-burg
Corbulo's Ditch

0   km   100

106

Ellewoutsdijk

In Roman times, large stretches of land along the coast consisted of peat bog. It was thought for a long time that this was not habitable, although Caesar insisted in his writings that the Menapii lived there (see page 22). Indeed, some parts were cultivated in the Late Iron Age. This means that land was drained by means of ditches, so that the top layer of soil dried out and changed into fertile agricultural land. This process continued into the second and third centuries AD, until the region became swamped due to extensive flooding (see page 139). As a consequence, archaeologists had to dig up the remains of the bog settlements from under layers of medieval marine clay.

This makes locating the bog settlements a real archaeological challenge. Moreover, the peasants had been poor, which considerably reduces the chances of finding any kind of unusual artefacts. Furthermore, it is quite difficult to recognize the traces of their habitation – that is, if there are any traces left: the area's submergence in salt water, combined with the methods used for harvesting peat in the Late Middle Ages, may have seriously damaged any traces of habitation that might have been preserved in the ground.

An excavation in 2001 in Ellewoutsdijk in the Netherlands brought a breakthrough. Traces were found there of nine farmsteads, three outhouses, several wells, and fences, that seem to have formed a cattle stockade. It has been ascertained by tree ring dating, that the hamlet existed for almost a century, from the middle of the first century to the middle of the second century AD. Because it was usual for most farmsteads to serve about one generation, it appears that two or three families lived in Ellewoutsdijk.

The houses were built on the banks of drainage canals, as it was there that the ground dried out most and was very solid. The farmsteads could be quite big – the smallest house measured 13 x 6 metres – and they had straight, well-built walls, obviously artisan work. As is usual for the Low Countries, the barn and living quarters were under the same roof. To create shelter from the dominant west wind and catch as much sun as possible, the farmhouses were built along an east-west axis.

Comparison with other agricultural settlements shows us that the barns in Ellewoutsdijk were rather small. We can deduce from this that the inhabitants lived mainly from agriculture. Indeed, the chaff from barley and wheat has been identified on the site, and a millstone, made from imported stone, has been found. With regard to animal husbandry, there were traces found of oxen, goats and sheep. The excavation of spinning apparatus proves that the wool was used to make textiles. The fact that very few horses were found, even fewer pigs, and no poultry whatsoever, suggests that the inhabitants of Ellewoutsdijk had very little contact with the Romans.

The plant residue in the goats' droppings shows that the animals ate types of grass that thrived on salt. They must have grazed on the salt meadows in the summer, and the plants harvested there, must have been their winter fodder. Evidence shows that, every now and then, the shepherds also emptied fish traps, and collected mussels. Although the relative absence of coins proves that the peasants were not linked into the monetary economy of the rest of the Roman world, they did not live in complete isolation either: the peas, spelt, and dill found in Ellewoutsdijk could only have been imported.

The largest farmstead measures 27 x 7 metres and would seem to have had three naves. Its height can be deduced from the A-frames on which the ridge beam rested. Because the poles were slanted, archaeologists could work out at which point they had crossed each other and, in this way, the height of five metres could be calculated. The use of these A-frames was not unusual: archaeologists also found them further north, around the mouth of the Meuse.

On the other hand, the process used in producing the hand-moulded pottery found at Ellewoutsdijk was closer to the traditions of the Flemish coastal region in the southwest. Because the River Scheldt ran further to the north and formed the border of the habitat of the Menapii, we may assume that the inhabitants of the excavated farmsteads belonged to that tribe.

One of the most remarkable discoveries was a pinewood pole, which the excavators found impossible to relate to the known Roman tree ring curves. Finally, it turned out that the wood had been twenty-five centuries old when Ellewoutsdijk became inhabited. It must have come from a piece of ancient forest that was perfectly preserved in the peat, only to come to the surface in Roman times when the peat was washed away.

9 A Frontier Zone in Peacetime

• The Army in Peacetime

During the civil wars of AD 69, Rome's principal temple, the Capitol, went up in flames. Many people believed that this omen foretold the end of the Roman Empire. And this forecast seemed to be coming true. In Gaul, Julius Sabinus thought he could found a Gallic Empire; rebellious Jews and Batavians continued their resistance with a new burst of energy; and in several places in the Empire, rival cities settled old scores. However, with the sound policies of Vespasian (r. 69-79) and his sons, Titus (r.79-81) and Domitian (r.81-96), Rome was able to recover.

Mask of a Roman horseman, found in the Corbulo canal at the place where it branches off from the Rhine, close to Leiden in the Netherlands. Because of the face's similarity to that of a well-known Dutch singer, it was nicknamed 'Gordon' (Leiden, Rijksmuseum van oudheden/National Museum of Antiquities).

Sound rule, however, was no guarantee of a quiet reign. The biographer Suetonius reports, in a (mainly negative) portrait of Domitian, that he controled the town officials and provincial governors so well, that they never were more honest and just.[130] However, that cannot only be seen as positive, because it also meant that the senators, for whom the administration of the provinces had always been quite lucrative, lost a source of income. This created bad blood between emperor and senators, and the atmosphere of mutual distrust only came to an end when Domitian was murdered in AD 96. For a while, it looked as if a new civil war might break out, but the old senator Nerva, who succeeded Domitian, designated a capable general as his successor. This was Trajan, and his accession to the imperial throne in AD 98 went smoothly. He was praised by the senators as the best emperor Rome had ever had. How the people in the provinces responded to the reinstatement of the senatorial incomes, is not recorded.

A legionary leads away a captive (drawing Graham Sumner).

Frisian pottery from Housesteads, Great Britain.

Bronze pendant from a horse harness mentioning LEG HISP IX, from Ewijk near Nijmegen, evidence of the stay of the Ninth Legion Hispana in the Low Countries after its departure from Britannia (Nijmegen, Valkhof Museum).[135]

The Empire now experienced a period of unrivalled prosperity, which continued during the reigns of Trajan's successors, Hadrian (r.117-138), Antoninus Pius (r.138-161), and Marcus Aurelius (r.161-180). This was Rome's golden age, and that applied also to the frontier zone of Germania Inferior, where Romanization now really took off, about a century after Gallia Belgica.

And yet, in this time, too, there were occasional disturbances. Some of these conflicts can be identified. In AD 77, there was a Roman expedition against the Bructeri and, six or seven years later, this same tribe was given a pro-Roman king.[131] Domitian visited the Lower Rhine country and in the spring of AD 89, the army of Germania Inferior suppressed a revolt by the governor of Germania Superior. Trajan's honorary arch in present-day Benevento shows the chiefs of the German tribes swearing allegiance to Rome, which may happened during Trajan's visit to Germania Inferior. After this, we hear little about border violence. That everything was peaceful and calm, however, would be a misconception. For various reasons, there are very few sources about this period, and it is likely that there were indeed German incursions about which nothing has been passed down to us. These raids cannot have been very big and the Romans must have considered them a frequent aggravation that could never wholly be prevented. The construction of a camp at Ermelo, thirty-five kilometres north of the Rhine, proves that the Roman leaders still deemed it necessary to put on a display of strength.

Yet, it was possible to reduce the size of the Roman garrison. After the Batavian Rebellion, there were still four legions in Germania Inferior: the Twenty-First Rapax at Bonn (later: I Minervia), the Sixth Victrix at Neuss, and the Twenty-Second Primigenia in a new and smaller camp at Xanten, while the Second Adiutrix had been replaced at Nijmegen by the Tenth Gemina. As the recruits of the last unit came from northern Italy and southern France, it was very unlikely that they would sympathize with indigenous rebellions.

The auxiliaries were no longer levied from the local population. Thus, a Spanish cohort moved into the fort at Utrecht and, at Moers-Asberg, troops from the area of the Lower Danube relieved the Tungrian unit. In the seventies AD, these Tungri served on the Dalmatian coast, after that in the region around Budapest, and during the second century in Romania. Other Tungrian units left for Mauretania and Britannia. The Cananefates ended up in Algeria, where at Tipasa a tombstone has been found of a cavalryman with the name Adiutor.[132] There is also interesting evidence from the fort at Housesteads on Hadrian's Wall in northern England, where so much Frisian pottery has been found that it seems plausible that the Frisian auxiliaries there had taken a potter with them. Since many potters were women, it may well have been a soldier's girlfriend. In Vindolanda, another fort on Hadrian's Wall, the correspondence was found of one Flavius Cerialis, commander of a unit of Batavians, and his wife Sulpicia Lepidina.

The new levy of Batavian units also served outside the province, for example, in Britannia and the Middle Danube. The following epitaph of someone called Soranus is a reminder of this.

I am the man that was once known to everyone in Pannonia. From 1000-strong Batavians, I was the very best. Under the attentive eye of Hadrian, I succeeded in swimming across the deep water of the Danube in full military kit. With my arrow, I could cleave a launched arrow in flight. Nobody could outdo this feat: no Roman soldier with his spear and no Parthian barbarian with his bow.

Here I lie now, my deeds immortalized in stone. Is there anyone who might be able to rival my achievements? I do not think so, but, should they succeed, remember: I set the precedent, I was the first.[133]

In AD 83-84, the Emperor Domitian defeated the Chatti in the Taunus Mountains in Germania and annexed the Black Forest. One of the memorials to these events was a cavalry statue on the Roman Forum. It appears to have been no less than eighteen metres high and had a (now lost) inscription on its pedestal, in which the Emperor claimed to have advanced to the place where the Rhine divided into two branches.[134] Perhaps this is a rhetorical exaggeration, but it is conceivable that Domitian did indeed pay a visit to the Low Countries. It is certain that a road was constructed along the river during his reign.

In these years, the army base at Neuss was closed down, and Germania Inferior and Superior lost the status of 'military zone in the province of Gallia Belgica'. Now they became independent provinces. The Emperor Trajan transferred the Tenth Legion Gemina from Nijmegen to Budapest in the first years of the second century AD and sent (a subunit of) the Ninth Hispana to Nijmegen in their place. Perhaps it was these soldiers who repaired parts of Domitian's road. In Xanten, legion XXX Traiana replaced the old garrison.

Trajan's successor, Hadrian, was well known for his curiosity and he visited almost all the provinces of the Empire. Since he was also a conscientious administrator, he tried to correct abuses in situ. Here follows a somewhat rambling summary of what he did during his visit to the Low Countries in the summer of AD 121.

Setting out for the Gallic provinces, he gave support to all the communities with various forms of generosity. From here, he proceeded to the German provinces and, while he was eager for peace rather than for war, he trained the soldiers as if war were imminent, instilling into them the lessons of his own endurance; and he himself supervised the military life among the units, cheerfully eating camp fare out of doors – bacon fat, cheese, and rough wine – after the example of Scipio Aemilianus, Metellus, and his own adoptive father Trajan, giving rewards to many and honours to a few, so that they would be able to put up with harsher conditions than he was imposing. For he did, in fact, take army discipline in hand. After Caesar Octavian, it had been sinking, owing to the lack of attention given by previous emperors.

He set in order both the duties and the expenditure, never allowing anyone to be absent from camp without proper authorization, since it was not popularity with the soldiers but just conduct that won commendation for tribunes. He encouraged others by the example of his own good qualities, too: he would walk as much as thirty kilometres in armour; he demolished din-

Domitian (Toledo Museum of Art, Toledo, Ohio).

The *Historia Augusta*

In the early seventeenth century, the title *Historia Augusta* was given to a series of biographies of the emperors from the second and third centuries. The problem with it is that a large part has been fabricated. On the face of it, six authors have written the lives of the emperors, but from the language used, classicists have established that the collection was, in fact, compiled by one author, who appears to have lived in the 370s.

This man put a lot of effort into insinuating that his six alter egos lived about sixty years earlier. He purposely leaves gaps in order to create the impression that he is presenting to his readers a very old, disintegrating book. Furthermore, he does not shrink from quoting sources he has thought up himself, and then goes on to claim that these sources are unreliable. He has also completely made up certain facts. However, historians cannot dismiss this source of information as an ancient mockumentary with only literary value, because we have preciously few written sources about the second and third centuries. Fortunately, we can discern where the author has based his work on reliable information.

Trajan (Glyptothek, Munich).

Hadrian (Berlin, Altes Museum/ Old Museum).

ing-rooms in the camps, and porticoes, covered galleries and ornamental gardens; frequently he would wear the humblest clothing – putting on an ungilded sword-belt, fastening his cloak with an unjewelled clasp, and only reluctantly permitting himself an ivory hilt to his sword. He would visit sick soldiers in their quarters, would choose the site for camp himself, and he would not give the rank of centurion to anyone who was not robust and of good reputation, nor would he appoint anyone tribune who did not have a full beard or was not of an age to assume the powers of the tribunate with prudence and maturity; and he would not allow a tribune to accept any presents from a soldier. He cleared out every kind of luxury from all sides.

Finally, he improved their arms and equipment. As regards soldiers' age, too, he pronounced that no one should serve in camp contrary to ancient usage either at a younger age than his strength called for or at an age more advanced than humanity would permit. It was his practice always to be acquainted with them and to know their unit. Besides this, he made an effort carefully to familiarize himself with the military stores, examining the provincial revenues in expert fashion too, so that if there was any particular deficiency anywhere, he could make it good. But he strove, more than all emperors, never at any time to buy or to maintain anything that was unserviceable.[136]

This text is part of the so-called *Historia Augusta*, a somewhat dubious collection of biographies of emperors. Fortunately, the biography of Hadrian does have reliable parts, and this happens to be one of them.

Although the author gives a long list of the measures taken by Hadrian, he does not mention all of them. Archaeologists have established that, about the time Roman soldiers built Hadrian's Wall in Britannia, their fellow-soldiers in Germania Inferior improved their own border defences. A few forts were rebuilt in stone, Corbulo's canal was dredged, and a new road was constructed on top of the dyke on the south bank of the Rhine. Admittedly, a road along a dyke does not appeal to the imagination in the same way that Hadrian's building project in Britannia does, but in the Low Countries, with its endless stretches of flatlands, the Romans also emphasized where civilization ended and the realm of barbarism began.

It is conceivable that the Rhine-border fortifications coincided with the redistribution of land south of present-day The Hague, where, around this time, the fragmented fields and pastures changed into a regular patchwork landscape. This large-scale land reform must have been imposed from the top down and this suggests that the owners of traditional large estates no longer had the last word. At the same time, Voorburg (near The Hague) developed

Paying taxes (Trier, Rheinisches Landesmuseum/State Museum of the Rhineland).

into a modest town, where the taxes from the surrounding countryside were probably collected. It looks as if the need to supply food to the soldiers manning the renewed fortifications created the impetus for the development of a more efficient type of agriculture and for early urbanization.

It would also seem that Hadrian had sanctioned the recruitment of native people for the Roman army, as, from the time of his reign, more and more men from Germania Inferior and Belgica served in the Rhine legions. This was an obvious step to take. In the previous century, an increasing number of soldiers had acquired citizenship after their service in the auxiliaries. Their sons were then considered Romans and consequently were allowed to serve in the legions. The word 'native' used here is, therefore, somewhat misleading.

• *Civitates*, *Coloniae* and *Municipia*

The fact that men from the indigenous population were admitted into the legions meant that Hadrian did not see the people of the Low Countries as subjugated barbarians, but as fully-fledged members of the Roman Empire. In the century and a half that had passed since Caesar's conquests, more and more people had acquired Roman citizenship, some by serving in the auxiliaries, others by virtue of their posts as administrators.

A few towns underlined their Roman character by adopting the name of a member of the imperial family. The inhabitants of Cologne – officially named Altar of the Ubii – started the ball rolling. Because their city had been the birthplace of Agrippina, the wife of the Emperor Claudius, the inhabitants requested the ruler to allow them to rename it Altar of the Agrippinians – and permission was granted accordingly. The reconstructed town of the Batavi on the banks of the Waal was called after the Emperor Trajan; his family name was Ulpius, and from then on the town became known as Ulpia Noviomagus ('new market'), of which the modern name Nijmegen is a corruption. A generation later, the capital city of the Cananefates was given the name Forum Hadriani, which is present-day Voorburg. However, such a change of name did not have much significance. In a letter from Andalusia, in which Vespasian granted a request to change the name of a town, it states explicitly that all the existing rights and duties remained unchanged, and there are no indications that this was otherwise elsewhere.[137]

The Town That Never Existed

Even today, maps of the Roman Empire sometimes show a town called *Lugdunum Batavorum*, somewhere near the estuary of the Rhine. It is unlikely that a town with this name ever existed, because the western part of the Netherlands was the territory of the Cananefates. The Batavi lived more to the east.

The town of Batavian Lugdunum was, in fact, an invention of the late sixteenth century, when the Dutch Republic had become independent in the Eighty Years War against the Spanish. At that time, Dutch scholars discerned a parallel between their own insurrection against the Spanish and the Batavian Revolt against the Romans, and on historical maps, the land of the Batavi was shown as being more or less identical to the territory of the Dutch Republic. At the same time, the newly-founded Leiden University was looking for an impressive Latin name for its institution. *Lugdunum* seemed a plausible linguistic ancestor of *Leiden*. Thus *Lugdunum Batavorum* was born. (The real name of ancient Leiden was Matilo.)

Dynastic names such as *Claudia* and *Ulpia* do not occur in Belgica. Tongeren simply remained Atuatuca, Bavay was still called Bagacum, and Cassel retained the name Castellum Menapiorum. An explanation might be that the custom of changing the names of towns, which originated in the Near East, was brought to Germania Inferior by soldiers who were transferred from the eastern provinces. That would explain why dynastic names occur in the border provinces only and not further inland. This is the only explanation scholars have come up with, but it remains unsatisfactory.

Some administrative centres had the status of *colonia* and, as we have already seen, this meant that inhabitants had acquired Roman citizenship. Law cases were only conducted in accordance with Roman law, and native customs were not taken into consideration. Because Cologne received its body of laws from Claudius, the 'Agrippinians' also added his name to the name of their city, which consequently sported the proud name of *Colonia Claudia Ara Agrippinensium* (the Claudian colony at the altar of the Agrippinians). That was quite long-winded and therefore it was shortened to CCAA, a Latin acronym found, among other places, on the gate to the city.

Other administrative centres were sometimes referred to as *civitas* and others again as *municipium*. These categories had at least one thing in common, and that was the administration of justice: whoever went to court would first agree with his opponent on whether he wanted Roman or native jurisdiction. It is not known if there were any differences between *civitas* and *municipium*. In the 1920s, historians suggested that a *municipium* was a *civitas* which had been given certain rights by the emperor, but that cannot be true, because a *municipium* is, by definition, a town with ancestral rights. The emperor could not possibly grant them what they already had.[138] Historians have since revised their ideas, but the misunderstanding continues to crop up.

• The Roman Town

Except for officials, it would not have made much difference to most Romans if an administrative unit was registered as a *civitas*, *municipium* or *colonia*. A list from the second century AD, which sums up the characteristics that earmarked a place as a real town,[139] does not mention the administrative rank at all. It does, however, say that the magistrates had to have at their disposal a presentable meeting hall, and that a number of public services should be available, such as a theatre, a water supply (a public baths was included in this), and a gym. Finally, a town also had an economic function, so there had to be a market. In ancient times, the presence of temples was considered to be so usual that nobody thought to mention them. All these buildings were also present in the cities in the Low Countries.

The ideal Roman city was built in accordance with a gridiron plan, where the different squares represented blocks of houses. Even the inconsiderable town of Voorburg, with just a thousand inhabitants, had been built in accordance with this pattern. In the centre, two main streets crossed each other on a central square, the *forum*. Visitors knew that they could find the town hall and a temple for the principal gods here. If the city was very large, it had several market squares, but in the small towns of the Low Countries, the weekly market will have been held in the central square.

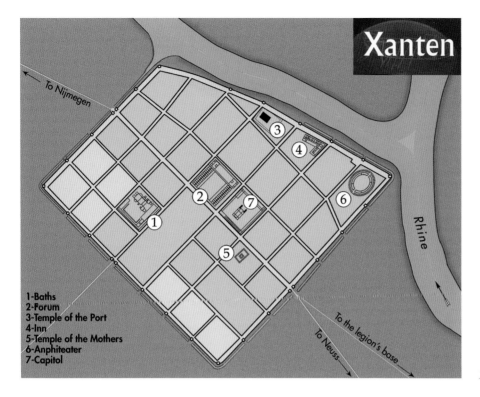

Xanten

To Nijmegen

Rhine

To the legion's base

To Neuss

1-Baths
2-Forum
3-Temple of the Port
4-Inn
5-Temple of the Mothers
6-Anphiteater
7-Capitol

Xanten in the second century AD.

You can still see such a market square in Bavay, the capital of the Nervii. On one side of the square, there was the *basilica*, a multifunctional hall where merchants did business, the governor administered justice, and the municipal council could meet. Its length of almost a hundred metres made the Bavay basilica one of the largest of the Roman world, larger than Carthage, for example. In many places there were simple altars where merchants could take oaths. In a time when most people were illiterate, there was not much point in registering agreements in writing. Instead, oaths were taken in the presence of the immortal gods or the emperor, who received divine honours, too. (Because they were not allowed to take oaths, Christians did not take part in normal economic life and could become social outcasts.)

The temples in the central square could be dedicated to any of the gods the Romans worshipped and there were quite a number. If the town had the status of *colonia,* then there was always a Capitol, a temple to Jupiter, Juno, and Minerva, just as in Rome. The present-day church of St. Maria im Kapitol in Cologne was, as the name indicates, built on such a temple. Besides this, Cologne had several other temples: among them the shrine of Mars, the Roman god of war, and another one to the eastern sun-god Mithras, who was popular among the soldiers. There must have been a sanctuary at the river port, dedicated to Rhenus, the river god, and to Portunus, the god of the port and river trade. Of course, there was still the altar for the imperial cult from which the town got its name.

The native gods had their temples, too. The high, square buildings were covered on all sides with a low, canopied roof resting on pillars. The best-known example is the temple built of natural stone at Elst, just north of Nijmegen. This was erected around AD 100, on the site of an older cult shrine. With its surface area of 23 x 30 metres and a height of about 17 metres (the measurements of a modern four-storey building), the new temple could hold its own with the temples of Italy. The largest temples of Pompeii were actually smaller.

It is certain that the native deity worshipped at Elst also appealed to the Romans, as among the archaeological finds was a traditional Roman sacrifice, a *suovetaurilia.* This con-

Remains of the Bavay basilica.

Two mayors on a relief from Seebronn
(Stuttgart, Lapidarium).

sisted of a pig, a sheep, and a bull, and was exclusively offered to the male and female deities of fertility, Mater Matuta and Mars. This is not to say that the Batavian deity worshipped in Elst was either Mars or Mater Matuta, as the remains of a small statue of Hercules has been found there, too.

Also on the central square, close to the most important temple of the town, stood the city hall. It is such a pity that this type of building has not yet been found in either the Netherlands or Belgium. Where these have been discovered in other places, bronze tablets with municipal laws, imperial announcements, and important decisions of the municipal council have sometimes been found as well. We might learn a bit more about the affairs that occupied local politicians. There's only one exception: in 2003, at Leersum (Netherlands), archaeologists found fragments of a bronze plate on which there was a small part of a text from a letter or a speech, but, unfortunately, the text is too fragmented to be comprehensible. We only know that the plate had been brought there by an ancient looter and cut into pieces to facilitate melting the metal. It is not known why these few pieces escaped the oven.

This text is the only one of its kind. For lack of more information, we have to limit ourselves here to the assumption that town councils in this part of Germania were administered in the same way as in other parts of the Roman Empire; i.e. by two mayors voted in for one year, and a meeting of councillors consisting of about eighty men. In contrast to Italy, where only the 'old rich' were considered sufficiently reputable for administrative functions, north of the Alps, successful merchants could also become town councillors.

There was yet another sort of administrative centre in Germania Inferior: the head-quarters built for the general in Cologne around AD 50. It later served as a palace for the governor. This *praetorium*, about three and a half hectares in size, towered imposingly high above the Rhine, and the façade along the river was meant to impress people on the other

*Reconstruction of the temple of Cuijk
(Alphen aan den Rijn, Archeon).*

bank. In the courtyard, which was lined with pillars, and in the rooms decorated with the most magnificent mosaics, the governor received his guests. Here, civil servants computed the provincial accounts, officers dropped in to discuss the security of the borders, and anyone appealing a sentence of the city magistrates had his case tried. One of the less customary events that took place here was when Vitellius was proclaimed emperor by his troops.

*Reconstruction of a house in Voorburg
(Alphen aan den Rijn, Archeon).*

Reconstruction of the Heerlen bath-house (Alphen aan den Rijn, Archeon).

The list of buildings that were typical for a town or city included a sports school or gym. Sometimes, these buildings were part of the public baths (*thermae*). The best example is the complex that was excavated at Heerlen in the Netherlands. Visitors could train on the playing field or in the outdoor swimming pool, then relax in the cold, tepid, and hot baths or in the sauna, and afterwards dine in the restaurant. For literate people there was a library.

A bathhouse such as the one at Heerlen presupposes a water supply and sewerage system. The water supply system is an undervalued triumph of Roman technology: it improved urban hygiene in a way that only our tropical doctors can really appreciate. The average

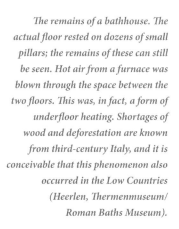

The remains of a bathhouse. The actual floor rested on dozens of small pillars; the remains of these can still be seen. Hot air from a furnace was blown through the space between the two floors. This was, in fact, a form of underfloor heating. Shortages of wood and deforestation are known from third-century Italy, and it is conceivable that this phenomenon also occurred in the Low Countries (Heerlen, Thermenmuseum/ Roman Baths Museum).

life expectancy in ancient times was around twenty-one years, as a third of all babies died in infancy and childhood diseases were fatal. Those who survived until the age of ten were out of the danger zone and could expect to live for another thirty-three years. In the Third World today, wherever a comparable demographic situation exists, the introduction of clean drinking water and a good sewerage system brings sensational results: a ten-year-old may then hope for another forty-three years of life, ten more than previously. In the towns of the Roman Empire, a comparable increase in life expectancy must have taken place with the introduction of public baths. However, only if we are not talking about the very big cities: there, their introduction had the opposite effect, as they were places where people were more likely to catch infectious diseases. Everyone bathed together, the healthy and the unhealthy, in a warm, damp atmosphere full of bacteria. On the other hand, where public baths afforded more room to the visitor, they were more hygienic and certainly contributed to extending life expectancy. This must have been the case in northwestern Europe.

Water works have been excavated in every Roman city in the Low Countries. We know of aqueducts in Nijmegen, Xanten, Cologne, and Tongeren. Wells are known from other sites. Pliny the Elder mentions one with special qualities.

Tongeren has a remarkable spring which sparkles with many bubbles and tastes of rust, although you only notice this when you have drunk from it. This water is strongly purgative and cures tertian fever and the pain of kidney stones.[140]

Alas, there is no source to be found anywhere in the area of Tongeren that meets this description exactly. Perhaps Pliny is referring to the springs of Spa or the healing properties of the waters of Aix-la-Chapelle. It is also possible that Pliny does not remember the qualities of the water very well, and is actually talking about the well near modern Tongeren that is now nicknamed 'Pliny's Well'.

The last item on the list of essentials for a town was a theatre. Cologne appears to have had one, but elsewhere travelling players used the amphitheatre, which was actually meant for animal and gladiator fights. However, this did not make much difference, as in many Roman plays it was graphically shown how the hero came to his end (with a prisoner under death sentence as stand-in). Most cities in the Low Countries had an amphitheatre. The one

The aqueduct at Xanten.

The Tongeren town walls.

Burial mound at Herderen.

Sarcophagus of a girl, buried with her tambourines (Nijmegen, Valkhof Museum - drawing by José Antonio Germán).

in Xanten has been partially restored.

The gridiron town was surrounded by walls. Those of Cologne were two-and-a-half metres thick and eight metres high, and their function was not only to keep enemy Germans out, but also to impress on them that Rome was almighty. No less imposing are the walls that were erected around Tongeren during the reigns of Trajan and Hadrian: six metres high, two metres thick, and more than four kilometres long. For that matter, it is a mystery why the walls were built in the first place, as there was no imminent threat of war.

The cemeteries were located outside the gates of the city, because Roman law prohibited the burial or cremation of people within the walls. The Low Countries had diverse traditions for the disposal of the dead. For instance, military graveyards were different from civil ones. Cremation was the most usual way, but young children were often buried. Generally speaking, the dead person was given a number of gifts to take with him or her. These could include brooches, crockery, a piece of sucking pig or, very occasionally, a weapon. The parents of the little girl from Nijmegen gave her tambourines to take with her. Elsewhere, there were no grave gifts: it depended on the region.

The graves were variously marked above ground. Some prominent people had a burial mound erected, as can be clearly seen along the roads from Tongeren to Bavay, Huy, or Maastricht. Other graves were only marked with a wooden sign or a small roof. That is, if they were marked at all, because in some places archaeologists have found cemeteries that were built on top of older ones, which suggests that the older graves had not been recognized as such. Finally, there were posers who threw their money about, like the officer Lucius Poblicius who, a little south of Cologne, had a fifteen-metre monument erected to his own memory with a statue of himself, in all his finery, including a toga.

• The Countryside

Voorburg, Nijmegen, Xanten, Cologne, Tongeren, Bavay, and Cassel were the administrative centres in the Low Countries. However, they were not the only settlements. To be sure, the old oppida had been eclipsed by the capitals of the administrative centres, but they had not all been abandoned. In other places, new centres of habitation came into being. For instance, in the neighbourhood of the military camps there were civil settlements where merchants, innkeepers, and the families of the soldiers lived. Along the coast you could find fishing villages and harbours, such as Boulogne in present-day France, and Domburg, Colijnsplaat, and Katwijk in the Netherlands. Charcoal-burners and hunters lived in the woods, mineworkers near the mines, and potters where there was good clay, such as Berg en Dal in the Netherlands. Here roof tiles were manufactured on a truly industrial scale. For a short while, there was also large-scale production of ceramics around Heerlen; to date, archaeologists know of no fewer than forty-six ovens.[141] The army also maintained a tile factory across the river.

Furthermore, people lived around ancient sanctuaries. Other settlements would evolve near a river crossing, such as Cambrai in France, Kortrijk in Belgium, and Maastricht in the Netherlands. Along the main communication routes there were also stopping places where soldiers and officials could get fresh horses and take a bath. There could also be a police station at such an inn, making it attractive for merchants and peasants to settle there. In this way, Liberchies and Heerlen grew up on the road from Bavay to Cologne.

Most settlements, however, were unpretentious hamlets, consisting of two or three farmsteads, sometimes located in the neighbourhood of a Roman country estate. The Roman officials referred to such countryside settlements using either the pre-Roman term *pagus* or the Germanic loan word *vicus*.

A well-known country estate lies near Voerendaal in the Netherlands.[142] Built in the second half of the first century AD on the site of a native village, two wings were added to the main building over the course of years, extending the width of the complex. The residents wanted for nothing: there was a bathhouse, under floor heating in the owner's living quarters, and even the servants' rooms were very comfortable. Some walls were decorated with frescos. It goes without saying that there were storerooms, granaries, barns, gardens, and stables. A low wall surrounded the property, which measured around 180m x 215m, and outside the wall there were cornfields.

Many peasants from the surrounding countryside worked as day-labourers on such an agricultural estate. Between them and the gentleman farmer there was a world of difference. While the latter was so rich that he never needed to work, the day-labourer did not have the guarantee of work at all. Even a slave had more security, as he knew that he had work and food every day, and could indulge in his own pursuits in the free time his master granted him. (The slave mentioned on the writing tablet found at Tolsum, Netherlands, had saved enough money to be able to lend it out, while others used what they had saved to buy their freedom.) On the other hand, the chance that a day-labourer could improve his lot was quite limited. Most of the population of the countryside were neither poor nor rich, and a great variety of farmsteads have been excavated.

There was extensive production of grain as the thousands of soldiers stationed on the Rhine needed more food than the farmers in the surrounding countryside could produce. Of the many Roman votive stones found, few are more representative of the economic reality of life in the Low Countries than this one from Nijmegen:

Marcus Liberius Victor,
a Nervian citizen, grain merchant,
fulfils his vow to the Mopatian Mothers
willingly and deservedly.[143]

Another indication of a flourishing grain trade is that one of the ships excavated at Woerden was carrying a cargo of grain. As grain could not be grown everywhere, regions where the soil was not suitable for grain cultivation, such as the Dutch river area, contributed in another

Grave of Lucius Poblicius (Cologne, Römisch-Germanisches Museum/ Romano-Germanic Museum).

Scene from a town in the countryside
(drawing by Graham Sumner).

way to an economy that was dominated by the needs of the army. This appears from the excavation of stud farms at Rijswijk and Wijk bij Duurstede. (Generally speaking, so many horse bones have been found in the river area, that there must be a connection to the Batavian cavalry units in the Roman army.) Nevertheless, grain was still the most important product. The cereal-growing farms on the fertile loess soil in Belgica were at the heart of its economy, and this region would continue to be one of the most prosperous parts of Europe for many centuries to come.

In order to facilitate the production of grain, the peat bogs behind the dunes in Zeeland and Flanders were developed. These were cushions of centuries-old wet organic material, which rose just a few metres above sea-level. It was very simple to adapt this peat ground to growing crops, as a farmer only had to dig out parallel drainage ditches to transform his land into arable fields of pure compost. However, this process was not without risk, because, as the water drained off, the ground began to shrink and the level of the land gradually dropped below sea level. In the first and second centuries AD, nobody seemed to notice this phenomenon and there is evidence of continued widespread bog reclamation. Drainage ditches have been excavated in several places. West of Zaandam, even the traces of huts made of turf were found. These were possibly used by farmers or shepherds.

Draining the land led to great feats of water engineering. In Vlaardingen and Valkenburg, two towns in the Dutch coastal area, drainage culverts have been found: when the water in the stream was low, drainage water could be siphoned off. A valve prevented rising river water from flowing back through the pipe and flooding the fields.

• New Crops

The first generations of legionaries in Germania were from northern Italy, Gaul, and the Iberian Peninsula, and, as mentioned already, to please their palates various products such as figs, olive oil, fish sauce, wine, dates, and spices were imported from the south. Not all legionaries were prepared to eat the local fare of bacon, cheese, and egg sauce, even if the Emperor Hadrian thought it was good enough for him. Imports from the south were necessary as many products that the legionaries were accustomed to were not grown locally: even the local wild cinnamon was suspect in Pliny's eyes and could not hold a candle to the real thing.

Cinnamon is also grown in our world, at the very edge of our Empire, close to where the Rhine flows. I saw them planting it there between the beehives. It does not have the scorched colour the sun gives it, and therefore it misses this particular aroma.[144]

Fortunately, there were many Mediterranean products that did not need to be imported. The trees and plants from which they were picked could be grown successfully in Germania. A good example is the cherry tree, and Pliny, who was an expert, as he had an estate of his own in Campania, said the following about it:

Before the victory of Lucullus in the Mithridatic War [70 BC] there were no cherries in Italy. He imported them first from the Black Sea region and in the course of 120 years they crossed the Ocean as far as Britannia. It must be said that, in spite of all possible care, nobody has ever managed to cultivate them in Egypt.

Apronic cherries are the reddest, Lutatic the darkest, while Caecilian are perfectly round. The Junian cherry has a pleasant taste, but only if eaten under its tree, since it is so tender that it cannot withstand the rigours of transportation. However, the best of all are the hard cherries that are called 'Plinians' in Campania, and in Belgica and on the banks of the Rhine, 'Lusitanians'. These have a third colour, which is between black, red, and green, so that it seems that they have been ripening for ages.[145]

The people of the Low Countries had picked and eaten wild cherries as far back as the Stone Age. With the arrival of the Romans, the fruit began to be cultivated, as appears from the fact that cherry stones were found in settlements, especially military bases. Since cherries were difficult to store and transport, these cherry stones must have come from fruit trees that were cultivated nearby.

Another innovation was the grape-vine. The Belgian tribes had already been importing Italian wine before they had been subdued by Caesar, but grapes were unknown until the Romans introduced them and began the production of wine. That this actually happened is evidenced by, among other things, the excavation of a wine sieve in Rosmeer, halfway between Tongeren and Maastricht. (The fact that, back then, wine could be made in the Low Countries, leads us to believe that in those days the climate was a little warmer than it is now.) However, the soldiers did not only drink local wines, as amphorae from northern Italy, Provence, and even the Greek islands have also been found. Furthermore, archaeologists have excavated wine-barrels whose wood originated in the valleys of the Rhône and the Moselle. Once empty, these barrels were given a second lease of life, as they were used to line the walls of wells.

The Romans also brought with them the first walnut and almond trees. Again, it was soldiers who ate them, as the shells have been mainly found in and close to forts. The cultivation of beetroot (for both the leaves and the root) was another novelty from this period, and this also applies to apricots, chickpeas, medlar fruit, pear, and plum. The peach is dubious:

Reconstruction of a Roman garden (Xanten, Archäologischer Park / Archaeological Park).

archaeologists have found peach stones – again in military settlements – but it is possible that these came from imported preserved fruit. Besides fruit, the assortment of herbs was enhanced with the addition of chives, coriander, mint, celery, fennel, and rue. There is also some evidence that the Romans taught the people of the Low Countries to eat asparagus.

Under the Romans, the variety of animal species in the Low Countries also increased. Among others, they introduced the peacock and the mule, which became a very useful draught animal for peasants. The diet of the local people was enriched with guinea fowl, Roman snails, fallow deer, chicken and, of course, chicken eggs. A case apart is the rabbit. It has been claimed that this animal from the Iberian Peninsula did not arrive in the Flemish and Dutch dunes until after the Roman era, because we find mention of it for the first time in sources from the High Middle Ages. However, the Romans did inadvertently have a hand in spreading this 'instant source of food'. They kept rabbits in enclosed gardens. After the disintegration of the Roman Empire, the rabbits escaped from these gardens in large numbers and once in the wild, they became veritable pests and a threat to the dykes.

All things considered, the military camps were *the* place where new crops and animals were introduced. The gardens in the towns must have also played a role. These were larger and more significant than one would expect. Excavations in Nijmegen, for instance, have revealed layers of black garden soil within the walls, which points to the fact that horticulture was carried out inside the town itself. For us, it is counter-intuitive that important agrarian changes began inside towns and not on farms in the countryside. This was due to the fact that, in those days, the division between town and countryside was not as sharply defined as it is today.

• Taxes, Trade and Craft

As we have seen, the development of Germania Inferior did not keep pace with that of Belgica. It was almost a century after the foundation of southern towns such as Cassel, Thérouanne, Bavay, and Tongeren that the towns of Voorburg, Nijmegen, and Xanten began to develop in the north. One of the other differences was that Gallia Belgica was a net tax exporting zone, while Germania Inferior belonged to the regions where the government invested more than it got back.

As the native population of Germania Inferior was not very large, the tax the Romans collected there fell very far short of what was needed to maintain the large armies stationed in the region. Consequently, the central government had to pour money into the province. On a balance, therefore, Germania Inferior received a lot more money than it paid into the exchequer, and thus profited from the occupation.

In fact, there was so much money pumped into the province that the towns grew too rapidly and eventually became so large that the products grown in the surrounding countryside could not support them. The number of inhabitants in Nijmegen increased to as many as 5000, more than the Batavian economy could feed. Many people in Nijmegen were entrepreneurs selling products and services geared to tease money out of the fat purses of the soldiers and auxiliaries. These must have included items crafted from precious metals, slaves, prostitutes, and gladiatorial games. This dependence on the army made the economy of Nijmegen very vulnerable. And indeed, things went wrong. Archaeologists have discovered the burn layer of a great fire that must have spread across the city in about AD 180. Because the Ninth Legion had left by this time, the city lacked the financial means to recover from this disaster. Thus, Germania Inferior may have benefited in the short term, but eventually, it remained a weak province.

At the same time, the Roman occupation of Belgica put a heavy financial burden on that region. Very little money flowed in from the central government, and yet the Belgians

had to pay taxes. However, in the long run, Belgica did better than the region along the Rhine, because a more varied and therefore healthier economy developed. And, as already discussed, the fact that taxes had to be paid in ready cash stimulated trade and industry, and the region began to flourish. The Belgian corn supplies to the Rhine army have already been mentioned, but there were other activities, such as the trade in geese reported by Pliny, who visited Belgica in AD 75:

Isn't it amazing that this animal, in spite of having wings, comes walking to Rome from the land of the Morini? Along the way, geese that have become tired are placed in front, so that the

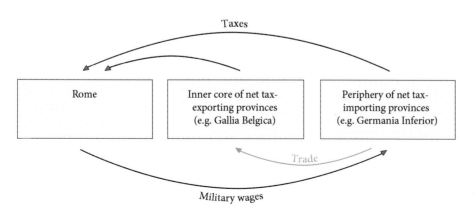

Overview of the tax and trade flows in the Roman Empire. The arrows indicate the flow of revenue to and from Rome; the lighter line shows inter-regional trade. The grain trade with Germania Inferior was essential for Gallia Belgica, as it financed the taxes that had to be paid to Rome.

125

Grave of a slave-trader from Nickenich (Bonn, Rheinisches Landesmuseum/ State Museum of the Rhineland).

other animals instinctively push them ahead.

White geese engender extra profit because of their feathers. In some places they are plucked twice a year, which stimulates the growth of a new covering of feathers. The down that is closest to the skin is softer and, in this regard, the geese from Germania are the most admired. There the geese are pure white, but they are also smaller. They are called gantae. *The price of their feathers is around five denarii a pound. That is why commanders of the auxiliaries have often been accused of having sent away entire cohorts from sentry duty to hunt these birds.[146]*

The down was used in Roman clothing, for example as feather boas, or for trimming collars. Another Belgian product that arrived on the Mediterranean market was soap.

Soap is an invention of the Gauls and is used to dye their hair red. It is made from tallow and ashes – the best sort is made from beach ash and goat tallow. There are two varieties, solid and liquid, and both of them are used more by men than by women.[147]

A product that can be compared to soap is perfume. The following inscription comes from Cologne:

For Sextus Haparonius Justinus,
perfume merchant.
His brothers had this tombstone erected.[148]

The excavation of hundreds of perfume bottles in the city of Cologne, which also had a thriving glass industry, makes it conceivable that the perfume that was later christened *Eau de Cologne* was bottled here. Whether the perfume itself was manufactured in Cologne is not yet known with certainty, but this is quite likely.

Besides trade, industry also profited from the incentive that came from the tax imposition. Native craftsman became acquainted with new tools. Carpenters learnt to use the claw hammer, the square, certain kinds of saws, and the plane. For other craftsmen, there were the plumb line and the spirit level, and the potter's wheel entered the pottery industry. The Morini and the Menapii were famous for their salt production, an activity that the Canane-fates and the Frisians also engaged in, and the Nervii had an excellent reputation as wool producers.

In order to come by good straight pieces of wood, the plane tree was imported from the south. It seems that Pliny did not quite understand the usefulness of this tree:

And who would not be justifiably amazed by the fact that a tree which is appreciated only for its shadow should be imported from a completely different part of the world? That is what happened with the plane tree, which was first imported into the Diomedes' Island in the Ionian Sea to decorate his grave, subsequently crossed over to Sicily and was one of the first trees presented to Italy. Meanwhile, the plane tree has reached the Morini. There it occupies land that tax has to be paid on, so that the tribes pay tax on shadow![149]

As it happens, this does not refer to the plane tree we know today, because this is the result of a cross between the tree mentioned by Pliny and the American sycamore. The ancient tree was less resistant to the winter cold and never came further than the southern Low Countries. In the Netherlands, oak wood had to be used, which facilitated the building of quite impressive structures all the same. Research into the provenance of the wood used in Roman ships proves that it had often come from oak trees cut down in the area of the Middle Rhine, while wood from the northern part of the Netherlands was used for certain parts of the boats. This suggests that the Roman shipbuilders believed that wood from different places had different qualities.

Furthermore, the mining industry in the Low Countries developed by leaps and bounds. Zinc had already been mined in Stolberg in Germania before the arrival of the Romans, copper and lead came from the Eifel mountains, and in the Taunus mountains there was a gold-mine. The exploitation was now intensified and the products found their way into the Belgian metal industry. Limestone from Tournai was used in the whole region of the Scheldt. The inhabitants of the towns in the Rhineland preferred to use tuff from the Eifel for support walls and limestone from Lorrain for decoration. Besides that, marl was quarried in the area of Valkenburg (east of Maastricht). Pliny knew more about it:

They use a saw to quarry a white sort of stone that looks like wood and is easy to process. This is used for making a variety of roof tiles or, if required, a type of roof covering that is known as peacock-style.[150]

Transit trade was also carried on. Germans from the region along the Elbe who wanted to sell amber, horses, lead, textiles, and slaves, exchanged them with the tribes on the east bank of the Rhine, and they, in turn, did business with the Romans from Germania Inferior and Belgica. The Romans then sold the material in the cities in the south. The tribes immediately across the Rhine supplied hides, oxen, furs, and blond female hair, which the Italian wig-makers loved to process. A recent excavation in Apeldoorn illustrates that, thirty kilometres north of the Rhine, there was a large-scale iron works. We have to conclude that most of the inhabitants of the north and east of the Netherlands, who were politically independent, were nevertheless completely absorbed into the Roman economy.

Trade on the North Sea must have been very busy, too. Evidence of this can for example be found in the amount of pottery from Britannia in Voorburg. As we have seen, the Chauki and Frisians plied their trade in the North Sea, and this trade route was to become particularly important from the third century AD.

• Native Religions: Votive Stones as Evidence

Up to now, the native religions have only been mentioned en passant. It is difficult to give a systematic account of this interesting subject, because the data (written sources and archaeological artefacts) are not sufficient to come to conclusions. We would love to have at our disposal the pagan equivalent of the Christian author Augustine of Hippo's *Confessions*, but there are no texts in which an adherent to one or other of the ancient polytheistic religions describes his or her spiritual journey.

A simple example can illustrate the problems. We know that the Aduatuci thought that Caesar had the assistance of the gods. That is at least something, but it is no great help to us when it comes to understanding how 'different' the gods were perceived by the Belgian tribes, and how easy it was for a person to be considered divine. Was the case of Caesar unique or was it quite usual for the Aduatuci to ascribe great deeds to a god? We cannot answer this question – and this is nearly always the case. We have some evidence to describe the outside phenomena of ancient religion, but cannot understand its 'inside', its significance to the believers. We are forced to confine ourselves to a presentation of the evidence, while bearing in mind that a description of the evidence must never be confused with a description of the religion itself.

A perfume bottle (Cologne, Römisch-Germanisches Museum/Romano-Germanic Museum).

The remains of a typical farm, excavated in Apeldoorn, not far from the kiln.

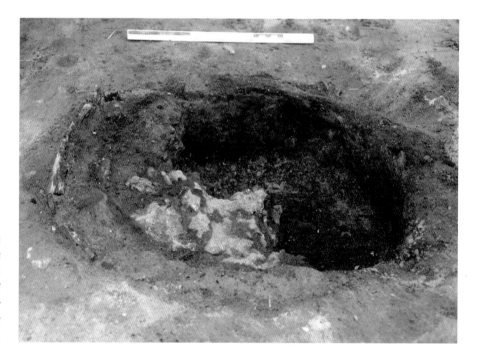

The remains of a bloomery from Apeldoorn, which was used to melt iron. The slags are still visible. This kiln dates to the second half of the second century AD: a comparatively early example of Germans producing iron for the Romans.

How complex the problems can be, appears from our first category of evidence: the votive stones. Frequently, these texts only say that a man has kept his promise to dedicate a monument to a god or goddess. The last words are always that he did it "willingly and deservedly", usually abbreviated to LM (*libens merito*). Only occasionally does it say what the god has done.

One of the Nehalennia altars (Leiden, Rijksmuseum van oudheden/National Museum of Antiquities).

Marcus Secundinius Silvanus,
pottery merchant trading with Britannia,
has willingly and deservedly honoured his debt
to the goddess Nehalennia
for the protection she afforded him.[151]

Secundinius probably experienced this divine protection during a crossing of the North Sea, as the Nehalennia sanctuary was situated at the mouth of the Scheldt. In this particular case, there is a little more information to help our research, because we know from another inscription that this Secundinius came from Cologne, where his family owned a wholesale pottery business.

So, it is possible to reconstruct a small part of the cult of Nehalennia.[152] It would appear that, during a storm, the seafarers invoked the goddess and promised her a votive stone if she helped the sailors to return home safely. After the rescue, the captain bought an expensive piece of natural stone and had the standard formula inscribed on it. It looks as if the believers made a deal with the goddess ("I will give you a votive stone if you save me") and,

The Aufanian Mothers (Bonn, Rheinisches Landesmuseum / State Museum of the Rhineland).

Magusanus with the attributes of the Roman demigod Hercules: a club, a three-headed hound, and over his head and shoulders a lion's skin (Bonn, Rheinisches Landesmuseum/State Museum of the Rhineland).

in the past, researchers have interpreted this more than once as the principle of *do ut des*, "I give so that you give". The fact that this was not a religious doctrine but a legal principle was conveniently ignored. In fact, we have too little evidence to be able to draw conclusions. The fact is that we do not know if other sacrifices had to be made, or if processions took place, and whether, from then on, a certain type of behaviour was expected of the person saved. We are simply in the dark as to how the votive stones fit into the entire cult of Nehalennia.[153]

However, because of the location of the sanctuary and the presence of merchants' inscriptions, we do have *some* things to go on when trying to understand this cult. The same cannot be said of the cult of other gods and goddesses known from votive stones. Around 1300 of these, mostly from the second half of the second century AD and the first quarter of the third, bear the inscription "for the Mothers", but we have scarcely any idea who these Mothers were! There are numerous different types, such as the Alaferhuic Mothers, the Aufanian Mothers, the Cartovallensic, the Rumaneheic, and the Vatviaic-Nersihenic Mothers. Some Mothers seem to have limited their activities to a particular tribe, like the Hamavehic and the Hiannanefatic Mothers of the Chamavi and the Cananefates.

It is a colourful collection of names. Unfortunately, it is not possible to ascertain if the natives believed that the Mothers actually protected them at all. It is true that many votive stones dedicated to them express thanks for help given, but it must not be ruled out that there were others who were given a stone when they withheld the exercise of their evil influence. In other words, the Mothers could have been guardian goddesses or, like fairies in the tales, they could have played a more ambiguous role.

To sum up: the hundreds of inscriptions teach us little about the gods and goddesses venerated in the Low Countries. We know from them that the Alaisiagae sisters and the goddesses Beda and Fimmilena were popular among the Tubantes in the east, that Haeva and Magusanus were mainly venerated by the Batavians, and that Sunuxal was worshipped by the Tungri. However, this is just a litany of names. It is the equivalent of a Catholic calendar of saints without the corresponding hagiographies.

However, there is one category of native gods about whom we do know more. These are the gods who were put on a par with Roman gods. On inscriptions, they have a double name, such as Apollo Grannus, Mars Lenus, or Mercurius Cissonius. The Batavian god Magusanus was always compared to Hercules, a masculine demigod from the Mediterranean pantheon who served as a role model for human men. Evidently, the Batavian god had characteristics in common with this macho god, but it is difficult to say which. Besides, there is an extra complication here: one and the same Roman god could be identified with several native gods. An example of this is that both the gods Cissonius and Gebrinius (of whom we know nothing, incidentally) can be called 'Mercurius' in Latin.

Meanwhile, the huge number of inscriptions that have been found makes it possible for us to draw up a list, in order of popularity, of the gods from Germania Inferior and Belgica, and to compare them with those in the other parts of the Roman Empire, such as central Italy. We should set one thing straight, before we start: the frequent mention of Nehalennia is a misrepresentation, because nearly all votive stones have their origins in just two sanctuaries. Yet, we can establish from the table that the same gods were not universally venerated. Thus, the Olympic pantheon of gods, which modern introductions to the classical tradition refer to so often, played absolutely no role in the Low Countries. Venus, the goddess of love, who was so popular in the Mediterranean region, just about makes it on to the list of the top fifteen most popular gods and goddesses in Belgica; but in Germania Inferior, she fails even to qualify. Therefore, there are substantial regional differences, and only Jupiter, the supreme god, and Mars, the god of war, belong to the group of gods who were most venerated everywhere, with Hercules coming in a good third.[154]

Moreover, a table like this raises some questions. From the numbers, it appears that, all over the Empire, there were five or six gods who were truly popular. However, in Italy, the

The most popular gods in three parts of the Roman Empire, compared with the popularity of Jupiter.

Latium		Germania Inferior		Belgica	
Mars	194	'Mothers'	168	Mercury	139
Venus	101	Jupiter	100	Mars	136
Jupiter	100	Nehalennia	67	Jupiter	100
Fortuna	92	Mercury	43	Liber Pater	84
Hercules	71	Mars	37	Apollo	52
Silvanus	45	Hercules	34	Hercules	41
Diana	44	Fortuna	21	Sol / Mithras	37
Sol / Mithras	43	Juno	16	'Mothers'	30
Victoria	40	Diana	16	Minerva	19
Cybele	36	Sol / Mithras	16	Diana	13
Juno	30	Apollo	11	Juno	13
Ceres	28	Minerva	11	Fortuna	8
Isis	25	Isis	8	Victoria	8
Mercury	25	Silvanus	8	Venus	5
Apollo	24	Victoria	7	Silvanus	3

Dedication to Mars Thingsus, Beda, and Fimminella from a fort on Hadrian's Wall, erected by Tubantes (Housesteads).

rest of the gods in the pantheon also had quite a following. For the also-rans in the northern provinces, however, votive stones were seldom erected. This may mean that the Tungri, Nervii, Batavians, and Ubii restricted their selection more than the Romans in the south. Northern polytheism appears to have been narrower. It could also mean, of course, that, besides the core group of five or six gods, they venerated others that did not appreciate votive stones.

One thing that stands out is the huge popularity of Mercury and Liber Pater (Dionysus) in Belgica, where not even one god with an indigenous name turns up. It is plausible, however, that by Mercury they meant, in fact, a native god such as Lug, Esus, or Teutates, and that an indigenous wine-god is disguised behind the Latin name Liber Pater. But this is no more than a possible hypothesis and it raises the question of why the inhabitants of Germania Inferior gave no Latin names to their own gods. All suggestions welcome.

• The Native Religion: Other Evidence

The possibility that, behind a votive stone for a familiar Roman god or goddess, an unknown indigenous deity may be hidden is also a problem that arises when it comes to our second category of evidence: images. Hundreds of statuettes of Mediterranean gods made from metal or terra alba have been found in native settlements. The owner of such a statuette, however, may not have seen in it an image of Mercury or Minerva or Mars: in fact, he or she may not have considered it a cult object at all. Another possibility is that a native god, who, in an inscription, was put on a par with, say, the goddess Fortuna, had a particular appearance that lent itself for veneration with a statuette of the goddess of fertility, Cybele. This could explain why statuettes of this eastern goddess have been excavated much more often than might be expected from the number of times she is mentioned on votive stones.

The problem of the Roman and native representation also arises with regard to the so-called Jupiter-Giant columns that have been found in the Rhineland among the Treveri, the

Inscription for the Syrian sun god Elagabal. The inscription tells us that Lucius Terentius Bassus, standard-bearer with the auxiliaries, erected this small monument in honour of the sun 'Heliogabalus' and Minerva, for protecting the life of the Emperor Antoninus Pius (Woerden, …Stadsmuseum/Municipal Museum).

Tungri, and the Nervii. These are column-shaped monuments. The shaft is often decorated with images of all sorts of gods, while the top is crowned with a statue of the supreme god Jupiter who, seated on a horse, is slaying a monster. There were many Greco-Roman myths about the battle of the gods against horrible giants, but images of the supreme god riding a horse are unknown. Despite his Roman appearance, it seems that the Jupiter on these columns has been inspired by a Belgian or German myth unknown to us. Some historians have tried to link this unknown myth to the stories about the German god Woden and his eight-legged horse, but it is unknown if this famous god was already venerated in the Roman Low Countries. The identification would be more convincing if we had just one dedication to, say, 'Jupiter-Uoden', but such an inscription has never been found.

Even when the name of the deity is on an image, the interpretation can still be problematic. Above the inscriptions for Nehalennia, there is often a woman depicted, sitting on a throne in an apse flanked by pillars. In the Greco-Roman world, apses were traditionally reserved for lesser deities like water nymphs, which makes it plausible that the goddess herself is depicted here, and not a priestess. She has a basket of fruit on her lap and there is a wolfhound sitting on the ground beside her. Sometimes she is depicted with one foot resting on a ship. We cannot know if she is trampling on or protecting the ship, although the fact that the sculptors have not indulged in a realistic rendering of a wrecked ship suggests the latter. The fruit basket is a mystery: is it a reference to the Apple Island (Avalon) – the land of the dead from Celtic legend? Is it a fertility symbol or a symbol of the transience of human existence? And what about the hound: is it a watch-dog, man's best friend, or a threatening animal – a "hound of the sea", as mentioned by Albinovanus Pedo?

Besides all these uncertainties, there are other big drawbacks when studying inscriptions and images. They only give information about the religion of those who were rich enough to pay for a block of natural stone, and who could read and write Latin. Moreover, most of the votive stones have been erected by men and, therefore, the information we get from them is not particularly representative of the population in general. (For that matter, this can be said of almost all texts from Antiquity and the Middle Ages.)

We are not restricted in this way when it comes to the third category of evidence: the study of ancient fairy-tales and popular traditions. Indeed, these can relate to the poor as well as to the rich, and to women as well as to men. Unfortunately, going down this road has not brought many results. It has been said that Mother Hulda from Grimm's fairy-tales represents the goddess Hludana, who is mentioned on a couple of inscriptions. Mother Hulda was able to create snowfall, which in turn suggests that Hludana was a weather goddess. This could be true, but, no matter how we look at it, it is still pure speculation. An extra disadvantage is that most fairy-tales and popular traditions were only written down during the Renaissance or even later.

The study of ancient pagan myths and sagas is a fourth source of information. Some of these stories, which were written down in the Middle Ages by Scandinavian and German writers, contain a historical story-line that can be traced back to Antiquity. That is why they have been used in an attempt to describe the Germanic religions in the Roman era 'from the inside out'. This has worked for the regions east of the Low Countries. It seems that the Germans who migrated from the Elbe to the west venerated gods that strongly resemble Norwegian-Icelandic mythology. The results of this research, however, are not applicable to Belgica and Germania Inferior, because the Germans from the Elbe only came west in Late Antiquity.

Greek and Roman writers are the fifth and last type of evidence. However, they are unreliable when it comes to describing non-Romans. Tacitus writes that Isis was very popular with the Suebi, for example,[155] and that probably means that there was a native goddess who, just like her Egyptian sister, was pictured with wings, or while holding a child to her breast. Again, it is not possible to say with certainty which German deity Tacitus was referring to here.

Jupiter-Giant column
(Tongeren, Gallo-Romeins museum/
Gallo-Roman Museum).

In general, Greek and Roman writers were always fascinated by the wildness of Germania Inferior and its inhabitants. When they talked about the religion of the Low Countries, they continuously mentioned sacred groves, but this said as much about the Romans themselves as about the indigenous peoples. Of course, it is quite plausible that the inhabitants of the Low Countries worshipped sylvan deities, but it is just as plausible that the Roman writers, in their obsession with forests on the fringes of the world, put too much emphasis on these cults. The place of the sylvan god Silvanus, at the bottom of the list of top fifteen gods, does not tally with the frequent mention of sacred woods, although this may – to make things even more complex – be evidence for the changing nature of this deity.

To sum up, we can say that inscriptions, images, medieval texts, folklore, and the stories told by Greek and Roman writers open small windows on the ancient religions. Only when a shrine can be identified and excavated will we be in a position to know more. The discovery of medical instruments in a temple in Velzeke, a town in Nervian lands, makes it plausible that a healing god was worshipped there: the Roman god Aesculapius or a native equivalent.

Another example is the excavation of the sanctuary of Magusanus in Empel near Den Bosch (Netherlands).[156] Many votive gifts have been found in the temple complex, including used weapons. Magusanus was, as we know, a macho deity who had much in common with the Roman god Hercules. However, weapons were not a usual votive gift in the Roman world and, therefore, we can assume that the cult in this form had existed before Roman times, when small arms were thrown into the water as an offering. When the Batavi settled here, they adopted this custom. Probably veterans of the Batavian auxiliaries left some of their weapons here out of gratitude for the protection the god had afforded them during their career. After all, religious rituals often have to do with a transition from one phase of life to another.

However, the artefacts excavated in Empel are quite unique. In this case, as in the wor-

Statue of Isis with the child Horus (Aardenburg, Archeologisch museum/ Archaeological Museum).

The German Religion

We have a very poor knowledge of the religion of people outside the Roman Empire. Well-known names of gods such as Woden, Baldur, and Donar are only mentioned for the first time in the Middle Ages, after the mass migrations of the fifth and sixth centuries, so that we cannot assume that these names were current in ancient times.

Archaeology does not help us very much here, although it is clear that the inhabitants of the lands on the other side of the Rhine often represented their gods as long, wooden poles with the carved features of a human being (see photo on page 68). It is difficult to discover which deities were venerated in this way. Another aspect is the ritual offering of personal arms, whereby weapons were cast into swamps and rivers. This custom among the population of Germania Inferior predates Roman times.

Not only weapons, but also coins, garment clasps, and other metal objects were thrown into the water. In Velserbroek (west of Amsterdam) a ritual offering site has been discovered on a sand bank that regularly became flooded. This spot formed a link in the route through the swamp, so it is possible that, at this place, travellers asked the gods for a safe journey. This ritual centre had more than local significance and was possibly one of the main Frisian cult site.

ship of Nehalennia, the finds have only revealed a small part of the story to us. Other questions remain unanswered. For example, how did the demobilized auxiliaries feel during the presentation of offerings? Were they the only people taking part in the ceremonies? Which myths were current about Magusanus? Did the cult have a moral appeal? Which offerings were brought and under what circumstances? Were there processions? How did the prayers and hymns sound? It is unlikely that we will ever know.

• Still: the Edge of the World

For most of the second century, the borders of the Roman Empire were secure. Romanization continued apace, until, in AD 212, the Emperor Caracalla granted all free male inhabitants of the Empire Roman civil rights. Whether intentionally or unintentionally, one of the consequences was that it broadened the basis for recruitment into the legions, where, after all, only Roman citizens were eligible to serve. However, rumour had it that Caracalla took this step solely for fiscal reasons. The only proof we have of this accusation is a remark made by Cassius Dio,[157] who, in the last parts of his *Roman History*, leaves no opportunity to portray Caracalla as a despot. Dio's insinuation cannot possibly be true, however, as the richest inhabitants, who were, after all, those who paid the most tax, had already been citizens for quite some time. The true reason is presumably that the Emperor, a well-travelled man, concluded, with justification, that the Empire was sufficiently Romanized. This was certainly the case in the Low Countries.

There was one small hitch, however: most Romans living in the Mediterranean area did not see it that way. Even though the inhabitants of Germania Inferior lived just like any other Roman – and even though emperors such as Trajan, Hadrian and Caracalla had realized this – Italian and Greek citizens of the Empire continued to describe the Low Countries in the same old stereotypical terms. In his *Germania*, Tacitus extolled the virtues of the blond, mustachioed hunters, armed with spears, who came from the forests in the far north. They

Caracalla (Berlin, Altes Museum/Old Museum).

might be dressed in animal hides, but at least they still knew what it meant to be hospitable. He included the Batavi in this category of noble savages – his portrait of Julius Civilis is an example. And, by analogy, classicists and historians have thought that the Batavi were clad in animal skins and went hunting. That nothing could have been further from the truth was proven by the archaeologists who excavated weaving weights, spindles, and weaving shuttles in farm-steads all over the Batavian lands.

Tacitus was not the only writer who voiced obsolete ideas about barbarians on the fringes of the world. The poet Martial assumed that everyone would enjoy his poetry except those "with a Batavian ear".[158] Around AD 240, three centuries after the Romans had seen the Rhine for the first time, the Greek-speaking writer Herodian alleged:

Of the northern rivers, the Rhine and the Danube are the biggest. The former passes Germania and the latter Pannonia. In the summer they are deep and wide enough to be navigable but in winter because of the cold they freeze over and horsemen can cross them as if they are solid earth. What was formerly a flowing river becomes so firm and hard that it can support people and horses. Those who want to fetch water do not take a jug or other empty vessel with them, but an axe or a pick. When they have hacked it out, they pick up the block of water and take it with them as if it is a piece of stone.[159]

What Herodian says about the climate in the Low Countries is not completely untrue, but, by presenting an extreme example as representative, he creates the impression in the unsuspecting reader that the untamed fringes of the world are not very far away. In this respect, the text can be compared with Varro's description of marl and Pliny's account of the drifting islands.

The Italian and Greek Romans were completely indifferent to the world beyond the Alps. It was the same disdain that they had manifested half a millennium before, although then they simply divided up the world into their own civilization and the surrounding barbarism. The inhabitants of Belgica and Germania Inferior were certainly not the only butts of such prejudice, as appears from the descriptions of India written in the Roman era. Several travellers had gone to the Far East and their travel accounts were known in the west,[160] but members of the Greco-Roman elite were just not interested in recent literature. They preferred to read the descriptions of India from the time of Alexander the Great – the fourth century BC – as they had been written in better Greek!

This may seem strange to us, but it was not complete nonsense. Everyone who was anyone in the Roman Empire had learned Latin and Greek and, with that, had accumulated a cultural baggage that enabled him to speak with other prominent Romans wherever they might be. A Menapian who had attended school could communicate with someone from present-day Tunisia, Jordan, or Bulgaria. In order to make this possible, the school culture had to remain static. Consequently, for many centuries, everyone in the Roman Empire shared the same ideas, not only about the correct use of language, but also about the contrast between the Mediterranean civilization and the barbarians living at the edge of the world. This literary culture would continue to function as *the* characteristic which marked out the Roman elite, until it took on a more military character in the fourth century AD.

Milestone. Museum Swaensteyn, Voorburg.

10   From Gold to Iron to Rust

• Crisis Looming Ahead

In AD 180, the proverbially wise Emperor Marcus Aurelius died and was succeeded by his son, Commodus. Many writers in Antiquity mark this event as a watershed in the history of the Roman Empire, because succeeding emperors pursued weak foreign policies and turned out to be incompetent. No longer was Rome successful in holding back its enemies at the frontiers of the empire. Cassius Dio writes that the last parts of his history was about "an empire of gold that declined into iron and then rust".[161] His colleague Herodian took up the story at the point where, according to him, the rot had set in, and gave it the title *The Empire since Marcus*.

This is all somewhat exaggerated. It is true that there were enemy incursions, but during the reigns of Commodus (r.180-192), Septimius Severus (r.193-211), Caracalla (r.211-217) and their successors, the borders continued to be secure. And yet, something had indeed changed. Altogether the first seventeen emperors of the Roman Empire were in power for more than two centuries (30 BC – AD 180), while the following seventeen ruled for only a total of sixty-four years. Of the latter, only one died a natural death; of the first seventeen, there were eleven. From the first group of emperors only two had to personally conduct a foreign war, and from the second group, half of them. A third period lasted from 244 to 284, and there were more emperors than years. Practically all these rulers came to a violent end.

If we are to believe our sources, the reign of Marcus Aurelius also marked a turning point in the Low Countries, because the barbarians broke through the frontier limes about AD 172. An account of the event can be found in the *Historia Augusta*. One of the emperors dealt with is Didius Julianus, who would assume the purple for two months in 193. The following is told about his earlier career:

After his praetorship, he was given command of the Twenty-Second Legion Primigenia in Germania, and following that, he governed Belgica unimpeachably for a long time. Here, with auxiliaries hastily levied from the provinces, he fought against the Chauki, a people of Germania who dwell on the River Elbe, as they attempted to break through the border. For these services, on the recommendation of Marcus Aurelius, Julianus was awarded the consulship. He also won a crushing victory against the Chatti, after which he accepted the governorship of Dalmatia, and cleared it of hostile tribes on its borders. Subsequently, he governed Germania Inferior.[162]

The fragment does not say how the Chauki were able to penetrate as far as Belgica, but it is safe to assume that they came across the North Sea. After all, they had carried out a similar raid under the command of Gannascus in AD 47. Whatever was the case, the damage they caused was extensive. Estate farms around Tournai were abandoned and the inhabitants of Velzeke also deserted their houses. Arras was set on fire. The capital cities of the Morini and the Nervii, Thérouanne and Bavay, were so extensively damaged that they had to be rebuilt in the last quarter of the second century.

At Maldegem-Vake, one of the cavalry camps of Didius Julianus' auxiliaries has been excavated.[163] The wooden fortifications were built around AD 172 and provided accommoda-

Roof tile from Nijmegen, made during the governorship of Didius Julianus (Leiden, Rijksmuseum van Oudheden/ National Museum of Antiquities).

136

tion for cavalry troops who were recruited in the area of Tongeren. (Although we cannot be completely certain, it is possible to draw this conclusion from the large number of slingshots found, which came from the terraces of the River Meuse, east of the Tungrian capital.) After a few years, the camp was dismantled and defensive forts were built on the coast, such as those at Oudenburg and Aardenburg.[164]

We may add the Zeeland isles of Walcheren, Goeree and Voorne, where, in the sixteenth and seventeenth centuries, large ruins were visible, which must have become submerged later. More to the north, a small coastal fort has been excavated at Ockenburgh near The Hague. The line of fortifications continued from the mouth of the Rhine to Boulogne. The Romans spared neither effort nor money in the construction of this coastal line of defence, evidenced by the fact that tens of thousands of cubic metres of natural stone were transported here from the quarries at Tournai and the Eifel Mountains. The 'stonification process' had already started in the early 160's, and was completed during the reign of the Emperor Septimius Severus (r.193-211), when the entire Rhine limes had been strengthened.

For the time being, the preventive fortification of the limes was sufficient and Germania Inferior remained safe. Unfortunately, the enemies also pushed forward in other places: the Alamanni in southern Germania, the Marcomanni and Quadi on the Danube, the Persians in the East, and the Moors in the Atlas Mountains. Later, there would be more tribes such as the Picts from Scotland and the Laguatan nomads in Libya. For the time being, the Roman armies kept all the attackers at bay, and Septimius Severus took the offensive, even adding some territory to the Empire. However, he was to be Rome's last conquering emperor. The pressure on the frontiers was increasing irrevocably.

In the Low Countries they were quite accustomed to small-scale incursions by German warriors. The Roman armies usually retaliated by burning the homesteads of the raiders or by getting the neighbours of the offending tribe to do it for them instead. With Roman silver and gold it was always possible to incite one tribe to attack the other. However, the attack of 172 surpassed anything that had gone before, and it cost the Romans a lot of effort to keep everything under control. The increased number of coin hoards dating from this period, excavated in the zone north and east of the Rhine, suggests that diplomats must have paid large sums in bribes. An example is the hoard of coins found at Uitgeest, in the northwest of Holland.[165]

For the time being, the situation was manageable. However, the frequency of the predatory raids increased, and the number of successful punitive expeditions fell, even though the Romans pursued the invaders deep into free Germania. Plundering raids that went unpunished were an enticement to the Germans and, sometime after the year 235, the line of forts along the Lower Rhine was no longer sufficient to hold back the marauding tribes. Burn layers are evidence of large-scale destruction, and settlements deeper into the province appear to have been abandoned. Another marker is that the cult at Empel disappeared. This was no longer a low-intensity conflict between the Roman Empire and bands of German plunderers, but a full-blown war that was fought using every conceivable means. It was to take some time before Rome developed a new strategy to cope with the altered situation.

• New Tribes

The Germans who harassed the Roman Empire from the third century AD did not belong to the tribes that had been familiar to the Romans for many centuries. More powerful and aggressive enemies appeared on the other side of the Rhine: the Alamanni in the south of Germany, the Franks in Westphalia and the north of the Netherlands, and the Saxons along the German shore of the North Sea. As the name *Alamanni* ('all men') suggests, these were groups of warlords from old tribes who had banded together. The Franks ('war hungry')

Some coins from Uitgeest-Dorregeest, Holland.

A German with his hair in a Suebian knot (British Museum, London). Compare the drawing on page 51.

were a federation of Chamavi, Tubantes, Amsivarii, Chattuari, Bructeri, and Salians. The Saxons took over the pirating traditions of the Chauki.

The Frisians are a separate case. At this point, they disappear from our written sources. This has less to do with the fact that they were absorbed into a federation than that the sea threatened their country. It is not clear what happened to them. Although many of their mound dwellings were elevated further, it seems that the land remained largely uninhabited until the Saxons repopulated it. From the seventh century AD, the new mound dwellers were given the name 'Frisians' in Latin sources, after the region in which they had settled. Up to the present, this has remained the name of the inhabitants of this area, suggesting an ethnic continuity that does not, in fact, exist.

The Romans found all those new tribes very confusing. The writer of an inscription found at Augsburg did not know what to make of them, either, when, in AD 260, he referred to a group of plunderers as "either Semnones or Juthungians": he apparently did not know what the enemy were called. The fluid character of the ethnic relationships at this time makes it understandable that the Romans referred to all their opponents as barbarians. However, the use of this term does not do either their enemies or themselves justice. The Romans were actually excellent teachers, and from them the inhabitants of the regions across the Rhine had learnt a lot via trade and military service.

After all, the so-called barbarians had been part of the Roman economic system for centuries. We have a lot of evidence to prove this. To mention a few examples: fishing rights in the Wadden Sea were leased to the Romans; prisoners of war were sold to Roman merchants; the Romans bought all kinds of goods from the tribes. And it was not a one-way street. The Roman demand for these products led to the intensification of agriculture and industry in the regions across the Rhine. The farms at Wijster (in the northeast of the Netherlands) are typical: the inhabitants sold their products to Roman merchants or to middlemen and often turned their profits into gold or silver, which they hoarded.

Other Germans had learnt military skills from the Romans by doing service in special auxiliary units for foreigners. The squadrons of Usipetes, Tubantes, and Frisians are examples of these units. After their demobilization, the returning veterans obtained leading positions in their tribes, on account of their extensive military experience, and, of course, the wealth they had accumulated. In this way, differences in status and wealth began to arise in the once so egalitarian tribal societies. It now became customary for wealthy leaders to arrange marriages for their children with other equally rich leading families, and, in this way, family ties were formed between the different members of what was gradually becoming a tribal elite. These people were proud of their German origins – and, as time went on, this element began to manifest itself more and more. When we are talking about the first two centuries AD, we should use the word 'German' with caution, but from the third century, this term really applies.

The emerging tribes had a very warlike character. A German warlord had followers who would stand by him through thick and thin. In return, they were provided for and, very importantly, were given many presents. Gold, in particular, was a valued gift, and it was considered a great act of valour to seize this precious metal as booty during raids into enemy territory. The thirst for gold accounts significantly for German incursions into Germania Inferior, although population pressure and shortage of women also played a role.

The raiders carried weapons that looked typically barbarian to Roman writers. For example, the Saxons were notorious for their use of the *sax* or *scramasax*, a kind of machete. The Franks were known for their skill with the throwing axe, the *francisca*. In contrast to the Roman sword, which even a layman could use to murder someone, professional training was required in order to master the use of the throwing axe. Once he had acquired this skill, the owner was able to kill someone from a great distance. The Romans could condescendingly call this weapon 'barbarian', but it was anything but primitive.

• Economic Problems

The foes that Rome had to deal with from the reign of Marcus Aurelius formed a more serious threat than the enemies of the previous period. Rome tried to solve the problem by increasing the size of its armies, but this was very expensive. Still, the cost might have been no problem for them if an epidemic had not led to a decrease in taxpayers. The emperors refused to increase taxes and decided instead to create more money by debasing the silver in the coins. Since the time of the Emperor Nero, a denarius contained almost three grams of silver. Now, however, it was 2.25 grams. Septimius Severus reduced it further to 1.85 grams, and his son Caracalla had coins struck with one-and-a-half grams of silver. From then on, the value of the precious metal in the coins spiralled downwards. The resulting inflation meant that the value of a soldier's pay fell, and serving in the army was no longer considered an attractive career. Therefore, the emperor raised army pay, which was again financed by the creation of more money, again made possible by lowering the amount of silver in the coins. Thus ensued a very vicious circle.

The consequences were far reaching. Confidence in money disappeared, which meant that more and more business was transacted in kind: even the tax office accepted this method of payment. As a result, an incentive for economic growth was lost. Another consequence of the devaluation was that the funds for the maintenance of public buildings in the towns gradually evaporated (see page 82). The quality of urban facilities fell and the local elite withdrew to their estates. While the towns became less and less important in the third century, palatial mansions arose in the countryside. Gradually, merchants lost interest in the urban markets and, instead, travelled from estate to estate. This economic shift towards the countryside did not mean that western Europe became poor in the third century: for most of Gaul, it was rather a time of transformation.

However, in the northern regions, it would be better to speak of a crisis. The inhabitants of coastal Belgica and Germania Inferior were confronted with incredible problems. While many suffered from German predatory raids, others died in the struggle against an increasingly aggressive sea. This was a consequence of harvesting salt through cutting into the sand banks, which exacerbated the erosion caused by the tides. Furthermore, when the sea did break through, it was able to cause significant damage, because the cultivation of the cushions of peat had caused the land behind the dunes to sink (cp. page 107). The coasts of Flanders and Zeeland shifted kilometres to the east, so that Zeeland began to look like an archipelago. It is no coincidence that not one votive stone dedicated to Nehalennia can be dated after AD 227: the sanctuary had simply been washed away. More to the north, the

A francisca (Koninklijke musea voor kunst en geschiedenis / Royal Museums of Art and History, Brussels). Compare the drawing on page 166.

channel of water between the Wadden Sea and Lake Flevo gradually widened, swamping the cultivated salt marshes in the north. Although many habitation mounds along the Wadden Sea were built up higher, this obviously did not stop the inhabitants from fleeing the area, because the countryside became depopulated. As has been mentioned already, the Frisians disappear from our sources around this time. Floods can of course happen at any time, but this ecological disaster was clearly the result of human activity.

At the same time, we witness a drop in population figures in the Rhineland. In the area around Cologne, villages were left empty, a process that began slowly, but which gradually gained momentum, until it ended with the depopulation of the whole countryside after 274. The potteries of Berg en Dal (near Nijmegen), where roof tiles had been manufactured, closed down and a number of Batavian villages disappeared. Analyses of the ancient pollen tell us that trees slowly ousted grain and grassland plants. In other words, cultivated land became wild, abandoned by those cultivating it. Large parts of the area along the frontier had already been depopulated before 250, and we do not need to look far for the reason: German raids had forced the inhabitants to seek safer places to live. Germania Inferior would never again return to what it was. The only town that continued to prosper and grow was Cologne. Some twenty thousand people lived there, sheltered by the high protective walls of the city.

In Belgica, however, the economy was still healthy, apart from the Flemish coast. When the Rhine limes collapsed after 235, local troops were able to deal with it. Since our sources only focus on the deeds of emperors, details of this event have not been recorded: there was no historian to write an account of it, as Tacitus had done about the Batavian Revolt. Nevertheless, we do have proof that the land of the Lower Rhine was recovered: for example, road works were being carried out in the area of The Hague.

If it had stayed at just one incursion, this would not have been a problem. However, when the Franks realized that the Romans had withdrawn troops from the limes around AD 256 to fight against the Persians, they penetrated into Germania Inferior again and very quickly advanced into Belgica. Archaeology shows us the consequences. The forts on the Lower Rhine were temporarily abandoned. The population of Krefeld did not have time to cremate their dead, but instead threw the corpses into an underground temple. Trier was sacked. Only Cologne resisted successfully, thanks to its eight-metre high walls.

When the Emperor Gallienus got news of the incursions, he rushed to Gaul to lead the defence of the Empire from Trier, and forced the Franks to retreat. He did not do this by a military victory, since the legions were not at full strength, but by paying large sums of gold to a German king living far away in the east, with the request to attack the Franks in their homeland. This move was successful, and, near the end of AD 259, he could claim that he had restored peace in the border area.

Gallienus left the reconquest of the forts on the Lower Rhine to General Postumus. However, in the summer of 260, Postumus had to break off his campaign because he had received grave news from the east: Gallienus' father and fellow Emperor, Valerian, had been defeated by the Persians and taken prisoner. The suspension of the counter-offensive encouraged the Frankish warriors on the Rhine to cross the river once more. At the same time, the already mentioned "Semnones or Juthungians" pushed through to the south. Some months later, they reached the Adriatic Sea.

• The Gallic Empire

For the events of the following years, we have no choice but to consult the not-very-reliable *Historia Augusta*. The following description of the reign of the Emperor Postumus, comes from this.

Gallienus (Brussels, Koninklijke musea voor kunst en geschiedenis/Royal Museums of Art and History).

This man, most valiant in war and most steadfast in peace, was so highly respected for his whole manner of life that he was even entrusted by Gallienus with the care of his son Saloninus (whom he had placed in command of Gaul), as the guardian of his life and conduct and his instructor in the duties of a ruler. Nevertheless, as some writers assert – though it does not accord with his character – he afterwards broke faith and after slaying Saloninus seized the imperial power. Others, however, have related with greater truth, that the Gauls themselves bitterly hated Gallienus and because they were unwilling to endure a boy as their emperor, hailed as their ruler the man who ruled in trust, and dispatched soldiers to kill the boy. After this murder, Postumus was gladly accepted by the entire army and by all the Gauls, and for seven years he performed such exploits that he completely restored the provinces of Gaul.

Meanwhile, Gallienus spent his time in debauchery and taverns and grew weak in loving a barbarian woman. Nevertheless, he undertook a campaign against Postumus, during which he himself was wounded by an arrow. The Gallic tribes felt great love for Postumus because he had driven back all the German tribes and had restored the former security of the Roman Empire. However, when he began to behave with more strictness, in accordance with their custom of always desiring a change of government, they put him to death at the instigation of Lollianus.[166]

Gold coin with the triumph of Postumus (Bonn, Rheinisches Landesmuseum/Rhineland Regional Museum).

Not everything in this text is untrue, but it teems with inaccuracies. Thanks to the casual remarks of other authors, as well as archaeological finds, inscriptions, and coin legends, it is possible to correct the story. And so it has been established that Postumus was not Saloninus' guardian, that he came to power by another means, that he ruled for longer than seven years, and that he was not murdered on the orders of Lollianus. The latter was actually called Laelianus, and the official emperor of the Roman Empire was less debauched than the author of the *Historia Augusta* would have us believe. Finally, the remark that the Gauls always wanted a change of government is one of the clichés about barbarians that every writer in ancient times had to hand.

As governor of Germania Inferior, Postumus was responsible for conducting the war against the Franks. He turned out to be a competent general and he defeated the invaders somewhere in North Brabant (Netherlands). It must have been a very convincing victory, as, for many years, the Franks did not venture to cross the Lower Rhine again. Perhaps this period of peace also had something to do with the generous treatment of the defeated by the conqueror. For example, Postumus allowed a Frankish warlord and his followers to fight in the Roman army, albeit that they had to cross the Channel to Britannia to do so. This step was a sign of the times. Although it was not for the first time that non-Romans fought in the Roman armies, it was certainly one of the first times that they were recruited en bloc.

Postumus' victory had consequences which he could not have foreseen. Gallienus' son commanded the booty captured from the Franks to be transferred to him. As it was usual for the soldiers to share in the spoils, this demand triggered a mutiny, and the soldiers proclaimed their general emperor. Within a few months, the child was dead and Postumus became lord and master of Gaul and the two German provinces. He was also acknowledged as sovereign by the general who dedicated to the new ruler his victory over the "Semnones or Juthungians", after they had marauded through Bavaria. Not long afterwards, tokens of loyalty to Postumus also came from the Spanish and British provinces.

The Emperor Gallienus, who had lost his father and his son within a year, crossed the Alps to challenge the usurper, but Postumus avoided a pitched battle. It would seem that the Emperor then offered to avenge the death of his son by fighting a duel with his presumed murderer, but Postumus once again refused. Eventually, the two emperors made a pact that they would not fight each other, but would instead expend their energy on fighting the barbarians. Postumus honoured his pledge and, when rebels in northern Italy hailed him as emperor, he did not go along with it. On the other hand, Gallienus, who did not consider himself bound by his pledge, attempted to reconquer the Gallic Empire in 265. Once again, his opponent avoided direct confrontation and, when Gallienus was wounded in a fight, it brought this civil war to an end.

In the winter of 262-263, Postumus once again undertook a successful war against the Franks on the Middle Rhine, after which a period of peace dawned. It seems that, for this campaign, the Gallic Emperor used German allies who lived behind the Franks and the Alamanni, on the other side the Rhine. At least, that is the only explanation we can give for the fact that gold coins with a portrait of Postumus have been found in large numbers in the lands of the Thuringi, and nowhere else. Apparently, Postumus paid this German tribe to attack the Franks from the rear, while he launched a frontal attack. In all probability, the Thuringi also served on the Rhine limes, where Postumus rebuilt some forts.

His most important building project, however, was the series of fortifications in the north of Belgica. Postumus realized that the restored line of defence along the Rhine was not strong enough to keep out the Frankish warriors permanently. Once they had crossed the frontier, they could push on into Italy and Spain, as there were no troops anywhere in the hinterland. That had been proven in 256-258. In addition to the border troops along the Lower Rhine, Postumus set up watchtowers along the line Aardenburg – Velzeke – Mechelen – Tongeren – Maastricht – Cologne, and garrisoned soldiers in towns south of the line. In this way, there were always soldiers on hand, who could swiftly be moved to sections under threat at any time. Thanks to this strategy, the main road from Boulogne through Bavay and Tongeren to Cologne never fell into enemy hands, and the strategic loessial land, which was so important for the economy, was protected.

This policy of 'defence in depth', to use military jargon, seems to have been Postumus' personal invention. Nevertheless, if we look beyond that, there was nothing special or specifically Gallic about his new empire. Granted, it had its own emperor, its own armies, and its own coins. But the rest of the structure was typically Roman, with its governors, consuls, magistrates, and Senate. This was further confirmation that the Romanization of the Gauls had been completely successful. And it would not be an exaggeration to state that Postumus' empire was an expression of the self-confidence of the flourishing Gallic provinces, especially of the northern province where he came from. If the central government could not defend the Rhine frontier, then the Gauls would do it for themselves.

From Postumus' coins, it appears that he placed the empire under the protection of the demigod Hercules, or, actually, of Hercules Magusanus, the god of Empel. It is tempting to think that Postumus' veneration of a Batavian deity proves his Batavian origins, but that is not in the least certain. The thinking behind his worship of the demigod could also have been that the ruined shrine of the deity was near the place where he had won his first victory.

In 268, for reasons unknown to us, Postumus debased his coins, which up to then had been of comparatively high quality. This caused quite some unrest among the population. Laelianus exploited this, proclaimed himself emperor, besieged the mint in Cologne and made Mainz his residence. Postumus made short work of the revolt, but he refused to allow his soldiers to plunder the conquered city. This is the incident that the *Historia Augusta* is referring to when it writes that Postumus "began to act more severely". In a different way to that described by the *Historia Augusta*, it did indeed lead to his death: in 269, the first emperor of the Gallic Empire was murdered by his own troops, who were greedy for the loot they had been deprived of.

The Gallic Empire outlived its founder, Postumus, who was succeeded by Marius. Even before the summer of that year, Marius was, in turn, replaced by Victorinus. Only when Victorinus died in February 271, did the Franks and Alamanni risk crossing the Rhine once more. However, the new Gallic Emperor, Tetricus, swiftly marched against them and drove them back. Although the emperors replaced each other in quick succession, the Gallic Empire prevailed and remained vigorous and economically sound. Belgica and the Rhine prov-

Coin of Victorinus (Bonn, Rheinisches Landesmuseum/ Rhineland Regional Museum).

Coin of Tetricus from Velsen.

inces continued to be the power base of the emperors, just as they had been for Vitellius and Julius Sabinus in AD 69 and would be for the Merovingian dynasty in the fifth century.

• Disaster

In the summer of 274, the Gallic Empire came to an end. Aurelian, who had been recognized as emperor by the Senate in Rome from 270, crossed the Alps and, in an infamously bloody battle, defeated the army of Tetricus at Châlons-sur-Marne.

After this defeat, Aurelian's propaganda was all that was needed to morally break the Gallic Empire. The rumour was spread that the troops of Tetricus had mutinied, and that, in fear of his life, their emperor had started secret negotiations with his Roman counterpart. The two emperors were supposed to have agreed that Aurelian would spare Tetricus and his son, if the Gallic Empire was handed over to him. This sort of propaganda can only be effective if the conquered ruler is really spared. And this was the case here. During Aurelian's triumphal entry into Rome, Tetricus and his son were displayed in chains and clad in trousers – barbarian garb – walking behind the triumphator's chariot.[167] And so we see that the Romans in Italy were still convinced that, to the north of the Alps, only savages lived.

Aurelian proudly called himself *restitutor orbis*, 'restorer of the world'. And indeed, to all appearances, it seemed that the empire had been reunited and rebuilt, but that is a relative impression. For the German provinces and Belgica, Aurelian's successes were the greatest

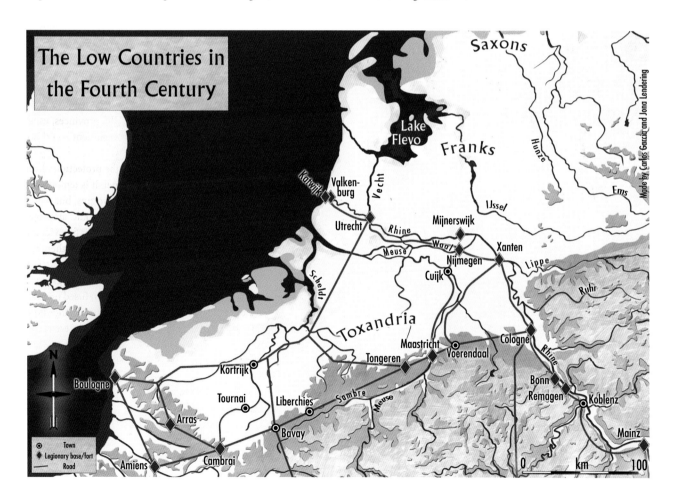

143

catastrophe in their history. Very many soldiers had been killed, leaving the Roman army seriously depleted. The German warlords seized their chance. The Roman forts on the Rhine were sacked and the watchtowers and garrison-towns built by Postumus could offer very little resistance. Hordes of German warriors, the likes of which had never been seen before, surged into Gaul. Cologne was plundered, Maastricht put to the torch, Tongeren gutted, Bavay levelled to the ground. Some deceased inhabitants of Tongeren never received a proper burial, such as the man whose skeleton was uncovered, lying on his back and with arms spread wide. The corpses of a family of six were thrown into a well with the carcass of a horse, and nobody was ever able to give them a decent funeral.

Saxon pirates also joined in the action, although it cannot be established, with any certainty, if it was they who were responsible for the fact that the fort at Aardenburg was evacuated, never to be occupied again. In the haste to build protective walls in several towns in present-day France, even old gravestones were recycled as building material. But it was often too late: Trier, Metz, Reims, and Paris went up in flames.

Extensive regions were abandoned by the inhabitants, such as the hinterland of Cologne, which was now completely depopulated. The provinces lying more to the south did not suffer as much as Germania Inferior and Belgica, but were subsequently faced with the fiscal measures taken by the Roman emperors, whose priority now was the defence of the empire along the Danube and in Syria. In the Gallic Empire, tax money had been spent on the armies defending Gaul, but, from now on, this was out of the question. Aurelian's 'restoring' meant, in fact, that the Gauls were under the yoke of an emperor who took absolutely no interest in their welfare. Worse still, Aurelian had broken the self-confidence of the Belgian people, who, from this time on, no longer felt themselves automatically to be Roman.

11 Militarization

● **Recovery**

Frankish plunderers, Saxon pirates, Roman tax collectors … the only ray of light in the catastrophic years after 274 was that the Franks were not (yet) sufficiently organized to settle permanently west of the Rhine. Their hordes roamed through Gaul and devastated villages and towns; but, once they had done their work, they moved on. They did not stay in Gaul.

At the same time, there was unrest in the Belgian coastal area, where peasants were arming and banding together to defend themselves. As soon as the Roman central authority was restored, this form of self-defence was regarded as rebelliousness. And in the *Historia Augusta* – a history written by the conquerors – the local leaders in the Rhineland, Proculus and Bonosus, are dismissed as tyrants. Clearly, the central government did not have much trust in the Romans along the northern frontier.

For three long years, the central government in Italy did not raise a finger to help Gaul. Only in 277 did the Emperor Probus intervene. When the Alamanni and the Franks heard of his arrival, they tried to return to their homelands on the Rhine, but, as they were laden down with booty, they could only make very slow progress. At the river, they found Probus' troops waiting for them and they were heavily defeated in the ensuing battle. Nonetheless, they were lucky: Probus allowed them to settle as peasants in the deserted areas, on condition that they would fight on the side of the Romans whenever there were new incursions into Roman territory. The proof of the wisdom of this measure was that it would be another three-quarters of a century before the Rhine frontier collapsed once more.

Probus went about organizing the defence of the northern border in somewhat the same way as Postumus had done. In the garrison-towns, soldiers forming the backbone of the empire's defence were stationed. Watchtowers protected the region south of the line Oudenburg – Tournai – Bavay – Tongeren – Maastricht – Cologne. However, he gave up the defence of the area between this line and the Lower Rhine. A no-man's-land emerged in which the homesteads of some German peasant farmers lay scattered here and there in the countryside. Chemical analyses reveal that the pottery found there was made of a type of clay not found in Belgica. It appears that these peasants originated in the northern Netherlands and Westphalia.

For a number of reasons, Rome began to lose its grip on Belgica. The inhabitants had become frustrated by the manner in which they were being punished for the Gallic Empire, and no longer automatically identified with Rome. Coupled with that, the new German immigrants felt more affiliation with the tribes on the North Sea. They continued to trade with their northern neighbours, as evidenced by, among other things, the excavation in the Low Countries of black burnished ware – a type of hand-turned ceramics made in Britannia. What is even more remarkable is that this pottery was not even of very high quality. It appears that, up to roughly the year 250, the inhabitants of the Low Countries were far more southern-orientated than thereafter. Archaeological evidence points to the fact that, after the year 300, they were trading equally with both northern and southern Europe.

A start could only be made with the reconquest of northern Germania Inferior when there was peace inside the Roman Empire itself. When that had been achieved, it then took

Probus (Vienna, Kunsthistorisches Museum/Museum of Fine Arts).

a little time to organize. The person who guaranteed peace was Diocletian. This efficient ruler had visited Tongeren before he came to power in 284. The writer of the *Historia Augusta* adopts the tone we have become familiar with in the meantime, and summons up the archaic word 'druid', because in his view, the people north of the Alps were still barbarians.

My grandfather told me the following anecdote, which he had heard from Diocletian. "When Diocletian was still in a minor post", he said, "he was staying in an inn in the land of the Tungri in Gaul. When he was haggling about his bill with the female inn-keeper, a druidess, she said to him: 'Diocletian, you are much too avaricious and far too mean'."

According to my grandfather, Diocletian replied, not in a serious way but jokingly: "I shall be more generous once I am emperor". To which the druidess is said to have answered: "Make no jokes, Diocletian, as you will be emperor after you have slain a wild boar."

Circumspect as he was, Diocletian laughed and was then silent. Nevertheless, every time there was an opportunity during a hunting trip, he always killed the boars with his own hands. And so it was that when first Aurelian took power, then Probus, after that Tacitus and finally Carus, Diocletian complained: "I am the one who always kills the boars, but others enjoy the meat."[168]

As is usually the case in this type of story, the hero takes literally a prediction that was meant metaphorically. The true meaning of the prophesy became clear when Diocletian killed a certain prefect with the name Aper ('boar') and took power.

The new emperor reorganized tax collection, and did so in such a way that the revenue – how could it be otherwise – increased. In order to ensure that the projected returns would, in fact, be realized, he threatened the peasants with heavy penalties if they did not work their land, or if they chose another livelihood. The peasant livelihood was, in fact, made hereditary in this way.

Another problem that Diocletian dealt with was the fact that the Roman Empire, which was now threatened on all the fronts, could no longer be governed by one man. Therefore, in 285, he appointed a co-emperor in the west, Maximian. But he did not stop at that: to ensure that the succession would not be decided by violence in the future, both emperors designated their heirs in advance. That meant that there were now two emperors (*Augusti*) and two crown princes (*Caesares*), and, consequently, there had to be four official residences. The official residence for the Low Countries was at Trier, where the ruins of the imperial basilica and baths are living witnesses to this time of prosperity.

In 293, Maximian's crown prince, Constantius Chlorus ('paleface'), showed himself to be a capable general by defeating the Franks in the Lower Rhine area. From that moment on, some forts were again put into service, and it is conceivable that, in these years, a new Batavian unit was put together. Now that the northern borders had been restored, the Romans could begin the re-conquest of Britannia, where a Menapian military commander, Carausius, had set up his own empire.

Maximian and Constantius also carried out some administrative changes: the borders of the province were adapted and, in Belgica, the Nervii and Menapi were given new capitals, namely Cambrai and Tournai. The old capital cities, Bavay and Cassel, had suffered too much damage during the Gallic Empire and were not able to function as before.

In 305, Maximian abdicated in favour of Constantius Chlorus, but the new Emperor unexpectedly died in the second summer of his reign, whereupon the troops proclaimed his son emperor in the west. This was Constantine, known as Constantine the Great.

We must, indeed, grant him a certain kind of greatness as, among other things, he succeeded in becoming supreme ruler of both the western and eastern provinces of the Roman Empire. Furthermore, he fortified the frontiers on all sides. His biographer Eusebius ran out of superlatives to describe Constantine's many victorious campaigns. He tells how Con-

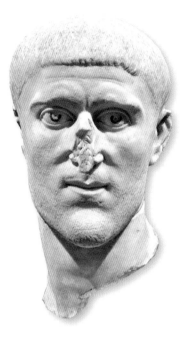

Constantius Chlorus (Berlin, Altes Museum/Old Museum).

Constantine the Great (Rome, Musei Capitolini/Capitoline Museums).

stantine fought against the tribes on the coast of the western Ocean, how he subjugated the barbarians of the remotest north, and, furthermore, how, in the south, he advanced as far as Ethiopia. Finally, he tells how Constantine turned his attention to the Indians in the East, whom he did not consider beneath his dignity.[169]

Of course, this is exaggerated, but it is a fact that Constantine, building on the work of his predecessors, secured the peace. He perfected the system of 'defence in depth', by stationing the border troops in real castles that could withstand a long siege. Other forts, such as Divitia opposite Cologne, served as bases for sorties. Nevertheless, it was not completely peaceful on the other side of the Rhine, as would appear from this inscription:

Guardsman Viatorinus served for thirty years and was killed by a Frank near Divitia in the land of the barbarians. The general of the garrison at Divitia erected this monument.[170]

Further north, a new wall was built around Xanten. In its heyday, the town had comprised thirty-nine blocks. In the meantime, it had shrunk so much that the new walls of the town encircled only nine blocks. Nijmegen got a military function once more: a garrison was stationed in a fort that was protected by a wall one-and-a-half metres thick. Because it was built from imported tufa, we can be sure that the Romans thought it important to keep this position. At the mouth of the Rhine, Valkenburg was restored, and so too were coastal forts such as Oudenburg.

Constantine and his successors also walled in the garrison-towns of the hinterland. One example is Tongeren. It is true that these towns were smaller than they had been in the second century, but they were still important enough to be defended. Along the roads between the Rhine frontier and the garrison towns, watchtowers were fortified. On the stretch of road between Tongeren and Cambrai alone, there were eight. A fort was built at the bridge at Maastricht, while, further downstream in Cuijk (just south of Nijmegen), both a bridge and a fort were erected. Together, these fortifications ensured that the Romans could always send reinforcements to the frontier.

The extensive network of fortifications, giving the country a military character, had its critics. It is true that the troops stationed on the outer borders of the Empire were only capable of temporarily holding back their enemies. If things got out of hand, there was nothing else for them to do but withdraw into their castles, hoping that the army in the hinterland could come to their rescue in time. Until then, their enemies could pillage the border zone to their hearts' content. Around the year 500, the historian Zosimus expressed the criticism as follows:

Impression of ancient Divitia, modern Deutz opposite Cologne (drawing by José Antonio Germán).

Constantine did even more to leave the door to Roman lands open for the barbarians. As I have already said, as a consequence of Diocletian's policy, the Roman Empire was protected on all fronts by towns, forts and watchtowers, and the whole army was garrisoned in all these fortifications. The barbarians were not able to get past these, because wherever they turned, they were always met by an army, ready to drive them back.

This security was undermined by Constantine, because he withdrew the larger part of the army from the border lands and stationed them in towns that did not need defending, while he took their protection away from the people who were at most risk from the barbarians.[171]

This criticism was not wholly justified. Certainly, there was a zone one hundred kilometres wide that was open for plundering, but that was the price that had to be paid for the security of the Empire as a whole.

There must have been tens of thousands of soldiers garrisoned in all these fortifications. Grain could no longer be produced in the hinterland, because that was more or less depopulated. Therefore, it had to be imported from Britannia by sea routes that had been used by the Frisians and the Chauki as far back as the first century, and that had been further developed in the dark days after the fall of the Gallic Empire. Warehouses were built inside the protective walls of the fort at Valkenburg and the 'Brittenburg' (see page 150) may, in fact, have been a grain silo or a lighthouse related to this trade.

A final ploy the Romans used in the defence of their borders was to make treaties with some German warlords obliging them to prevent their fellow Germans from making incursions across the border. The orator Libanius exults about the civilizing effect of this situation:

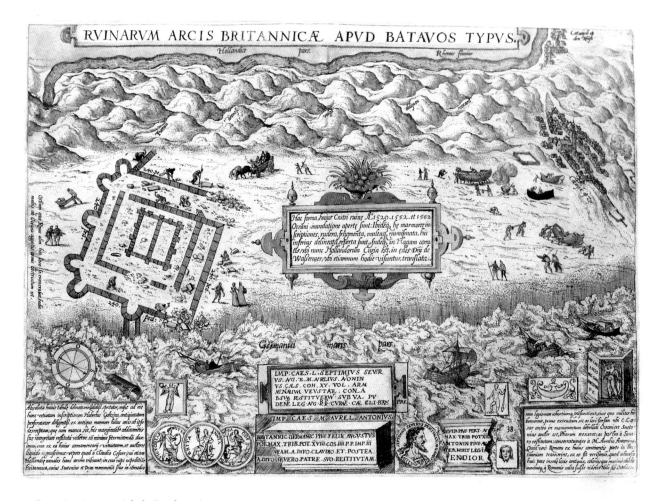

We gave them leaders who supervise their comings and goings. Because of this, they have moderated their bestial rage, learnt to apply common sense, abandoned their unbridled hunger for power, and learnt to fulfil their agreements.[172]

• The Language Border

The recovery of the northern frontier of the empire required significant investments, but these were worth it. For the period of the fourth century it remained peaceful. Confidence in the monetary system returned slowly, as appears from the wreck of a ship with a large cargo of coins. When the ship foundered it was probably on its way to Britannia to pay for the grain supplies for the Rhine army.

Nevertheless, there was never really unbroken peace. We know of a few German incursions, one of which was a particularly violent Frankish invasion in 355. The brief usurpation of one Silvanus, a high-ranking Roman officer with Frankish ancestors, contributed to the chaos, but General Julian, who was destined to become emperor, restored order. In 358 he allowed groups of raiding Franks to settle in Toxandria (the medieval duchy of Brabant). This was an agriculturally poor region to the north of the main road from Cologne to Boulogne. Various tribal brothers had preceded them there and, by the second half of the fourth

From time immemorial, the Dutch coastline and dunes have been shifting slowly eastwards. Because of this, in the sixteenth century at Katwijk, the remains of a Roman edifice, which had been buried under the sand dunes, became exposed on the beach. It is known as Brittenburg, *'the British Castle'. The etching, by the famous sixteenth-century cartographer, Abraham Ortelius, shows how the remains of the walls lay on the sand. Archaeologists have no idea what this building might have been. Examination of the site of the ruin was attempted, but nothing was found, because the remains of the walls had been washed away by the surf when the coastline changed. Very recently, however, the investigations have been resumed with the latest technologies (Wikipedia Commons).*

A Roman soldier from the fourth century. On his left, he carries a longer sword that the legionary on page 52 and an oval shield, while his helmet covers his entire head. The soldier wears a flexible armour of metal scales sewn on heavy linen, and his lower legs are protected by bronze shin-guards. The Romans were not above copying good ideas from their enemies: the shield boss is based on a German example (compare the illustration on page 51) and the form of the helmet is based on a Persian model (photograph by Jacques Maréchal).

century, the Franks had become the dominant group of inhabitants. One of the proofs of this is the large Roman mansion at Voerendaal (east of Maastricht). In the first half of the fourth century, this villa was still being fortified by its owner against German plunderers. There is evidence, however, that at a later date, the owner allowed German immigrants to build houses on his land. We can assume that, initially, these people worked as farm labourers. At some point, the owner left, and by the end of the fourth century, the descendants of the first immigrants moved to the main building.

Julian (Athens, National Archaeological Museum).

The Roman government seems to have been somewhat concerned by the presence of the immigrants. In 365, marriages were prohibited between the old inhabitants of the provinces and people of barbarian origin, but this statute would turn out to be a dead letter. Obviously, the Romans could do little to stem the tide of German land-seekers. Julian was very sensible not to ethnically cleanse Toxandria and to allow the Franks to settle there, even though it was under the usual conditions: that, in time of war, they would fight on the side of the Romans. Most of the troops in, for example, Nijmegen would have had German ancestors. Many were career soldiers, such as Arbogast, who was supreme commander of the Roman forces in western Europe between 388 and 394. His descendants were to rule the city of Trier in the fifth century.

Most Franks, however, were less Romanized and continued to use the old German language. In this way, the Rhineland and Toxandria were lost to Latin. The linguistic discrepancy was not the only difference between these regions and southern Belgica. In the south, rich Romans still lived in their villas and continued to play an important role in public administration. There was no such elite in the north. In the south, there were units stationed in the towns, who, when necessary, could immediately march north to repulse German warlords when they crossed the frontier; the north was much more vulnerable to such raiding parties. We may assume that the plunderers did not have much sympathy for the inhabitants of the northern region: after all, these people had betrayed their tribe by swearing loyalty to Rome.

Thus, in the second half of the fourth century a linguistic frontier came into being. Frankish was spoken in Toxandria, whereas, south of that, the language was Latin. This has echoed down the centuries and is the cause of the division between the Dutch-speaking Flemish and the French-speaking Walloons that exists in Belgium today. Contemporaries were aware of the fact that the Latin language was in retreat. When Sidonius Apollinaris, a prominent official from the fifth century, wanted to pay a compliment to a Frankish leader from south of the linguistic frontier, he wrote the following:

If there is anything still left anywhere of the splendour of the Latin use of language, now that this has disappeared from Belgica and the Rhineland, it rests in you. As long as you are un-impaired and can speak, the Roman language will not falter, even though Roman law stops at the frontier.[173]

Latin Changing

Linguists have ascertained that the Latin spoken by the inhabitants of Belgica was subject to the same changes as the Latin in the Mediterranean region. There, the sound of initial /k/ was pronounced more and more as a /tj/, so that place names in Belgica that contain the element *castra*, 'fort', changed into, for example, Chestres. Further north, place names such as *Kesteren* and *Kaestert* prove that this sound-change did not take place, which can only mean that Latin was no longer spoken there. Something similar can be said about Britannia, where several town names containing the element *chester* suggest that Latin was still used.

• The Rise of Christianity

Constantine owes his reputation not only to the fact that he restructured the border security of the Roman Empire, but also – and especially – to the fact that he was the first emperor to favour the Christians. The legend of his conversion in 312 is one of the best-known stories from Antiquity. Just before an important battle, he received a vision in which he saw a cross with the words "By this sign thou shalt conquer". This was the moment that Constantine is said to have converted to the new religion and, thanks to divine assistance (and the help of soldiers from Tongeren), won a glorious victory.

The military victory was a historical event, and so, too, was the vision, but they are not, in fact, related. The first reference to the vision is a speech delivered in 310 to commemorate the founding of Trier.[174] The speaker made it clear that, in the preceding summer, somewhere near Trier, Constantine had seen the solar god and Victoria, offering him wreaths. It would seem that Constantine reinterpreted this vision later in his reign, after he had conquered the eastern provinces with their large Christian minorities.

More and more people converted and were baptized. This applied also to the Low Countries, where excavations of artefacts such as an oil lamp with a cross, a signet ring with a fish and an anchor, or a helmet with a monogram of Christ indicate the growing popularity of the new religion. A particularly remarkable aspect of Christianization is the custom of up-ending the socles of Jupiter Columns with their images of pagan gods, and using them as Christian altars.

We have very few sources about the conversion of ordinary people, but the following inscription from Remagen in Germany, a poem, is more personal than we are accustomed to.

Here rests my sweetest wife Meteriola, who,
for a great many years, shared my suffering.
For twenty-three years she was my wife;
for eight years, seven months, and eighteen days
she was my sister in the Lord, our God Jesus Christ,
who considered me worthy to show me His ways,
which I can only try to follow.[176]

Reconstruction of a Roman helmet with the chi-rho sign, based on fragments found in the River Meuse (drawing by José Antonio Germán).

We know from our sources that, at an early date, there were bishops in the Low Countries. However, we know more about only some of those, like Maternus. He was a native of Trier, which was the residence of the Emperor Maximian, an active persecutor of Christians. To avoid problems, he moved to Cologne and became bishop there. In 313, after the end of the persecutions, Maternus attended the Synod of Arles, which indicates that he was a rich man, as otherwise he could never have financed the trip. Perhaps he was a relative of another Maternus, the immensely rich Cologne official whose tombstone from 352 states that he was a councillor, police commissioner, mayor, and financial superintendent.

Servatius from Tongeren lived a generation after Maternus. He, too, must have been a

Forgeries

Because there are so many collectors of objects from Antiquity and demand exceeds supply, there is a thriving market in forged antiquities. Generally speaking, the forgers are out to make money. However, that does not seem to have been the motive of the person who scratched Christian signs on Roman sherds and placed them on excavation sites in Nijmegen. For a short time, it looked as if this town on the River Waal had had a Christian community at the end of the second century. But in 2005, it became clear that the 'evidence' had been manipulated. In this case, the misrepresentation came to light, but we have no idea if there are many more forgeries displayed inadvertently as genuine objects in our museums.

wealthy man, for in 343 he took part in the Council of Sofia. In 350, we hear of him again as one of the most important speakers at the Council of Rimini. In his own city of Tongeren, Servatius dedicated a church to Mary, which is possibly one of the buildings excavated under the present-day Basilica of Our Lady. Here, archaeologists have discovered the remains of two earlier basilicas; the first must have been built after 275 and the other was never finished.[177] The interruption of the building activity is consistent with information offered by Gregory of Tours. Writing in the late sixth century, he tells us that the inhabitants of Tongeren were sinners; Saint Peter warned Servatius that barbarians would punish the Tungri, and that he had better leave. This is of course the legendary stuff, but Servatius did in fact move to Maastricht, where he died in 384. He was buried in the Late Roman cemetery outside the ancient city, on the road to Tongeren.

The best known of all Christian leaders in fourth-century Gaul was, however, Martin of Tours. He began his career as a cavalry officer in one of the armies on the northern border of the Empire, stationed at what is now the town of Amiens in France. Like many of his contemporaries, he sympathized with Christianity, without being baptized. (At that time, it was believed that, at baptism, one's sins would be forgiven. Therefore, many people postponed baptism and confession until they were on their deathbed.) Martin's biographer, Sulpicius Severus, tells the following well-known story about the event in 335 that made the eighteen-year-old cavalry officer decide to be baptized after all.

Although not yet reborn in Christ, he, by his good works, acted the part of a candidate for baptism: he gave assistance to the wretched, he supported the needy, he clothed the naked, and he reserved nothing for himself from his military pay, except what was necessary for his daily sustenance. Even then, not being deaf to the message of the Gospel, he did not worry about the morrow.

One time, when he had nothing except his arms and his simple military dress, he happened to meet at the gate of the city of Amiens, in the middle of winter, a poor man who was naked. That winter was more severe than usual, so that the extreme cold proved fatal to many. The poor man was entreating passers-by to have compassion upon him, but all continued on, paying him no attention.

Martin, a man full of God, recognized that he was destined to help this man to whom others showed no pity. Yet, what should he do? He had nothing except the cloak in which he was clad, for he had already parted with the rest of his garments for similar purposes. Taking, therefore, the sword with which he was equipped, he divided his cloak into two equal parts, and gave one part to the poor man, while he again clothed himself with the remainder. Meanwhile, some bystanders began to laugh, because he was now a sorry sight, being only partly dressed. Many, however, who were nobler of spirit, groaned deeply because they themselves had done nothing similar. They especially felt this, because, being richer than Martin, they could have clothed the poor man without reducing themselves to nakedness.

The following night, when Martin had resigned himself to sleep, he had a vision of Christ arrayed in that part of his cloak with which he had clothed the poor man. He was told to look at the Lord with the greatest attention and to acknowledge the robe he had given. Before long, he heard Jesus saying with a clear voice to the multitude of angels standing round – "Martin, who is still but a catechumen, clothed me with this robe". After this vision, the saintly man was not puffed up with human glory, but recognized the goodness of God in what had happened, and, when he was eighteen, he hastened to receive baptism. He did not, however, immediately retire from military service.[178]

In fact, he stayed in the army for more than twenty years, as, in 356, he succeeded in arranging the capitulation of an enemy army for the Emperor Julian, whose northern campaign has been mentioned already. After that, Martin retired to one of the first monasteries north of the Alps, but he was not to stay there very long, as, in 372, he was asked to become bishop of Tours, a post that was usually filled by rich men like Maternus and Servatius.

By continuing to lead an ascetic life as bishop, and to work for the alleviation of the poor, he showed his contemporaries what he felt it was to lead a Christian life. Even in life he was considered to be a saint. Many took inspiration from him, and this helped Christianity to spread quickly. In 383, it was the most important religion in most of Gaul. When Magnus Maximus carried out a coup d'état in that year, he hastened to be baptized with a view to making himself liked by the people.

In 385, Magnus Maximus called a synod at Trier. One of the subjects to be discussed was the trial of Bishop Priscillian of Ávila in Spain, an ascetic whose doctrines had been condemned earlier. One of the few people to defend the man was Martin, who demonstratively stayed away from the imperial dinners. Only once did he join the dinner guests, but it is unlikely that Magnus Maximus found much pleasure in his company, although Sulpicius Severus claims the opposite.

Cunera of Rhenen

Saint Cunera is venerated in the town of Rhenen, just north of the River Rhine. Her biography, a rhyming chronicle of considerable length from the fourteenth century, connects her life to the expedition of her niece Ursula, who was martyred in Cologne with no less than eleven thousand pious virgins. Although this story collapses under close historical examination, Cunera herself is a different matter.

The poem about her life mentions that in 337 AD, when Ursula's expedition had come to a bloody end, Cunera was brought to the castle of a man who was known as "the king of the Rhine". She was soon given responsibility for the household, much to the chagrin of the queen, who then strangled her. Subsequently, the queen was driven to suicide by her husband. At the end of the seventh century, Cunera's grave was discovered by Bishop Willibrord of Utrecht, a missionary from Britannia. He built a church on the site, which became a popular place of pilgrimage.

The story is embellished with some miraculous occurrences but the basic facts are quite credible. The most convincing point is that Rhenen was, indeed, an important Frankish settlement, and there are parallels of literate Christian captives who were elevated to responsible positions. Nor is it unlikely that Cunera's tomb was venerated after her death.

The guests present, who had been invited as if to a festival, were men of the highest and most illustrious rank. There was the prefect, who was also consul, named Evodius, one of the most righteous men that ever lived; and two courtiers who were possessed of the greatest power, the brother and the uncle of the Emperor. Between these two, the presbyter of Martin had taken his place; but he himself occupied a stool that was set quite close to the Emperor. About the middle of the banquet, according to custom, one of the servants presented a goblet to the Emperor. He ordered it rather to be given to the very holy bishop, expecting and hoping that he, the Emperor, should then receive the cup from his right hand. But Martin, when he had drunk, handed the goblet instead to his own presbyter, because, in his opinion, there was no one worthier to take the next drink after himself, and that it would not be right for him to ignore the presbyter in favour of either the Emperor himself or those who were related to him. And the Emperor, as well as all those who were then present, admired this conduct so much that this very thing, by which they had been undervalued, gave them pleasure.[179]

This last statement can not have been true, as Martin's theatrical way of indicating that Priscillian should have been judged by church authorities alone, made no impression on those present: the synod passed the death sentence. The Emperor had him beheaded – the first Christian to be condemned to death by other Christians. Other bishops were more effective in their attempts to prevent violence. Two years later, a similar incident took place in Milan, where Bishop Ambrose declared that "the emperor is not above the church", and openly defied an order from the Emperor of the west, Valentinian II. In 390, Ambrose demanded that the eastern Emperor, Theodosius, should do public penance for a massacre of citizens in Thessalonica. The behaviour of Martin and Ambrose shows that, at the end of the fourth century, the church had started to become a formidable political factor.

The imperial basilica at Trier, where Martin dined with Magnus Maximus.

12 Transformation

● The Franks Assume Power

No one travelling through the Low Countries in the year 400 would have predicted that great changes were on the way. To be sure, some things had already changed. The old economic system, where Belgica produced the grain that fed the armies in Germania Inferior, had disappeared, and the main trade routes now ran via the North Sea. Christianity had become the dominant religion, and the linguistic frontier had shifted to the south. Society had become more militarized and members of the elite preferred to project the image of efficient military men, rather than of well-read civil magistrates. A new type of animal, the dromedary, had recently been introduced into the fauna and was used by both the army and wealthy citizens as a beast of burden. Yes, there were certainly changes – and significant changes, too. However, in many respects it was still business as usual. The cavalrymen in the garrison-towns and the border troops on the Rhine were well-trained and continued to function efficiently; military roads and bridges were kept in excellent condition; the once dangerous Franks had been made loyal to Rome. Of course, there were always Germans breaking through the limes in search of good agricultural land to settle on, but they quickly became assimilated and were definitely not seen as a threat. Everything seemed well under control.

However, the Roman peace was rudely broken in 405 when the Visigoths moved into northern Italy. This Germanic group used to live north of the Lower Danube and had settled in the Balkans after 378. Now that they were on the move again and threatened Italy. The supreme commander of the Roman forces in western Europe, Stilicho, withdrew units from the northern provinces to help him defend the threatened area. He must have been aware that German tribes would cross the Rhine as soon as they knew that they would meet little opposition, but he took the risk anyway. After all, it would not be the first time that the northern frontier of the empire had been breached, and it had never failed to recover. We know of incursions in the years 69-70, around 240, and in 256-258, 274-277, and 355-358.

Unfortunately, Stilicho's hope against hope turned out to be in vain. In the winter of 406/407,[180] various tribes crossed the Rhine, and the calculated losses became disastrous. The following description, embellished with quotations from Virgil and *Psalm* 83, comes from the collection of letters of the Christian scholar Jerome.

I would like to say just one thing about our misfortune. Innumerable extremely violent tribes now occupy all the Gallic regions. Quadi, Vandals, Sarmatians, Alans, Gepids, Herulians, Saxons, Burgundians, Alamanni, and – oh, wretched society – Pannonian enemies [the Ostrogoths] have ravaged everything they could find between the Alps and the Pyrenees and everything enclosed by the Ocean and the Rhine. 'Assur also is joined with them.' Mainz, once a great town, has been overrun and devastated. In the church there were thousands slaughtered. After a long siege, Worms has ceased to exist. The prominent towns of Reims, Amiens, Arras, Thérouanne of 'the people at the end of the world', Tournai, Speyer, and Strasbourg, have become part of Germania. The provinces of Aquitaine, Novempopulana, Lugdunensis, and Narbonensis, have been plundered and destroyed. Only with tears in my eyes, can I describe the fate of Toulouse. It was the admirable action of the holy Bishop Exsuperius that guaranteed that the city was not reduced to ashes. The Spanish provinces, which will soon experience this peril too, tremble at the memory of the invasion of the Cimbri.[181]

The only people that Jerome does not mention are the Franks, who had fought on the side of the Romans. It would appear that Rome still had authority north of the Alps, and, if Stilicho could have concentrated his attention on restoring order, the crisis might have passed. But that was not to be. The armies of Britannia proclaimed their commander Constantine emperor and crossed over to mainland Europe, where the Gallic towns also recognized him as sovereign. The official emperor, Honorius, emerged victorious from the civil war, but, in the meantime, the plundering Germans had reached Spain. They would never leave the empire again.

That is not to say that the Roman diplomats were powerless. As usual, the barbarians were hungry for land and only Honorius could give it to them. By not doing so, he forced them to make concessions. Eventually, a compromise was reached whereby the immigrants promised to do military service in the Roman armies and, in return, received the land they had asked for. This meant, however, that some people had to be dispossessed, but there were also empty villas that could be reoccupied in this way. The new system would go on functioning adequately for more than another half-century.

The new gentlemen-farmers very quickly realized that the best way to keep their businesses going was to adapt to their surroundings. For example, because they had to deal with Romans, it was essential for them to learn to speak Latin. Furthermore, if they did not want to be ostracized by their neighbours, they had to convert to Christianity. For the leaders of the immigrants, there was an extra incentive to integrate: they were accepted into the state administration and could climb high on the provincial administration ladder, even to the post of governor or general. The Roman Empire, for centuries a reliable assimilation machine, could still absorb former enemies and transform them into loyal citizens.

At least, that is what happened in the Gallic and Spanish regions. For the Lower Rhine, it was too late. Since the Roman armies had left Britannia, the island was unsettled and attacks from Saxons, Picts, and Scots had continued. These attacks must have disrupted the grain trade with the Continent, and consequently the Romans were forced to withdraw troops from Belgica and the Rhineland. One of the abandoned fortifications was the fort at Oudenburg. As a consequence, the coast was now open to attacks from Saxon pirates, who settled in the valley of the Scheldt. From there, they organized forays into Britannia, or, alternatively, put themselves up for hire as mercenaries to fight there. When they became aware that there was very good pastureland across the Channel and that viticulture was also possible, they crossed the water and settled permanently in Britannia. The setting up of these German settlements is a bloody story, but it was the logical conclusion to a process of cultural influence that had already begun a long time before. In the course of the fifth and sixth centuries, all the North Sea coastal regions were to take on a Saxon appearance.

After the disintegration of Britannia, it became impossible for the Romans to restore the Rhine forts. And yet, this did not mean the end of Roman influence, as the garrisons that were left behind – for example, in Nijmegen and Xanten – remained nominally loyal to the emperor. At the same time, the commanders began to see their castles more and more as their own property, and gradually became independent. A generation later, the Frankish leader Chlodio succeeded in uniting the local leaders of Belgica and the Rhineland under his authority. The details cannot be reconstructed, but the result speaks for itself: the emergence of a Frankish state. It is true that Chlodio's troops sometimes fought against the Romans, but the Franks were more often allies of the Empire.

All in all, it is difficult to ascertain who, in fact, was at the helm in the Low Countries at this time. A Frankish warrior could perhaps consider Chlodio to be king and sovereign ruler, but in Italy people possibly thought that it was the emperor who still waved the sceptre in the countries north of the Alps. The ambiguity is very nicely expressed in an inscription wherein someone refers to himself as *Francus ego, cives Romanus, miles in armis*, "I am a Frank, a Roman citizen, and a soldier in the army".[182]

In the course of time, more and more Franks moved to the south. Chlodio extended his power as far as the Somme,[183] the descendants of Arbogast reigned from Trier, and other Frankish leaders became masters of Cologne, Metz, and Mainz. Some groups kept their own language, but in Belgica the unavoidable happened: Chlodio's Franks merged with the local inhabitants and started to speak Latin, the language of the Gallo-Roman population. (The proverbial *lingua Franca* is Latin.) Many Franks also received baptism, but it is not clear just how many.

Chlodio was succeeded by Merovech. What we know of him is that he fought for the Roman Emperor when in 451, the Huns, led by the notorious Attila, invaded Gaul. The Frankish king made such an impression on his contemporaries that his descendants were called 'Merovingians'. His son Childeric, who came to power in around 457, was confronted by the chaos that went hand in hand with the disappearance from western Europe of the Roman administrative structure, a process that is usually referred to as the fall of the Roman Empire. This typification is overdone and misleading, as the Empire survived in the eastern Mediterranean region; there was a Roman emperor still residing in Constantinople, who claimed that he also ruled over the west. The military rulers that assumed power in Gaul in the fifth century recognized this claim, and even minted coins with the portrait of the emperor.

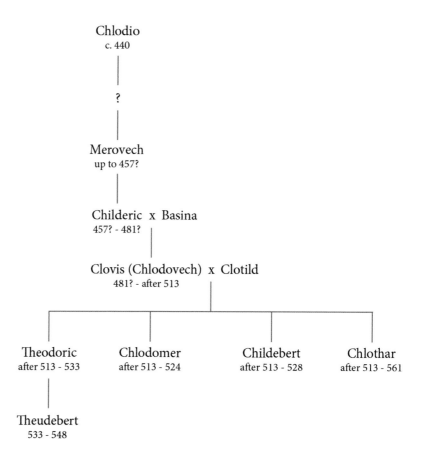

The First Merovingians.

That does not, however, take away from the fact that the changes were very real. From his capital at Tournai, Childeric slowly built up a genuine state and took over the existing civil service as much as possible. This made it easier for his non-Frankish subjects to accept the altered relationships. That this orientation towards the traditions of the Roman Empire was explicit policy, is proved by Childeric's choice of capital: not in the middle of Frankish lands – for example, in Tongeren – but on a spot where it was easy for him to receive guests who arrived from the Mediterranean world. It is striking that the Mediterranean writers never refer to him as a usurper or as a sovereign ruler, but always as the ruler of an area within the Roman Empire.

Childeric died in 481. The country he left behind, including the Rhine towns, formed the nucleus of the Frankish Empire and would become known as Austrasia: in reality former Belgica and Germania Inferior together.

His grave was discovered in 1653 in Tournai. Scholars have said that the sacrificed horses and the treasure of gold found with the grave prove that he was a heathen, because a Christian would not have been buried with such objects. This conclusion is, however, questionable: we know of comparable burials of baptized German leaders.

But although the Franks did their very best to pass for Romans, the Romans did not regard them as equals. While the commanders of the Roman armies realized very well how much the Merovingian rulers valued their friendship with the ancient superpower, there were always governors who still lived in the world described in Roman literature. To them the distinction between Romans and barbarians remained important. Take, for instance, how Childeric's contemporary Sidonius Apollinaris portrays the Franks as no better than animals. His sketch of them does contain elements of truth, but when he speaks about the hairdo of the Franks, it is as if we find ourselves in a topsy-turvy world. Not to mention what he says about their military tactics.

These monsters have red hair which falls over the forehead from their high crown, while the back of their head is bald and shines nakedly. Their watery eyes are white and have a blue shine. Because their faces are almost completely clean-shaven, they run their comb through their modest moustaches instead of through their beards. They wear tight clothes that are stretched high across their big male parts, so that their sturdy knees are exposed. A wide belt girds their slender loins.

It is a sport for them to throw their fast axes through the air from a great distance and to know in advance where they will land; to turn their shields so fast and to leap so quickly ahead that they will get to their enemies before the spear they have hurled. In childhood, their warlike behaviour is already that of an adult.[184]

German barbarity was not always given a negative twist. The Christian writer Salvian, likewise a refined man without military experience, tries to make it clear in the following fragment that the population of Africa was so terribly sinful that it was their own fault that they had been subjugated by a horde of barbarians.

For just as all sorts of trash run together in the hold of a big ship, so too, in a manner of speaking, do all the sins of the world converge in the Africans' way of living. I know of no depravation that they do not possess in abundance. Conversely, although the heathens and the savage tribes have their own special vices, their lifestyle, as a whole, is not reprehensible. The tribe of the Goths is treacherous but chaste, that of the Alans is not moral but less perfidious. The Franks are unreliable but hospitable; the Saxons are savage in their cruelty but admirable in their chastity. In short, all the tribes have their own bad ways, just as they also have their good ones. But, when it comes to the Africans, I would not know of one quality that is good.[185]

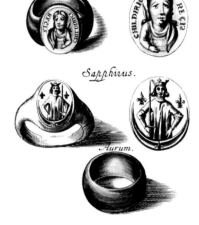

Engraving of some objects from Childeric's grave in Tournai. The originals were stolen in 1831.

Although the barbarians are not described here in very negative terms, the stereotyping is still present: evidence that the literary culture that bound together the Roman government elite, still existed. But what was once of the greatest importance if one wanted to make a career, had, by the fifth century, become less relevant. The remarks by Salvian and Sidonius Apollinaris emanate from the death throes of a dying classical culture.

• Implosion

One of the reasons why the Merovingians could extend their power was that, in the fifth century, the Roman government was beset by more urgent problems than the defence of the north. The first of these was the increasing power of the Vandals, one of the tribes that had crossed the Rhine in 406/407. They had been allocated land in Andalusia but had trekked on into Africa and in 439 had besieged Carthage, a rich city surrounded by extensive imperial domains. As we have just seen, Salvian blamed the victims.

The fall of Carthage meant the end of the supplies of free grain and olive oil that fed the city of Rome, the armies of Italy, and the imperial court. Because the people still had to be fed, the emperor decided, on the one hand, to impose taxes in kind and, on the other hand, to remunerate the leading officials with the yield of certain pieces of land. This was not a complete reversal of policy as there were precedents for both measures. Nor was it the end of coinage as, later, coins would still play a role both in tax collection and the payment of salaries. Nevertheless, it was clear that something very basic was changing.

At the same time, the government began to look for ways to economize. The state ac-counts-book was uncomplicated: in one column there was a list of estates and other taxable goods, and in the other column, a list of officials who had to be paid from the tax revenues. Therefore, the income tax yields were already earmarked, so that it was not such a big step for the emperor to take when, in the year 444, he decreed that the officials could collect the proceeds from the various estates themselves.[186] This construction, in fact, heralded the end of the official tax-collecting service.

Another development was the removal of basic rights from the population in the coun-tryside. This process had already begun more than a century before. The peasants were then given to understand that, in order to guarantee the stability of the tax revenues, they were not allowed to change their way of making a living. That decrees such as this were passed and applied at various times and that the penalties became more and more severe only proves that the peasants were consistently lax in their observation of this law, but the fact remains that, in the course of time, the official position of the peasants gradually worsened. They were tied to their land and had to give up part of their harvest to an official. They had become serfs.

The peasants did not take this submissively. We know that some of them banded into gangs and marauded through the provinces, plundering and pillaging – in many ways re-sembling the barbarian hordes. Quite often, peasants who had run away joined up with German bands, adding to the ambiguous identity of these groups: Romans *and* Germans.

The emperors attempted to turn the tide, but all efforts to reconquer Carthage came to nothing, which was a further blow to the prestige of the Romans. And yet there were some successes, such as the victory over Attila's Huns in 451, when an imperial army, reinforced by Visigoths, Burgundians, and Franks defeated a very dangerous enemy. As long as the em-perors could rely on the support of the descendants of the Germans who had settled inside the limes, it remained possible to defend Gaul and the provinces of the Danube.

In 468 another attempt to recover Carthage failed. Furthermore, a conflict ensued be-tween the Romans and the Visigoths, who, no longer intimidated by the authority of the emperor, now began the conquest of Spain. With this, the last vestiges of Rome's prestige evaporated, and it is not surprising that in 474, Gundobad, who was supreme commander of the Roman forces in western Europe, gave up this position in order to become King of the Burgundians. Nobody actually noticed when, two years later, one of the military leaders deposed the child who was the official emperor. One emperor – the one in Constantinople – was sufficient: western Europe could easily be delegated to its military leaders.

However, in the meantime, it had become considerably impoverished, as evidenced by the fact that the volume of inter-regional trade had fallen sharply and the towns had gone into decline. Incidentally, the dromedaries were no longer needed as beasts of burden, bringing to an end this remarkable episode in history. The prevailing chaos provided an opportunity for the Merovingians to extend their power southwards. In around 486, Childeric's son, who is usually called Clovis although his real name was Chlodovech, moved the southern border of the Frankish lands from the Somme to the Loire. The resistance offered by Syagrius, the son of the last general appointed by a Roman emperor, was in vain. However, the extension of the Frankish lands can be seen less as a conquest by Clovis than as a consequence of the implosion of Roman power. It was, of course, to the advantage of the Franks that Belgica, which Austrasia had absorbed, was still quite prosperous. Although the economies of Belgica and Germania Inferior had been shrinking since the middle of the third century, they had already adapted to the decline and had developed the North Sea trade. All things considered, Austrasia had the means to continue doing relatively well economically, at a time when the southern towns were in free fall. So, the Merovingians could expand their power.

Beyond the Somme, the Franks encountered a society where the peasants were serfs and government officials received their remuneration in the form of lands given on loan. These would also become important features of the society of the Middle Ages, which economically, socially, and politically differed considerably from that of (Late) Antiquity. Contrary to common belief, the origin of these changes is not to be found in the Frankish conquest. Serfdom and lands held in loan were not German inventions: the dynamics lay in the Roman Empire.

• The Baptism of Clovis

The Merovingians were not the only ones who profited from the power vacuum that arose when the Roman state apparatus disappeared in the fifth century. As has been said, other Frankish warlords conquered the towns along the Rhine. The Alamanni settled in the Alsace, the Vandals annexed Sicilia, the Burgundians subjugated the Rhône Valley, the Visigoths pursued their campaigns in Spain, and the Ostrogoths took over power in Italy. At the same time, the Saxons conquered parts of Britannia. What was once governed by one emperor was now divided among all sorts of different leaders, with one thing in common: they had loyal troops at their disposal who were mostly descended from German immigrants.

One of them was Clovis, the son of Childeric of Austrasia. He is one of the most important persons during the transition from Antiquity to the Middle Ages, but we do not have much information about his career. The problem is that we only have one real source, the *History of the Franks* by the sixth-century Bishop of Tours, Gregory. He is without doubt a very entertaining writer, but at times he is very inaccurate, especially when he speaks about events that took place before his own time. And this is the case with his account of Clovis, whom he so admired. Therefore, we must not set too much store by what he says.

Gregory claims that, five years after the death of his father, i.e. 486, Clovis wrested the land between the Somme and the Loire from the son of the last Roman magistrate. Five years later – in 491 – he was supposed to have beaten the Thuringii on the Upper Weser. Another five years later, in 496, Gregory reports that Clovis went to war with the Alamanni in

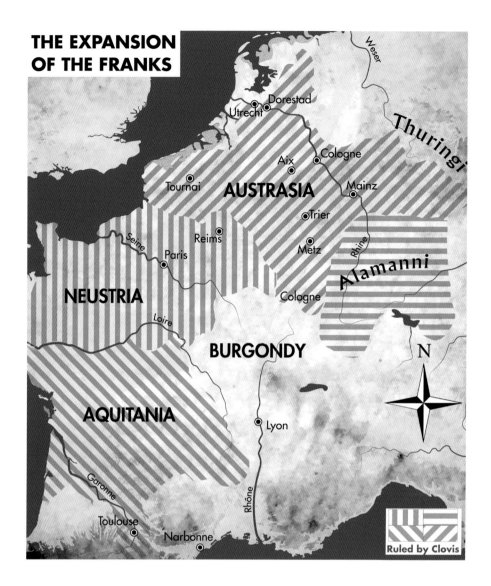

THE EXPANSION OF THE FRANKS

Thuringi

Weser

Dorestad

Utrecht

Aix

Cologne

AUSTRASIA

Mainz

Tournai

Trier

Alamanni

Reims

Metz

Rhine

Paris

Seine

NEUSTRIA

Cologne

Loire

BURGONDY

N

AQUITANIA

Lyon

Garonne

Rhône

Toulouse

Narbonne

Ruled by Clovis

the Alsace. (The last two campaigns could only have taken place if Clovis had already taken control of the Frankish states on the Rhine, but it is not clear how and when this happened.)

It is obvious from Gregory's use of five-year intervals between these events, that we must not take his chronology at face value. We can, however, supply a more likely date for the victory of the Alamanni, as, according to Italian sources, this took place in 507. After this, Clovis pushed the Visigoths back from the Loire to the Pyrenees. Finally, Gregory states that the great conqueror died in 511. This date is demonstrably false, as the *Book of Popes*, the official collection of papal biographies, reports that the king was still in the land of the living in the year 513.

However, although we may question the chronology of Gregory's historical work, it is certain that, at his death, Clovis ruled the entire region north of the Pyrenees and Alps, with the exception of the Rhône Valley, where the Burgundians still had an independent state. We also know that he worked closely with the Christian Church in the last years of his life. According to Gregory, Clovis' wife, Clotild, was responsible for this.

Queen Clotild continued to pray that her husband might recognize the true God and give up his idol-worship. Nothing could persuade him to accept Christianity. Finally war broke out against the Alamanni and in this conflict he was forced by necessity to accept what he had refused of his own free will.

It so turned out that when the two armies met on the battlefield, there was great slaughter and the troops of Clovis were rapidly being annihilated. He raised his eyes to heaven when he saw this, felt compunction in his heart and was moved to tears. 'Jesus Christ,' he said, 'you who Clotild maintains to be the Son of the living God, you who deign to give help to those in travail and victory to those who trust in you, in faith I beg the glory of your help. If you will give me victory over my enemies, and if I may have evidence of that miraculous power which the people dedicated to your name say they have experienced, then I will believe in you and I will be baptized in your name. I have called upon my own gods, but, as I see only too clearly, they have no intention of helping me. I therefore cannot believe that they possess any power, for they do not come to the assistance of those who trust in them. I now call upon you. I want to believe in you, but I must first be saved from my enemies.'

Even as he said this, the Alamanni turned their backs and began to run away.[187]

When the queen learned that her husband wanted to be baptized, she asked the Bishop of Reims, Remigius, to give the king religious instruction. The other Franks also promised to reject paganism. At last, the big day dawned:

The public squares were draped with coloured cloths, the churches were adorned with white hangings, the baptistery was prepared, sticks of incense gave off clouds of perfume, sweet-smelling candles gleamed bright and the holy place of baptism was filled with divine fragrance. God filled the hearts of all present with such grace that they imagined themselves to have been transported to some perfumed paradise. King Clovis asked that he might be baptized first by the bishop. Like some new Constantine he stepped forward to the baptismal pool, ready to wash away the sores of his old leprosy and to be cleansed in flowing water from the sordid stains which he head borne so long. As he advanced for baptism, Remigius addressed him in these pregnant words: 'Bow your head in meekness, Sicamber. Worship what you have burnt, burn what you have been wont to worship.[188]

In the way in which this story is told, it simply cannot be true. Gregory's account is too clearly modelled on the Constantine legend. Moreover, Gregory himself refers to the fact that, at an earlier moment, Clovis had demanded respect for the property of the Church, during his conquest of the land between the Somme and the Loire. He even put to death with his own hands a warrior who had not handled holy objects with due respect.[189] It is quite possible that Clovis was already a Christian, bearing in mind that the only information that confirms Gregory's picture of a still pagan Clovis, is the grave of his father Childeric, which, as we have seen, cannot be taken as evidence about his faith.

That being said, Gregory's story nevertheless contains an element of truth, because from the time of Clovis' government, the Merovingians and the Church would work closely together. The kings supported the Church and its missionaries, while the literate monks and bishops helped the king in the administration of state. One of the things they did, for example, was draw up Frankish Law.

The Frankish rulers were fortunate. They could never have profited from the disappearance of the Roman administrative machinery if northern Gaul had not been their power base. True, this region was not very wealthy, but its trade orientation towards the North Sea made it less vulnerable to the crisis that had sounded the death knell of the Roman Empire. It was not the first time that the prosperity of the North had been converted into political power. Vitellius and Postumus had also used it to their advantage. This time, its effects

The Lord of Morken: reconstruction of a Frankish warrior from the sixth century whose grave has been found in the western Ruhr area (drawing by Johnny Shumate).

would last longer: Austrasia would form the nucleus of the Frankish Empire for another three centuries.

• The Triumph of Austrasia

Clovis had four sons, who ruled the empire between them after the death of their father. We have no sources that tell us how this division of the Frankish kingdom worked out. We have to glean it from such items as letters, in which mention is made of who administered justice in a particular town. However, it is certain that the relatively rich Austrasia was not administered by only one ruler, and that the rulers of the sub-kingdoms did not govern one continuous region. According to this system, the eldest son, Theodoric, ruled in eastern Austrasia and in Auvergne. In spite of the sometimes uneasy relationships between the four brothers, the system worked. In 534, the Merovingian rulers together set off to fight the Burgundians, whom they defeated and subjugated. Two years later, they reached the Mediterranean.

The most powerful Merovingian ruler in the sixth century was Theodoric's son and successor Theudebert (r.533-548), the king of the larger part of Austrasia and Burgundy. When the Roman Emperor Justinian sent an army from Constantinople to reconquer Italy from its Ostrogoth rulers, Theudebert seized the opportunity to prove himself. In 539, he crossed the Alps and defeated both of the warring parties. Justinian even feared that the Frank would proceed to the Balkans, but Theudebert was too practical to allow himself to be tempted by such a venture. And yet, something had changed. After his Italian campaign, he emphasized the Frankish autonomy by having gold coins minted, not with the image of the emperor, but with his own likeness on them. This made a big impression on his neighbours and Theudebert could expand his sphere of influence to the Saxons, Thuringii, and Bavarians.

The power of Theudebert indicates, once again, the comparative prosperity of Austrasia, which would remain at the heart of the Merovingian kingdom. This was partly because, just as in the fifth century, the economy of the region between the British Channel and the Lower Rhine was healthier than in the Mediterranean region, where things went from bad to worse in the sixth century. Wars followed each other in quick succession, a terrible epidemic raged, and the towns declined further. Conversely, the towns in the north prospered – at least more or less. Cologne was still a centre of the metal industry; in Trier and Maastricht, pottery was manufactured; iron was mined in the Ardennes. The royal house seems to have taken

The Death of Hygelac

Theudebert achieved his first military successes when he was still crown prince. At one time a group of Danes sailed up the Rhine or the Waal, reached the area to the southeast of Nijmegen and began a plundering raid there when Theudebert surprised them. The Frankish prince defeated the invaders first on land, and, subsequently, on water, after which he retrieved all the loot. Gregory of Tours calls the murdered Danish leader Chlochilaicus, and this warrior is identical to the Hygelac who, centuries later, was mentioned in the Old-English saga, *Beowulf*. That a Danish hero who died in Austrasia is mentioned in a text from England, illustrates how close the ties were between the peoples living on the North Sea.

A Theudebert coin.

responsibility for the maintenance of the roads, for it has come down to us – although in a late source – that, at the beginning of the seventh century, Queen Brunhilda ordered the Roman roads to be repaired. Compared to the Mediterranean region, Austrasia was booming. There was commercial activity on some scale, and at the point where the River Lek branches off from the Rhine, close to the old limes fort of Levefanum, the town of Dorestad grew to become one of the most important trade centres in Europe.

Austrasia would maintain its influence for a long time to come. Several bishops propagated the Christian state cult: Amandus in Flanders and Lambert in Maastricht, while the Northumbrian missionary Willibrord built a small church within the remains of the ancient fort of Utrecht. In this way, the country became better organized, and it remained comparatively strong when the Merovingian dynasty was replaced by the Carolingian, which also originated in Austrasia. The best-known ruler from this family was Charlemagne (r.768-814). We have enough sources to establish that his kingdom was governed by about forty powerful families, among which the Austrasians were overrepresented. When the Carolingian Empire had to be carved up between the three grandsons of Charlemagne in 843, each of them saw to it that they were given a piece of Austrasia.

With the Treaty of Verdun, which divided Charlemagne's empire into three kingdoms, the unity of the Frankish Empire came to an end, and with it the central position that Austrasia had held for three centuries. Austrasia's success was due to a factor that is stubbornly ignored by the authors of our written sources: the northwest of Europe remained relatively prosperous in a period of general malaise. Thanks to the first phase of the Roman presence in Belgica, at the beginning of our era, it had a varied economy; thanks to the crisis after the fall of the Gallic Empire, it had begun trading with the countries on the North Sea; thanks to being settled by the Franks in the middle of the fourth century, it was spared destructive invasions in the fifth. When the Roman government disintegrated, the Low Countries were ready and willing to take advantage of the situation. And so, what had once been on the periphery of the Mediterranean world, could now become the centre of the first European empire.

Epilogue

In 2009, the Germans commemorated the battle which had taken place in the Teutoburg Forest 2000 years before. The celebrations began when the Chancellor, Angela Merkel, opened three magnificent exhibitions being held in Haltern, Kalkriese, and Detmold. On the face of it, nothing seemed to have changed since 1909, when the battle was commemorated in a similar way. However, at that time, the exhibitions sent out a different message: namely that Germany was born of the German victory over the Romans in AD 9. Nowadays, scholars are no longer so sure that this was the case.[190] The tenor of the 2009 exhibitions was that the conflict should be seen in the framework of the pan-European process of Romanization.

Most visitors will have realized that, in this way, the organizers were, in fact, thumbing their noses at the politicians: "You are very eager to hold an exhibition? Fine! But then we feel free to explain why there is actually very little to commemorate." One of the contributors to the catalogue made his point by writing, "Despite repeated claims by the historically illiterate, it is wrong to see the Battle of the Teutoburg Forest as a historical watershed."[191]

The 2009 Battle of Teutoburg Forest was, therefore, a different one from that of 1909. Our view of the past is continuously changing. In the nineteenth century, nationalism had centre stage, and the conflict between the Germans and the Romans was seen as the root of the poor relations between Germany and France. Nowadays we can perceive the globalization processes at work. In 1909, the accent lay on reading sources, and archaeology was an ancillary science to history; today, the centre of gravity lies with archaeology. In the past, history teachers were the main instrument for the transfer of knowledge; today re-enactors are increasingly important. There was a time when it was believed that the Roman Empire collapsed under the pressure of barbarian invasions; now we think that it imploded. And, where once it was thought that national heroes like Ambiorix, Arminius, and Julius Civilis were the driving forces behind the historical process, scholars now take a wider view of historical causality.

Our vision of the past is coloured by who we are ourselves. We can only get answers to questions that occur to us, and we can only understand the answers that correspond to our own mindset. This means that the past reveals itself to us as in an echo chamber. Furthermore, a human life is short and a scholar only has a finite amount of time in which to exploit his or her expertise. Consequently, there are only a limited number of questions that can be researched. Not only is our knowledge of the past very incomplete, but only a fraction of the known past can be scientifically examined.

Therefore, our image of ancient times is the result of choices made in the present. The most fashionable subject of our time, the cultural cross-fertilization along the borders of the Roman Empire, would never have become so popular if the old nationalism had not given way to international co-operation. In the Netherlands, for example, shipwrecks discovered near the Roman limes forts receive quite some attention, while there is scant interest in shipwrecks from the Middle Ages, although these provide evidence as to the origins and development of the types of ships that enabled the Netherlands to rule the seven seas in the seventeenth century. Histories focused on nation states, which are essentially nineteenth-century constructs, are now secondary to histories based on new, supranational constructs.

Such choices are inevitable, especially now that the amount of data is so rapidly expanding. As noticed in the introduction to this book, a twenty-five-metre high paper tower could be built from the reports written by Dutch archaeologists since 2000, while there are similar numbers for Germany and Belgium. Scholars must explain their choices and premises, but hardly do so. This lack of transparency is already damaging the credibility of the academic world.

But it need not be the last word on this subject. Museums can give more attention to scholarly policy choices and the way in which archaeological interpretations arise. They could also explain why some historical interpretations are considered more valid than others. Now that, more and more, archaeology is being given its place in large, infrastructural projects, space has been created for this kind of in-depth study. A lovely story is that of Woerden in the Netherlands, where a number of the artefacts found during the building of a parking garage are on display in a quite impressive exposition on the site. If the incorporation of archaeology into the urban infrastructure continues, the big museums can devote themselves to explaining the choices made and the interpretative methods applied.

Finally, which choices formed the basis of this book? First and foremost, the authors believed that research into the subject matter had to be broad, both geographically and chronologically. Geographically: by covering the whole region between the rivers Weser and Somme. The borders of the nineteenth-century national states are precisely that: borders from the nineteenth century. Chronologically: by allowing the story to go further than is customary. In this way, justice could be done to the economic and political power of Belgica/Austrasia, which adds a very interesting facet to the story. Ancient history must not be separated from later history.

In the second place, the authors believe that the Roman past of the Netherlands should be studied by both archaeologists *and* historians. That is why we have pointed out a number of misconceptions that have arisen because archaeologists are not familiar enough with the work of historians and vice versa.[192] This lack of knowledge of each other's work can be partly explained by the lamentable fact that, in universities, archaeologists and historians of Antiquity are seldom housed in the same institute. (Historians of Antiquity usually work closer with classical scholars; at least that is the case in the Netherlands.)

Another explanation is that, at the moment, Dutch historians do not do any intensive study of the Roman history of their country. It is inevitable that national history receives less attention than the history of pan-European processes, but ignoring your own past altogether is exaggerated, and the authors of this book hope to have shown that there is no reason for this reluctance. Germania Inferior is too interesting to ignore.

Appendix 1:
Rulers in the Low Countries

Roman Emperors

Augustus	died 14
Tiberius	14-37
Caligula	37-41
Claudius	41-54
Nero	54-68
Galba	68-69
Vitellius	69

First Gallic Empire

Julius Sabinus	69-70

Roman Emperors

Vespasian	70-79
Titus	79-81
Domitian	81-96
Nerva	96-98
Trajan	98-117
Hadrian	117-138
Antoninus Pius	138-161
Marcus Aurelius	161-180
Commodus	180-192
Pertinax	193
Didius Julianus	193
Clodius Albinus	193-197
Septimius Severus	197-211
Caracalla	211-217
Macrinus	217-218
Heliogabalus	218-222
Alexander Severus	222-235
Maximinus Thrax	235-238
Gordian III	238-244
Philip the Arab	244-249
Decius	249-251
Trebonianus Gallus	251-253
Gallienus	253-260

Second Gallic Empire

Postumus	260-269
Marius	269
Victorinus	269-271
Tetricus	271-274

Roman Emperors

Probus	277-282
Carus	282-283
Carinus	283-285
Maximian	285-305
Constantius I Chlorus	305-306
Constantine the Great	306-337
Constantine II	337-340
Constans	340-350
Magnentius	350-353
Constantius II	353-360
Silvanus	355
Julian the Apostate	360-363
Jovian	363-364
Valentinian I	364-375
Gratian	375-383
Magnus Maximus	383-388
Valentinian II	388-392
Eugenius	392-394
Honorius	395-407
Constantine III	407-411
Honorius	411-423
Johannes	423-425
Valentinian III	425-455

Merovingian kings of Austrasia

Chlodio	about 440
Merovech	until 457?
Childerik	457?-481?
Clovis	481?- after 513
Theodoric I	after 513-533
Theudebert I	533-548

Appendix 2:
Legions along the Rhine

I Ad	I Adiutrix	XVI	XVI Gallica
I G	I Germanica	XX	XX Valeria Victrix
I M	I Minervia	XXI	XXI Rapax
V	V Alaudae	X	X Gemina
VI	VI Victrix	XXX	XXX Ulpia Victrix
IX	IX Hispana		
XIV	XIV Gemina	The surnames of the legions XVII, XIIX	
XV	XV Primigenia	and XIX are not known.	

	Until 13 BC	9 – 9	10-28?	28?-43	43-69	70-83	83-103	103-121?	121?	130-274
Nijmegen	Unknown					X	X		IX	
Xanten	Unknown	XVIII	V, XXI	V, XXI	V, XV	XXII	XXII	VI	XXX	XXX
Haltern		XIX								
Neuss				XX	XVI	VI	VI			
Cologne	XIX	XVII	I G, XX							
Bonn				I G	I G	XXI	I M	I M	I M	I M
Mainz	I G, V	I G, V	XIV, XVI	XIV, XVI	IIII, XXII	I Ad, XIV	I Ad, XIV	XXII	XXII	XXII

Appendix 3:
A Visit to Germania Inferior

If you want to visit the Roman remains in the Low Countries, you can see the most important monuments and museums in less than a week, provided that you have a car. Although the people speak Dutch, French, or German, they all speak English too; nearly every museum has explanatory signs in more than one language.

Day 1

- Brussels, *Koninklijke musea voor kunst en geschiedenis* (Royal Museums of Art and History): the national archaeological collection of Belgium (kmkg-mrah.be/cinquantenaire-museum/).
- Tongeren, *Gallo-Roman Museum* and ancient Roman walls (gallo-romeinsmuseum.be).
- There are good hotels in Tongeren and Maastricht.

Day 2

- Heerlen, *Thermenmuseum* (Roman Baths Museum): the largest visible excavation in the Netherlands (thermenmuseum.nl/).
- Cologne, *Römisch-Germanisches Museum* (Romano-Germanic Museum): very large collection (museenkoeln.de/homepage/default.asp?s=169)
- Cologne, *praetorium* (museenkoeln.de/archaeologische-zone/)
- Continue to Xanten.

Day 3   (or 7, if you make the detour mentioned below)
- *Kalkriese*, museum and park: site of the Battle of the Teutoburg Forest (kalkriese-varusschlacht.de/).
- Haltern, *Westfälisches Römermuseum* (Roman Museum of Westphalia): on the site of the legionary base in the valley of the Lippe (lwl-roemermuseum-haltern.de). There are plans to rename it Aliso.
- Return to Xanten.

Day 4 (8)

- Xanten, *Archäologischer Park* (Archaeological Park): reconstructed city, with an excellent museum (apx.lvr.de/).
- Nijmegen, *Museum Valkhof*: finds from several sites in and around Nijmegen (museumhetvalkhof.nl/).
- There are several hotels in Nijmegen and Arnhem.

Day 5 (9)

- Alphen aan den Rijn, *Archeon*: reconstructions of buildings from the Iron Age, the Roman period, and the Middle Ages (archeon.nl/).
- Leiden, *Rijksmuseum van oudheden* (National Museum of Antiquities): Dutch national collection (rmo.nl/).

If you want to return to Brussel, you may like to add the small archaeological museums of Aardenburg, Oudenburg, and Velzeke. If you have more time to spend, you may consider making a detour:

Day 2

- Heerlen, *Thermenmuseum* (Roman Baths Museum): the largest visible excavation in the Netherlands (thermenmuseum.nl/).
- Arlon, *Musée archéologique* (Archaeological Museum): with a splendid collection of local sculpture (ial.be/).
- Pétange, *Titelberg*: a Belgian oppidum, perhaps the main settlement of the Treveri.
- Hotel in Trier.

Day 3

- Trier's two Roman bathhouses, basilica, Roman bridge, amphitheatre, 'black gate', Viehmarktplatz excavations.
- *Rheinisches Landesmuseum* (State Museum of the Rhineland): very large museum (landesmuseum-trier.de/).
- *Bischöfliches Dom- und Diözesanmuseum* (Episcopal museum of the Cathedral and Diocese) (bistum-trier.de/museum/)
- Hotel in Trier.

Day 4

- *Villa of Nennig.*
- Archaeological Park of *Belginum*: a rural settlement (belginum.de/).
- Hotel in Mainz.

Day 5

- Mainz' theatre, gate of the Roman fortress, underground temple of Isis.
- *Rheinisches Landesmuseum* (State Museum of the Rhineland): large collection of sculpture and inscriptions (landesmuseum-mainz.de/)
- *Römisch-Germanisches Zentralmuseum* (Central Museum for Roman and Germanic Culture): general museum of ancient art (rgzm.de/).
- *Museum für Antike Schiffahrt* (Museum for Ancient Seafaring): several wrecks and two full-scale reconstructions (web.rgzm.de/36.html).

Day 6

- Bonn, *Rheinisches Landesmuseum* (State Museum of the Rhineland): fine collection (rlmb.lvr.de/).
- Cologne, *Römisch-Germanisches Museum* (Romano-Germanic Museum): very large collection (museenkoeln.de/homepage/default.asp?s=169)
- Cologne, *praetorium* (museenkoeln.de/archaeologische-zone/)
- Continue to Xanten.

Acknowledgements

No writer works alone. From the many people who contributed to the Dutch versions of 2000 and 2010, we who would like to thank Hein van Dolen, Wim van Es, Paul van der Heijden, Richard Kroes, Jasper Oorthuys, Marco Prins, Sigrid van Roode, Hetty van Rooijen, Robert Vermaat, Jan van Vliet, Frans Wendel, Simon Wynia, and the people of Ambo Publishers and Athenaeum – Polak & Van Gennep Publishers, both in Amsterdam.

The text was translated into English by Marie Smit-Ryan. Her job was made more complex because we adapted the text to a new audience, unacquainted with the topography of the Low Countries, and because we used the occasion to update the text. We received useful advice from Wouter Vos (Hazenberg Archeologie) and Duncan B. Campbell. Eric Norde (RAAP Archeologie) contributed the photos of the Apeldoorn excavations, Martin Veen (province of Noord-Holland) sent the photos of the Uitgeest-Dorregaard hoard Ruurd Halbertsma (National Museum of Antiquities) provided advice about Caesar's bust and help with photos of the Velsen finds, and Jacques Maréchal took the photo of the re-enactors on page 151. New maps were drawn by Carlos García, new drawings were made by José Antonio Germán, Johnny Shumate, and Graham Sumner. Finally, we would like to thank Rolof van Hövell tot Westerflier and Karwansaray Publishers for creating this beautiful book.

Unless indicated otherwise in the notes (pages 178ff), the rather free translations in this book were made by Marie Smit-Ryan and Jona Lendering. Use has been made of several existing translations:

- Caesar, *The Gallic War*, translated by C. Hammond (1999)
- Dio, *Roman History*, translated by E. Cary (1914-1927)
- Gregory of Tours, *History of the Franks*, translated by L. Thorpe (1974)
- *Historia Augusta*, translated by A. Birley (1976)
- *Historia Augusta*, translated by D. Magie (1921-1932)
- Suetonius, *The Twelve Caesars*, translated by J. C. Rolfe (1913-1914)
- Sulpicius Severus, *Life of St Martin*, translated by A. Roberts (1894)
- Tacitus, *Histories*, translated by K. Wellesley (1975)
- Varro, *On Agriculture*, translated by W.D. Hooper and H.B. Ash (1934)
- Velleius Paterculus, *Roman History*, translated by F.W. Shipley (1924)

These existing translations have been adapted. Distances have been converted from stades to kilometres, place names and titles have been harmonized, and so on.

Literature

- R. Aßkamp, *2000 Jahre Römer in Westfalen* (1989)
- J. Bos, *Archeologie van Friesland* (1995)
- T. Bechert, *Römisches Germanien zwischen Rhein und Maas. Die Provinz Germania Inferior* (1982 München)
- T. Bechert and Willem Willems, *Die römische Reichsgrenze zwischen Mosel und Nordseeküste* (1995)
- A.V.A.J. Bosman, *Het culturele vondstmateriaal van de vroeg-Romeinse versterking te Velsen 1* (1997)
- C.R. Brandeburgh and W.A.M. Hessing, *Matilo – Rodenburg – Roomburg* (2005)
- D.J. Breeze, S. Jilek & A. Thiel, *Frontiers of the Roman Empire, Edinburgh* (2005)
- D.B. Campbell, *Roman Auxiliary Forts 27 BC - AD 378* (2009)
- M. Carroll, *Romans, Celts, and Germans. The German Provinces of Rome* (2002)
- B. Cunliffe, *The Ancient Celts* (1997)
- J.F. Drinkwater, *Roman Gaul* (1983)
- H. van Enckevort e.a., *Nijmegen. Legerplaats in het achterland van de Romeinse limes* (2000)
- H. van Enckevort & E.N.A. Heirbaut (eds.), *Opkomst en ondergang van Oppidum Batavorum, hoofdplaats van de Bataven, Opgravingen op de St. Josephhof in Nijmegen 1* (2010)
- W.A. van Es, *De Romeinen in Nederland* (1980)
- S. Fichtl, *Les Gaulois du Nord de la Gaule* (1994)
- T. Fischer, *Die Römer in Deutschland* (1999)
- M. Gysseling, 'Germanisering en taalgrens' in: *Algemene geschiedenis der Nederlanden 1* (1981)
- P. van der Heijden & M. Sier, *Wonen op veen. Ellewoutsdijk in de Romeinse tijd* (2006)
- W. Hessing e.a., *Romeinen langs de snelweg. Bouwstenen voor Vechtens verleden* (1997)
- P. van der Heijden, *Romeins Nijmegen. Luxe en ondergang van Rome aan de Waal* (2008)
- W. de Jonge e.a., *Forum Hadriani, van Romeinse stad tot monument* (2006)
- H. Kenzler, S. Burmeister, S. Berke, e.a., *2000 Jahre Varusschlacht. Imperium – Konflikt – Mythos* (2009)
- G. Klose & A. Nünnerich-Asmus (eds.), *Grenzen des römischen Imperiums* (2006)
- D. Lamarcq e.a., *De taalgrens* (1996)
- H. van Londen, *Midden-Delfland. The Roman Native Landscape Past and Present* (2006)
- R. Nouwen, *Tongeren en het land van de Tungri. 31 v. Chr.-284 n. Chr.* (1997)
- N. Roymans, *Tribal Societies in Northern Gaul. An Anthropological Perspective* (1990)
- N. Roymans, *Romeinse frontierpolitiek en de etnogenese van de Bataven* (1998)
- N. Roymans and T. Derks, *De tempel van Empel. Een Herculesheiligdom in het woongebied van de Bataven* (1994)
- M. Sier (ed.), *Ellewoutsdijk in de Romeinse tijd* (ADC Rapport 200) (2003)
- W.J.H. Willems & H. van Enckevort (eds.), *Ulpia Noviomagus. Roman Nijmegen. The Batavian Capital at the Imperial Frontier* (2009)
- Chr. Wickham, *The Inheritance of Rome. A History of Europe from 400 to 1000* (2009)
- E.M. Wightman, *Gallia Belgica* (1985)

Notes

1 Furthermore, the explosion of data has meant that, in the two years that have gone by between the publication of the revised edition in Dutch and this English translation, certain parts of the book have become outdated. We have used the opportunity to review the text, bringing this English version more up to date.

2 Pliny the Elder, *Natural History* 2.169a; Avienus, *The Coast* 114-129, 380-389, 404-415.

3 Cp. Herodotus, *Histories* 3.115, where he doubts the reports of earlier authors.

4 Strabo, *Geography* 17.1.19 (attributed to Eratosthenes).

5 Polybius, *World History* 3.22.

6 A discussion of the surviving fragments can be found in B. Cunliffe, *The Extraordinary Voyage of Pytheas the Greek* (2001).

7 Pliny the Elder, *Natural History* 37.35-36.

8 Ephorus of Cyme, quoted in Strabo's *Geography* 7.2.1.

9 Quoted by Pliny the Elder, *Natural History* 4.95.

10 Sidonius Apollinaris, *Panegyric on Majorianus* 239.

11 See page 94.

12 Caesar, *Gallic War* 1.1.1-3 (trans. Carolyn Hammond).

13 On this subject, see M. Gysseling, 'Germanisering en Taalgrens' (Germanisation and language border) in: *Algemene Geschiedenis der Nederlanden* 1 (1981).

14 Caesar, *Gallic War* 4.10.1-2 (trans. Carolyn Hammond).

15 Caesar, *Gallic War* 2.4.1-6, 8-10 (trans. Carolyn Hammond).

16 Caesar, *Gallic War* 6.16.

17 Caesar, *Gallic War* 2.1.2-4 (trans. Carolyn Hammond).

18 Caesar, *Gallic War* 2.15.4-6 (trans. Carolyn Hammond).

19 Caesar calls the river the *Sabis*. Because this vaguely resembles the word *Sambra*, it used to be thought that the battle took place on the banks of the Sambre. For the correct identification, see Pierre Turquin, 'La Bataille de la Selle (du Sabis) en l'An 57 avant J.-C.', in *Les Études Classiques* 23/1 (1955). The article is more than half a century old, but the erroneous identification continues to crop up.

20 Caesar, *Gallic War* 2.19.4-7 (trans. Carolyn Hammond).

21 Caesar, *Gallic War* 2.21.1-23.2 (trans. Carolyn Hammond).

22 Caesar, *Gallic War* 2.25.1-2 (trans. Carolyn Hammond).

23 Caesar, *Gallic War* 2.26.4-27.5 (trans. Carolyn Hammond).

24 Caesar, *Gallic War* 2.28.1-2 (trans. Carolyn Hammond).

25 Caesar, *Gallic War* 7.75.3.

26 Caesar, *Gallic War* 2.29 (trans. Carolyn Hammond).

27 Caesar, *Gallic War* 2.30.1-31.3 (trans. Carolyn Hammond).

28 Suetonius, *The Twelve Caesars*, Julius Caesar 54.2 (trans. J. C. Rolfe).

29 This matter has been discussed by N. Roymans e.a. (eds), *Late Iron Age gold hoards from the Low Countries and the Caesarian conquest of Northern Gaul* (2012 Amsterdam).

30 Caesar, *Gallic War* 2.35.1.

31 Cicero, *On the Consular Provinces* 19.

32 Virgil, *Aeneid* 8.727.

33 Cassius Dio, *Roman History* 39.44. Cp. Caesar, *Gallic War* 3.28-29.

34 Cassius Dio, *Roman History* 39.48.1-3. Cp. Caesar, *Gallic War* 4.11-15.

35 Cassius Dio, *Roman History* 39.48.3-5. Cp. Caesar, *Gallic War* 4.16-19.

36 Caesar, *Gallic War* 4.19.3.

37 Cicero, *Against Piso* 82.

38 Caesar, *Gallic War* 4.38.1-3 (trans. Carolyn Hammond).

39 Caesar, *Gallic War* 7.75.3.

40 Guido Cuyt, 'Geef aan Caesar wat Caesar toekomt...', in: *AVRA-bulletin* 7 (2006) 82.

41 Cassius Dio, *Roman History* 40.5-10 (trans. E. Cary). Cp. Caesar, *Gallic War* 5.24-53.

42 Caesar, *Gallic War* 6.5.4-6.4 (trans. Carolyn Hammond).

43 Cassius Dio, *Roman History* 40.32.2.

44 Caesar, *Gallic War* 6.30.1-31.3 (trans. Carolyn Hammond).

45 Historical maps that show islands in Zeeland, are usually based on much older maps that, in turn, are based on the passage quoted here from Caesar. What the countryside really looked like can be seen on palaeographic maps, such as J. Bazelmans, *Atlas van Nederland in het Holoceen* (2012).

46 Tactical sub-unit of a Roman legion.

47 Caesar, *Gallic War* 6.34 (trans. Carolyn Hammond).

48 Florus, *Epitome* 1.45.8.

49 Varro, *On agriculture* 1.7.8 (trans. W.D. Hooper and H.B. Ash).

50 Julius Honorius, *Cosmographia* 1-2.

51 Virgil, *Aeneid* 8.727. The expression proves that the third branch, the River Lek, was not very important in Antiquity.

52 Strabo, *Geography* 4.5.2.

53 Tacitus, *Germania* 29.

54 A. Vanderhoeven, 'The earliest urbanisation in Northern Gaul. Some implications of recent research in Tongres', in: *From the Sword to the Plough. Three Studies on the Earliest Romanisation of Northern Gaul* (1996) 189-260.

55 Livy, *Periochae* 141.2.

56 Strabo, *Geography* 4.4.2.

57 Julius Obsequens, *Omens* 71.

58 Cassius Dio, *Roman History* 54.20.4-6.

59 F. Kemmers, *Coins for a Legion. An Analysis of the Coin Finds from the Augustan Legionary Fortress and Flavian Canabae Legionis at Nijmegen* (2006).

60 Cassius Dio, *Roman History* 54.22.

61 Suetonius, *The Twelve Caesars*, Vitellius 8.1.

62 B. Makaske, G.J. Maas and D.G. van Smeerdijk, 'The age and origin of the Gelderse IJssel', in: *Netherlands Journal of Geosciences* 87/4 (2008).

63 Cassius Dio, *Roman History* 54.32.2-3.

64 Cassius Dio, *Roman History* 54.33.1-2

65 Julius Obsequens, *Omens* 72.

66 Cassius Dio, *Roman History* 54.33.3-4.

67 Pliny the Elder, *Natural History* 22.8.

68 Cassius Dio, *Roman History* 55.6.2.

69 J.-S. Kühlborn, *Germaniam pacavi. Germanien habe ich befreidet. Archäologische Stätten augusteischer Okkupation* (1995).

70 Cassius Dio, *Roman History* 55.10a.2-3; Velleius Paterculus, *Roman History* 2.104.2; Tacitus, *Annals* 1.63.4.

71 Velleius Paterculus, *Roman History* 2.104.3-108.1.

72 Augustus, *My Achievements* 26.4.

73 Velleius Paterculus, *Roman History* 2.117-119 (trans. F.W. Shipley).

74   Cassius Dio, *Roman History* 56.19-22.

75   Suetonius, *The Twelve Caesars*, Augustus 23.2.

76   Velleius Paterculus, *Roman History* 2.120.3-6.

77   Florus, *Epitome* 2.30.36-39.

78   Velleius Paterculus, *Roman History* 2.120.1-2.

79   Tacitus, *Annals* 1.3.6.

80   Suetonius, *The Twelve Caesars,* Tiberius 18-19.

81   Tacitus, *Annals* 1.50-51.

82   Tacitus, *Annals* 1.60.2-62.1

83   Press release of the Gallo-Roman museum, Tongeren, 7 May 2009.

84   Pliny the Elder, *Natural History* 16.5.

85   Tacitus, *Germania* 34.

86   Tacitus, *Annals* 1.70.

87   Tacitus, *Annals* 2.23-24.

88   Albinovanus Pedo, quoted in Seneca the Elder, *Suasoria* 1.15.

89   Pliny the Elder, *Natural History* 4.97.

90   Pliny the Elder, *Natural History* 16.1-4.

91   Pliny the Elder, *Natural History* 16.203.

92   *Corpus inscriptionum Latinarum* 13.8830.

93   Pliny the Elder, *Natural History* 25.20-21.

94   Tacitus, *Annals* 4.72-73.

95   Tacitus, *Germania* 37.

96   Tacitus, *Germania* 29 (quoted on page 000).

97   Strabo, *Geography* 4.4.2.

98   W. de Clercq, *Lokale gemeenschappen in het Imperium Romanum. Transformaties in rurale bewoningsstructuur en materiële culture in de landschappen van het noordelijk deel van de civitas Menapiorum (provincie Gallia-Belgica, ca 100 v.Chr.-400 n.Chr.)* (2009, 'Local Communities in the Roman Empire. Transformations in the Structure of Rural Habitation and Material Culture in the Lands in the Northern Part of the "civitas Menapiorum" (province of Gallia-Belgica, around 100 BC – 400 AD'.

99   P. Stuart, *Langs de weg. De Romeinse weg van Boulogne-sur-Mer naar Keulen, verkeersader voor industrie en handel* (1987, 'Along the Road. The Roman road from Boulogne-sur-Mer to Cologne, traffic arterial road for industry and trade').

100 Suetonius, *The Twelve Caesars*, Caligula 43.

101 Suetonius, *The Twelve Caesars*, Caligula 46.

102 S. Wynia, 'Gaius was here', in: H. Sarfatij, W.J.H. Verwers and P.J. Woltering, *In Discussion with the Past, Archaeological studies presented to W.A. van Es* (1999).

103 A.V.A.J. Bosman and M.D. de Weerd, 'Velsen: The 1997 excavations in the Early Roman Base and a Reappraisal of the Post-Kalkriese Velsen/Vechten Dating Evidence', in: F. Vermeulen, K. Sas and W. Dhaeze (ed.), *Archaeology in Confrontation. Aspects of Roman Military Presence in the Northwest* (2004).

104 Cassius Dio, *Roman History* 60.8.7.

105 Tacitus, *Annals* 11.18.1.

106 Tacitus, *Annals* 11.18.2-3.

107 Cp. Appian, *Iberian Wars* 85 (Scipio Aemilianus at Numantia); Plutarch, *Crassus* 10.3 (Crassus against Spartacus).

108 Tacitus, *Annals* 11.19.

109 Tacitus, *Annals* 11.20.3.

110 J.S. van der Kamp, *Vroege wacht. Archeologisch onderzoek van twee eerste-eeuwse wachttorens in Leidsche Rijn* (2007 'Early Watch. Archaeological Investigation of Two First-Century Watchtowers in Leidsche Rijn').

111 Velleius Paterculus, *Roman History Roman History* 2.120.2 (quoted on page 56).

112 Cassius Dio, *Roman History* 54.20.4, 54.32.2, 54.33.1; Tacitus, Annals 1.51 and Histories 4.37.

113 Tacitus, *Annals* 13.54.

114 Tacitus, *Annals* 14.46.2.

115 Tacitus, *Histories* 4.14.1-2 (trans. K. Wellesley).

116 Tacitus, *Germania* 22.

117 Tacitus, *Histories* 4.78.1 (quoted on page 103).

118 Tacitus, *Histories* 4.15.2 (trans. K. Wellesley).

119 Tacitus, *Histories* 4.16.2-17.1 (trans. K. Wellesley).

120 Tacitus, *Histories* 4.18.2-3 (trans. K. Wellesley).

121 Tacitus, *Histories* 4.21 (trans. K. Wellesley).

122 Tacitus, *Histories* 4.33.4 (trans. K. Wellesley).

123 Tacitus, *Histories* 4.60 (trans. K. Wellesley).

124 Tacitus, *Histories* 4.66 (trans. K. Wellesley).

125 Tacitus, *Histories* 4.78.1 (trans. K. Wellesley).

126 Tacitus, *Histories* 4.79.2-4 (trans. K. Wellesley).

127 Tacitus, *Histories* 5.19.1-2 (trans. K. Wellesley).

128 Tacitus, *Histories* 5.22.1-3 (trans. K. Wellesley).

129 Tacitus, *Histories* 5.23.3-24.1 (trans. K. Wellesley).

130 Suetonius, *The Twelve Caesars*, Domitian 8.2 (trans. J. C. Rolfe).

131 Pliny the Younger, *Letters* 2.7.2.

132 H. Brunsting, 'Adjutor, de Canninefaat', in: *Westerheem* 6 (1957, 'Adjutor, the Cananefate').

133 *Anthologia Latina* 1.660.

134 *Corpus Inscriptionum Latinarum* 6.1207.

135 Cp. D.B. Campbell, 'The Fate of the Ninth. The curious disappearance of Legio VIIII Hispana', in: *Ancient Warfare* 4.5 (2010) 48-53.

136 *Historia Augusta*, Hadrian 10.1-11.1 (trans. A. Birley).

137 *Corpus Inscriptionum Latinarum* 2.1423.

138 Aulus Gellius, *Attic Nights* 16.13; cp. F. Millar, *The Emperor in the Roman World* (1977) 398-400.

139 Pausanias, *Guide to Greece* 10.4.1.

140 Pliny the Elder, *Natural History* 31.12.

141 J. Hoevenberg, *De opgraving en levensgeschiedenis van een opmerkelijke Romeinse pottenbakkersoven in Heerlen-Centrum* (1996, 'Excavation and life of a remarkable Roman oven in the centre of Heerlen').

142 W.C. Bratt, 'De Grote Romeinse Villa van Voerendaal', in: *Oudheidkundige Mededelingen uit het Rijksmuseum van oudheden* 34 (1953, 'The Large Roman Villa of Voerendaal').

143 *Corpus inscriptionum Latinarum* 13.8725.

144 Pliny the Elder, *Natural History* 12.98.

145 Pliny the Elder, *Natural History* 15.102-103.

146 Pliny the Elder, *Natural History* 10.53-54.

147 Pliny the Elder, *Natural History* 28.191. Cp. Martial, *Epigrams* 8.33.19-20.

148 *Corpus inscriptionum Latinarum* 13.8354.

149 Pliny the Elder, *Natural History* 12.6.

150 Pliny the Elder, *Natural History* 36.159.

151 *Corpus inscriptionum Latinarum* 13.8793.

152 P.Stuart and J.E. Bogaers, *Römische Steindenkmäler aus der Oosterschelde bei Colijnplaat* (2001).

153 But see T. Derks, Gods, *Temples and Ritual Practices. The Transformation of Religious Ideas and Values in Roman Gaul* (1998) 217-227.

154 Cf. http://tinyurl.com/kkllrw.

155 Tacitus, *Germania* 9.

156 N. Roymans and T. Derks, *De tempel van Empel* (1994, 'The Temple of Empel').

157 Cassius Dio, *Natural History* 78.9.4.

158 Martial, *Epigrams* 6.82.

159 Herodian, *History of the Empire since Marcus* 6.7.6-7.

160 They are quoted by Christian writers.

161 Cassius Dio, *Natural History* 72.36.4

162 *Historia Augusta*, Didius Julianus 1.6-2.1.

163 W. Dhaeze, *Het Castellum van Maldegem-Vake. Studie van het verdedigingssysteem en de bevoorrading* (MA thesis, Univesity of Ghent 2000; 'The Castellum of Maldegem-Vake. Study of the Defence System and the Provisioning').

164 R.M. van Dierendonck, 'The Roman Wall-Paintings and the Character of the Roman Settlement at Aardenburg (The Netherlands)', in: C. Martin (ed.), *Aventicum V. Pictores per Provincias, Cahiers d'Archéologie Romande* (1987).

165 P. Vons, 'A Second-Century Roman Hoard of Corroded Denarii from Uitgeest' in: *Berichten van de Rijksdienst voor het Oudheidkundig Bodemonderzoek* 37 (1987) 123-152.

166 *Historia Augusta*, Thirty Pretenders 3.1-7 (trans. D. Magie).

167 *Historia Augusta*, Aurelian 34.2.

168 *Historia Augusta*, Carus, Carinus and Numerian 14.1-15.3.

169 Eusebius, *Life of Constantine* 1.8.

170 *Corpus Inscriptionum Latinarum* 13.8274.

171 Zosimus, *New History* 2.34.

172 Libanius, *Speech* 59.132.

173 Sidonius Apollinaris, *Letter* 4.17.2.

174 *Panegyrici Latini* 7 (6) 21.4-5; cf. http://tinyurl.com/d2vtuo5.

175 *Codex Theodosianus* 16.8.3.

176 *Corpus Inscriptionum Latinarum* 13.7813.

177 A. Arts e.a., *Fase 3 van het archeologisch onderzoek in de O.L.V.-basiliek te Tongeren* (2008; 'Phase 3 of the archaeological excavations in the Basilica of our Lady at Tongeren').

178 Sulpicius Severus, *Life of St Martin* 2.8-3.5(trans. A. Roberts).

179 Sulpicius Severus, *Life of St Martin* 20.4-7 (trans. A. Roberts).

180 The date has been challenged: see M. Kulikowski, 'Barbarians in Gaul. Usurpers in Britain' in: *Britannia* 31 (2000).

181 Jerome, *Letter* 123.16 (with references to *Psalm* 83.8 and Virgil, *Aeneid* 8.727).

182 *Corpus Inscriptionum Latinarum* 3.3576.

183 Gregory of Tours, *History of the Franks* 2.9.

184 Sidonius Apollinaris, *Panegyric on Majorianus* 238-250.

185 Salvian, *The Government of God* 7.63-64.

186 Cp. C. Wickham, 'The Other Transition: From the Ancient World to Feudalism' in: *Past and Present* 103 (1984).

187 Gregory of Tours, *History of the Franks* 2.30 (trans. L. Thorpe).

188 Gregory of Tours, *History of the Franks* 2.31 (trans. L. Thorpe). 'Sicamber' is derived from the name of the Sugambri, the tribe that Tiberius had settled near Xanten.

189 Gregory of Tours, *History of the Franks* 2.27.

190 See page 60-62.

191 'Es ist falsch die Varusschlacht als historischen Wendepunkt aufzufassen, wie dies geschichtswissenschaftlich Unkundige gerade in diesen Tagen wiederholt propagieren': P. Kehne, 'Der historische Arminius und die Varusschlacht aus cheruskischer Perspektive' in: S. Berke e.a., *2000 Jahre Varusschlacht. Mythos* (2009) 111.

192 See, for example, note 19, note 45, pages 60-62, page 113, page 114, and page 130.

Index Locorum

General Index

186